Da

Research

The Complete
Research Paper Guide

Doing Research

The Complete Research Paper Guide

Dorothy U. Seyler

Northern Virginia
Community College

McGraw-Hill, Inc.
New York St. Louis San Francisco Auckland Bogotá
Caracas Lisbon London Madrid Mexico City Milan
Montreal New Delhi San Juan Singapore
Sydney Tokyo Toronto

This book is printed on acid-free paper.

This book was developed by STEVEN PENSINGER, Inc.

DOING RESEARCH: THE COMPLETE RESEARCH PAPER GUIDE

5 6 7 8 9 0 DOC   DOC 9 0 9 8 7

ISBN 0-07-056351-9

This book was set in Galliard by The Clarinda Company.
The editors were Steve Pensinger and Tom Holton;
the designer was Robin Hoffmann;
the production supervisor was Denise L. Puryear.
R. R. Donnelley & Sons Company was printer and binder.

Library of Congress Cataloging-in-Publication Data

Seyler, Dorothy U.
    Doing research: the complete research paper guide / Dorothy U.
Seyler. — 1st ed.
        p.   cm.
    Includes bibliographical references.
    ISBN 0-07-056351-9
    1. Report writing.   2. Research.   I. Title.
LB2369.S46   1993   92-3539
808'.02—dc20

Contents

Chapter 4
Understanding Sources and Taking Notes 107

Chapter 5
Presenting and Documenting Research 151

Preface

As its subtitle suggests, *Doing Research* offers a complete guide to preparing documented papers in the humanities, social sciences, and science fields. The MLA, APA, and footnote/endnote documentation styles (those used in the humanities, the social sciences, and some science fields) are thoroughly explained and illustrated. Explanation is supported by sample student papers illustrating MLA and APA forms (in the text) and footnotes (in the *Instructor's Manual*). Variations of APA style used in the earth sciences and the number system used, with many variations, in other science fields are also explained and illustrated so that science students can read documented sources and prepare documented papers in their specialized field. Illustrations of the various documentation styles are supported by detailed guidelines for formatting papers in the various disciplines and for handling numbers and preparing visuals. *Doing Research* will serve, then, as a reference text or handbook for research that students can use throughout their undergraduate writing.

Equally important, perhaps more important, *Doing Research,* as the title indicates, explains and illustrates the *doing* of research, the steps in the research process. Although faculty are necessarily—and appropriately—concerned that students demonstrate their ability to prepare completed papers that conform to scholarly research conventions, many students fall by the wayside long before struggling to complete their page of references. They cannot finish because they do not know how to get started, because they are overwhelmed by an academic library, because they do not understand the researcher's relationship to sources. A process that may seem obvious to instructors is decidedly not obvious to many college freshmen who are, for the first time, being asked to engage in academic writing. Because of the range of preparedness among students, some research texts are designed primarily as reference handbooks, while others are written as composition texts that provide few guidelines for students working outside the English classroom.

Doing Research is based on the belief that a thoughtfully organized, clearly written, and amply illustrated research text *can* guide the less prepared student through the writing process while not condescending to the more prepared student who needs help primarily with technical details of documentation and manuscript conventions. *Doing Research* strikes the proper balance between explaining the process and providing guidelines for completing the paper. This text does not just tell students, "Do not fill your paper with quotations"; it explains why that approach is unsuccessful and then illustrates alternative ways of handling borrowed material. And *Doing Research* shows students how to do their own research, how to incorporate primary sources and their own thinking into papers so that they begin to taste the pleasures of investigation and problem solving—what doing research is really all about.

This text is organized into chapters that correspond to what can roughly be called steps in the research process, moving from selecting a topic to searching for sources and preparing a bibliography to reading and note-taking to writing and documenting. This organization does not imply, however, that the research process can be completed successfully by merely checking off a series of unrelated steps. Rather, the recursive nature of research is stressed—and illustrated—in the text.

The documentation style illustrated in preparing bibliography cards (Chapter 3) and documenting research (Chapter 5) is the in-text citation style of the Modern Language Association (MLA). Thus those instructors who want to teach the research process in detail and want students to use—or at least be aware of—MLA style can assign Chapters 1 through 6 in order. Other documentation patterns are explained in Chapter 7. Consequently, students selecting a style other than MLA can use the appropriate section of Chapter 7 instead of the sections of Chapters 3 and 5 that illustrate MLA style. The guidelines for preparing a working bibliography have been placed at the beginning of a separate chapter (Chapter 3)—not mixed in with locating sources (Chapter 2)—so that students using a style other than MLA can read about finding sources without the constant intrusion of sample cards and source-citing guidelines in a style they are not using in their papers.

Several other features of the text's organization and content should be noted. Chapter 4 devotes ample space to the note-taking process and types of notes but only after a discussion of the researcher's relationship to sources and the development of a preliminary outline to guide the researcher's use of sources. Many students have difficulty framing a thesis and developing a preliminary plan that will direct them to a paper meeting the expectations of a research assignment. This chapter explains how sources are to be used to fulfill different types of research assignments so that writers can move beyond the fruitless exercise of merely copying ideas from six sources on a topic. Chapter 4 also presents an annotated bibliography and a review-of-the-literature essay, projects that can be seen as part of the understanding of sources or as finished projects in their own right.

The technicalities of referring to authors and titles, presenting quotations and visuals, handling numbers and punctuation, and documenting sources are presented when they need to be introduced: in Chapter 5 *before* guidelines for writing the paper. If the single greatest difficulty students have is framing and then developing an appropriate thesis, the second greatest difficulty most face is presenting the results of research clearly and without awkwardness. Although not all elements covered in Chapter 5 will be relevant to every writer or every paper and the specifics of format cannot be learned all at once, students need to review this material and have a general understanding of formatting conventions so that they can avoid drafting a paper that will need extensive revision, or one that fails to take advantage of options such as tables or figures.

Chapter 6 organizes writing the research essay into a clear process of drafting, revising, editing, and proofreading; provides detailed guidance on writing opening, body, and concluding paragraphs, on revising, and on editing; and concludes with two annotated student essays, one a literary analysis, the other a study of advertising that includes primary research.

Users of the text will observe that rather than providing a separate, brief section on using a word processor, this text integrates discussion of word processing at each appropriate stage—note-taking, drafting, and completing an edited paper. Readers will also find that the numerous examples throughout the text are drawn from a wide range of disciplines and that several of the examples are returned to from chapter to chapter so that students can see how a researcher actually progresses from selecting a topic to finding sources to developing a preliminary outline and so on. The text gathers additional helpful information into two appendices, one listing many common abbreviations, the other providing a list of reference sources, including online databases, by discipline.

Finally, *Doing Research* concludes with two design features to aid student researchers: blank perforated pages that can be used for keeping a research journal and a pocket on the inside back cover that will hold bibliography cards or notes. This is a text that says to researchers, "Keep me by your side throughout your project, and I will help you complete a paper that will make you justly proud."

No book of value is written alone. Friends and colleagues have helped me with *Doing Research,* and I am happy to thank them publicly. My editor, Steve Pensinger, deserves first recognition for his faith in my ability to handle this project and for putting up with any anguished cries (surely only one or two!) over the project's perceived difficulty that I may have emitted. I am also grateful to my colleague Richard Wilan who read the chapters in draft and discussed them with me, and to Michael Hughes, assistant professor of sociology at Virginia Polytechnic Institute and State University, who helped me understand the kinds of papers assigned in the social sciences and who obtained papers from psychology students illustrating APA documentation.

My gratitude is due once again to the library staff at the Annandale campus of Northern Virginia Community College, especially to reference librarians Marion Delmore, Ruth Stanton, and Janice Jeffries, who helped me locate needed information and who read Chapters 1 and 2 in draft to keep me straight on the intricacies of microform, CD-ROM, and online materials. Frances Bernhardt, coordinator of library services, was especially helpful in explaining the subtleties of preparing Dewey Decimal and Library of Congress classification numbers for individual books. Of course not one of these generous people is responsible for any flaws in the final version of the book. My friend Sue Walker, putting up with yet another discussion of my project, gave me the initial idea of providing students with "something extra" at the end of the text. And I should not overlook the help closest to home: my daughter Ruth read some chapters, was a dutiful sounding board, and gave good advice from a graduate student's perspective. I appreciate as well the advice and specific suggestions of the following reviewers: Robert Budd, Lansing Community College; Kathleen Shine Cain, Merrimack College; Robert M. Esch, University of Texas–El Paso; Gerry McBroom, University of New Mexico. Finally, I want to acknowledge the students who allowed me to use their papers; they worked hard on their essays and deserve to be proud to have achieved an audience beyond the classroom.

Dorothy U. Seyler

About the Author

Dorothy U. Seyler is Professor of English at Northern Virginia Community College. A Phi Beta Kappa graduate of the College of William and Mary, Dr. Seyler holds advanced degrees from Columbia University and the State University of New York at Albany. She taught at Ohio State University, the University of Kentucky, and Nassau Community College before moving with her family to Northern Virginia.

She has coauthored *Introduction to Literature* and *Language Power,* both now in second editions, and is the author of *Read, Reason, Write,* in its third edition, *The Writer's Stance,* and *Patterns of Reflection.* In addition, Professor Seyler has published articles in professional journals and popular magazines. She enjoys tennis and traveling, and writing about both.

Doing
Research

The Complete
Research Paper Guide

Getting
Started

*W*riters, and teachers of writing, are fond of assuring students that getting started is the hardest part of any writing task. If they are right, then you have your research assignment under control, because, by opening this guide, you have begun. Before you complain that you are not that naive, let us agree that doing research is a complex, challenging, and sometimes frustrating—but also rewarding—activity. If you will also agree that complex tasks are handled best when divided into parts or steps and when you seek help for the new or most difficult parts, then you should be feeling a little less anxious already. For the help is here: This handbook will lead you through the research process and explain how to handle each part of the task. Remember, too, that some anxiety is good; it is what gets you to the library, what keeps you reading to stay on schedule. To keep your anxiety from interfering with progress, take comfort that you will be guided through each step in your project; and as you see results from your work, your confidence will grow and the excitement of discovery will carry you forward.

WHAT DOING RESEARCH MEANS

Doing research means obtaining information about a subject so that you know something that you did not know before. Doing research *well* means obtaining the *best* information as a result of thinking clearly about what you need to know and what sources can best provide that information so that what you know when you are through provides the best possible understanding of the subject.

Clearly we do research all the time. When you are ready to purchase a car, you will (if you are smart) do some research. You may have been looking over friends' cars for some time, so you have some experience, some ideas, with which to start. Now you need to supplement that knowledge with information from a variety of sources: brochures available from car dealers, comparative evaluations in consumer magazines, conversations with people who own models you are considering. Your goal is to collect and analyze the best information so that you can make a wise choice in the car you purchase.

The success of personal market research is measured by how happy you are with your purchase. When research is engaged in, at least in part, for others—for a professional or business community—then, instead of acting on the research by making a purchase, the researcher acts by sharing the results of research in some way: at a meeting, in a memo or report, or in a more formal paper. Most of you have had at least one experience of presenting the results of research in a library, term, or research paper, a paper that involved the use of sources and some form of documentation acceptable to the academic community. You may also have shared your knowledge through a class presentation. Frequently in college courses, as well as in business and professional settings, both oral and written reports of research are expected.

Unfortunately, in the bustle of finding information and the strain of coping with the technicalities of presenting source material, student researchers sometimes lose sight of the purpose of doing research. As you embark on a research project, keep in mind that we do research to provide:

1. New knowledge
   The biochemical triggers of alcoholism
   An edition of a writer's formerly unpublished journal
   A comparison of shopping habits in urban, suburban, and rural communities

2. New understanding
   Better methods for preventing or treating alcoholism
   A reevaluation of a writer's works based on a study of the published journal
   A shopping-center plan based on the study of shopping habits

The research *paper* is the written presentation of the researcher's new knowledge or understanding. Many college research projects, especially projects in the sciences and social sciences that involve experiments, case studies, or questionnaires, contribute new knowledge to both researcher and readers. Other research projects provide readers with new insights or approaches (and the researcher with new knowledge) as a result of the student's unique way of examining a topic. All researchers are expected to find the best information, understand that information, and present it in an organized, fresh, and thoughtful manner. And you are expected to prepare a completed paper that conforms to a format of scholarly writing that has become standardized over many years by many thousands of scholars. As you give energy to the study of sources and the patterns of documentation, though, remember that the success of your project will grow out of your care in selecting and studying sources, your insight into the topic, and your clarity and thoroughness in presenting the results of your research.

Types of Research Projects

While research projects can be sorted on the basis of the results of research, distinctions can also be made on the basis of the researcher's purpose. Different purposes lead researchers to papers that are primarily *expository, analytic,* or *persuasive.*

EXPOSITORY

The expository, or informative, paper is sometimes called a report. The purpose is to impart information, to explain to readers what the researcher has learned from the study. Scholarly reports include summaries of books, annotated bibliographies, and reviews of the literature on a given topic. (See pages 138–40 and 141–50 for an annotated bibliography and a review of literature.) Market research and technical reports are important kinds of informative writing in business. Reports serve as starting points for further research or as decision-making guides. College students are assigned expository research papers when instructors want them to read widely, to acquire greater understanding of complex topics, or, as in a composition class, when the goal is to improve research skills. A good report in any field will reveal the writer's critical judgment in selecting and arranging the information so that the reader sees the topic as the researcher sees it.

ANALYTIC

The analytic paper goes beyond an organized reporting of information to an examination of the implications of that information. While a report on problems in American education will assemble the results of recent tests to show American students' weaknesses in math and science, an analytic paper will present and discuss causes for these weaknesses. Many literary studies are analytic. An analytic study of light and dark imagery in Shakespeare's *Romeo and Juliet* will explain how the imagery contributes to the development of the play's theme. Analytic papers explore causes (what led to the dinosaur's extinction), classify data (techniques used in print advertising), explain processes (how journalists decide what's news).

PERSUASIVE

The persuasive research essay uses information and analysis to support a thesis, or position on the topic. A persuasive paper on problems in American education may use recent test results and an analysis of their causes to support an agenda for change. More specifically, a comparative analysis of Japanese and American schools may support the view that Americans should adopt elements of the Japanese system. An analysis of character and narrative point of view supports the thesis that Margot Macomber intentionally shot her husband in Ernest Hemingway's "The Short Happy Life of Francis Macomber." A study of television violence leads to a call for restrictions on programming.

   The best way to understand these three kinds of research essays is to see them as stages along a continuum rather than as entirely separate forms of writing. The selection and arrangement of information in a report will necessarily reflect the writer's interests and attitudes. Further, since the causes of complex physical, social, and psychological phenomena are debated among the experts, analytic papers often need to be recognized as persuasive. Finally, and perhaps most in need of emphasis, persuasive papers written to gain the respect of colleagues in one's field must be presented with restraint, with fairness, and with appropriate logic and evidence. Nonetheless, the distinctions between the three kinds of research essays can be helpful to researchers, who need to have a clear sense of their purpose in writing.

What Research Writing Is Not

Research writing presents the results of a new study of a topic, is organized and focused by the researcher to fulfill a clear purpose, is developed in part by drawing on information from sources, and carefully documents those sources used. With these characteristics of research writing in mind, we can also say what does not qualify as research writing. The following list is a cautionary reminder of the kinds of writing that will not meet the requirements of research assignments.

1. A paper that merely strings together quotations from sources is not a new study of a topic and is not, therefore, a legitimate research paper.

2. An essay drawn entirely from personal experiences, thoughts, and feelings is not a research paper because it is not grounded in reading on a topic or gathering evidence.

3. An entirely theoretical paper without any data from sources is not research writing.

4. A paper in which information drawn from sources is not properly documented is not a legitimate, honest research paper. (Of course a borrowed or purchased paper is also unacceptable.)

The Rewards of Research

Good writing is more likely to result when writers keep in mind the nature of the writing to be undertaken. Writers may also profit from reviewing the benefits of their writing, especially as they "gear up" for the task of doing research. A few minutes' reflection on the benefits of your project may help you get started with the positive attitude that can lead to a first-class project you will be justly proud to share with others.

NEW KNOWLEDGE/NEW UNDERSTANDING

Remember that the purpose of research is not just to complete a project and get a grade but to learn something you did not know before. When you finish, you should have acquired new information and perhaps a whole new perspective on the subject studied. In many disciplines, one of the final steps to a doctorate is the "defense of the dissertation." The graduate student has to discuss his or her research project with faculty members. This should be an exciting occasion as the student is initiated, as it were, into a community of experts in the field. As you work on your project, discuss what you are learning with anyone who will listen so that you develop a sense of pride in your new expertise.

RESEARCH SKILLS

Each time you take on a research assignment, you refine your research skills—skills, as observed at the beginning of the chapter, that you use in your private life and may use in your work as well. Much of research is asking the right questions and then finding ways to get the answers. These are basic problem-solving skills that are needed throughout our lives. More specifically, each time you complete a research assignment, you refine your skills in this particular kind of academic writing. Skills are sharpened only with practice. Even research papers become easier each time through.

PARTICIPATION IN THE ACADEMIC COMMUNITY

Every time you do research and present your results in a paper or discuss your project with classmates, you take an active part in the community of scholars. Even if you are not making a major contribution to knowledge, you are nonetheless offering your new understanding, your own special perspective, on the topic you have studied. Do not underestimate your contribution. Many instructors learn as much from the fresh insights of their students as they do from their continued study of scholarly sources. As you labor over the correct forms of documenting sources in your paper, keep in mind that you are learning the code for research writing of the scholars in your discipline. Each discipline has its specialized language (quasars and quarks; ids and egos; paradoxes and puns) *and* its way of presenting the results of research. Prepare your results with care so that you can feel a part of the scholarly community.

STEPS IN THE RESEARCH PROCESS

As you read through the following outline of steps in the research process, keep in mind that complex intellectual activities rarely fit neatly into a rigid sequence. No one can map, with certainty, your thinking processes, the ideas that will cause you to refocus your study and return to the library. Still, there is a basic process that remains much the same regardless of the particular topic or specific objectives of the assignment. And having an overview of the process will give you a sense of where you are headed as you begin your project. The following six steps provide that overview.

Step 1. Select and limit. Select and limit a topic consistent with assignment guidelines. Clear up any confusion about the assignment by asking questions of the instructor. Review some sources as necessary to aid in limiting a topic. Also consider purpose or type of research, audience, and required length or number of sources or amount of data when selecting.

Step 2. Focus and plan. Choose an approach or focus for your research. Decide on a tentative thesis, hypothesis, or question to answer. Think, talk, and read to complete this step. Write a statement of purpose or research proposal.

Step 3. Gather sources. In a systematic manner, locate potential sources in the library or in other appropriate places and/or collect data from original research.

Step 4. Read and think. Read and evaluate source materials and/or study original data. Record relevant information and ideas on note cards. Learn about the topic. Think about what needs to be covered and what you need to learn to complete your study. Develop a preliminary outline. Obtain additional information if necessary. Think some more.

Step 5. Organize and draft. Plan in detail the structure of your paper. With note cards arranged according to the proposed structure, write a first draft.

Step 6. Revise, edit, and format correctly. Revise the draft and edit to remove errors. Prepare the completed paper in an appropriate format with correct documentation of sources according to the expected style.

FINDING A WORKABLE TOPIC

As Step 1 states, to get started you need to select and limit your research topic. The key to success in your project is finding a *workable* topic, workable in a number of senses. No matter how interesting or clever the topic, it is not a workable one if it does not meet the guidelines of your assignment, so you need to start with a thorough understanding of the writing context created by the assignment.

Understand Purpose, Audience, and Constraints

We have established that research writing can be loosely classified as expository, analytic, or persuasive. As soon as you are given an assignment, determine the type of project called for. If you are asked to explain the chief solutions being proposed for the Southwest's diminishing water supply, then you must recognize that the instructor wants a report, not an argument in favor of one solution. If the assignment stipulates a comparative analysis of the Freudian and behavioral models of mental illness, then you know your task is to analyze how these two schools of psychology differ in their explanations of mental disorders and in their approaches to treatment. You cannot report on only one model, nor are you to argue that one is superior to the other. Finally, if your assignment requires that you take a stand on the question "Is *Death of a Salesman* a tragedy?" then you must accept that an argument is needed and that just reviewing other writers on the subject will not fulfill the assignment's guidelines.

A sense of audience is also important. Even though, in most cases, your actual audience is the instructor who has assigned the research project, you should still give some thought to the implications of that audience for you as a writer. If you are doing research in a specific discipline, then imagine your instructor as a representative of that field, a reader who has knowledge of the subject area but is willing to listen to fresh ideas. If you are learning about research in a composition course, then your instructor may advise you to write to a general reader, someone who reads newspapers and magazines and knows what today's issues and problems are but may not have the information and perspective you have. Specialized terms and concepts need definition and illustration for a general reader but not for a "colleague." In some courses students discuss at least parts of their projects with classmates, or present their papers in a seminar class. Thus you may actually have the multiple readers you have prepared for in your thinking about audience.

The required length of the paper, the time given for the project, and the availability of sources are three constraints you must also consider when selecting a research topic. Most instructors establish guidelines regarding length. Undergraduate research papers generally range from six to twelve typed pages of text. (Instructors in upper-division courses in which the only grades will be for one paper and a final exam will expect much longer papers.) Knowing the expected length of a paper is crucial to selecting an appropriate topic, so if an instructor does not specify, be sure to ask. Suppose you must write on one of the American novelists on the syllabus. You enjoyed Hemingway's *The Sun Also Rises* and decide to do something on Hemingway. Your paper, though, is to be six pages and is due in three weeks. Do you have the time to explore some element of Hemingway's style, for example, that would have to be based on an analysis of many novels? Time alone should constrain you to limit your paper to a topic on *The Sun Also Rises* or to a study of this and one other novel.

Along similar lines, be careful about selecting topics that are dependent on source materials obtained only through interlibrary loan or the mails. If you have only a few weeks for a project, you might not obtain government reports, for instance, in time to use them in your study. (Fax machines and databases that provide full texts of articles can reduce the waiting period for many but not all source materials located outside your library.)

Finally, we can list several kinds of topics that are best avoided because they usually produce disasters, no matter how well the student handles the rest of the research process.

1. *Topics that are irrelevant* to your interests and to the course. If you are not interested, your writing is likely to be uninspired. If you insist on selecting a topic far removed from the course content, you may create some hostility in your instructor, who will wonder why you are unwilling to become engaged in the course.

2. *Topics that are broad subject areas.* These result in general surveys that lack appropriate detail and support.

3. *Topics that can be fully researched with only one source.* You will produce a summary, not a research paper.

4. *Biographical studies.* Short undergraduate papers on a person's life usually turn out to be summaries of one or two major biographies in the library.

5. *Topics that evoke a strong emotional response from you.* If there is only one "right" answer to the abortion issue and you cannot imagine counterarguments, don't choose to write on abortion. Probably most religious topics are best avoided.

6. *Topics that are too technical for you* at this point in your college work. If you do not understand the complexities of the federal tax code, then arguing for a reduction in the capital gains tax may be an unwise topic choice.

Use Strategies to Generate and Limit Topics

Instructors vary in their control of topic selection. Some will assign topics, perhaps handing out a list of acceptable topics from which students
may choose. If your instructor restricts topics, consider this a benefit, for
your instructor has simplified a difficult step in the research process.
Even so, you may still need to use some of the strategies discussed here
to help you choose a topic from the list and develop your own approach
to that topic.

More often, research assignments do not list specific topics but call
for papers on course-related subjects. While working within assignment
guidelines, try to write about what interests you. For example, in a modern American history course you might be asked to explore the impact of
any federal law passed in the twentieth century. If you have an interest in
the 1920s, then you could choose to study the impact of Prohibition on
that era.

When you are free to write on any course-related topic, use whatever
strategies help you select a workable topic. Here are some suggestions.

Think About the Course

As soon as a research project is assigned, start thinking about topic possibilities. Although you will eventually need to go to the library, you
might use your time best by starting with what you already know or are
learning in your course. Look over class notes and think about subjects
already covered that have interested you. Or take a different approach
and reflect on topics that you could benefit from studying in detail. For
example, in your art history course you must write about one artist who
can be shown to be representative of his or her period or school of painting. Rather than choosing to write on your favorite impressionist, why
not select a surrealist so that you can learn more about surrealism? What
you discover may very well help you on the final exam, and your choice
might set you apart from other students in the class.

Some people can perform concentrated, productive thinking in their
heads, but others are aided by thinking on paper. You might try freewriting, brainstorming, or asking questions.

Freewrite.   Freewriting forces you to get some ideas on paper, for
the "rule" is that you cannot stop writing until you have filled a page or
written for, say, ten minutes. The student considering a paper for her art
history course might begin her freewriting as illustrated in Figure 1.

I need to select an artist for my research paper. My favorite is Van Gogh, but he's so special — maybe he doesn't make a good representative of a school. I could write about Monet, but everybody likes the impressionists and besides I think I can handle this term.

What should I be studying? What about the expressionists? The surrealists? Dadaism? These terms run together in my thinking right now. Maybe picking someone from one of these schools would help me understand the differences, because I'll have to be able to define these categories. Let's see - who are some artists? Dali? Miró? Escher? What about Chagall? I like his cow jumping over the moon. Is this surrealism or magic realism? Maybe I can approach this topic by explaining characteristics of some of the school's subcategories and then show elements of the subcategories in different Chagall paintings.

Figure 1 Sample of Freewriting.

Brainstorm.   Many people find brainstorming, another strategy that stimulates thinking and imagination, preferable to freewriting, perhaps because of its resemblance to making shopping lists. Indeed, as a method of searching for a topic, it is similar to making a shopping list—of possibilities, in this case—and it works much the same way. When starting to make a list, you might think you need only a few items at the store, but as you jot them down, others come to mind. And that is the idea: to range through possibilities, letting one idea generate another. Suppose your assignment is to study any current problem and then to explain and defend the best solutions to the problem. What problems concern you? You might get started by generating a list similar to the one in Figure 2.

Many problems worth investigating are listed in Figure 2. Now you need to analyze the list, perhaps grouping similar kinds of problems and crossing out those you reject—and thinking about why you are rejecting them. In other words, have a "conversation" with yourself about the list. Your conversation might look like Figure 3.

This brainstorming has actually combined listing, analyzing, and debating about ideas and interests—a kind of freewriting—to help you reach the decision to study a local environmental problem. When thinking about current problems, try to get beyond just those that are dominating the news. You may want to consider both college-based and community or statewide issues as alternatives.

Ask Questions.   One way to generate a narrowed topic from a broad subject is to ask questions. Contemplating Prohibition, you might generate these questions:

Who wanted Prohibition?

Who opposed it?

Who benefited from it?

What forces created the climate for its passage?

What were the consequences?

What reasons were given to support the law? To oppose it?

Where did the temperance movement originate? Where was it most influential?

When was the law passed? When rescinded?

Why did people defy the law?

Note that these questions use all the questions we associate with the journalist's list: *Who? What? Where? When?* and *Why?*

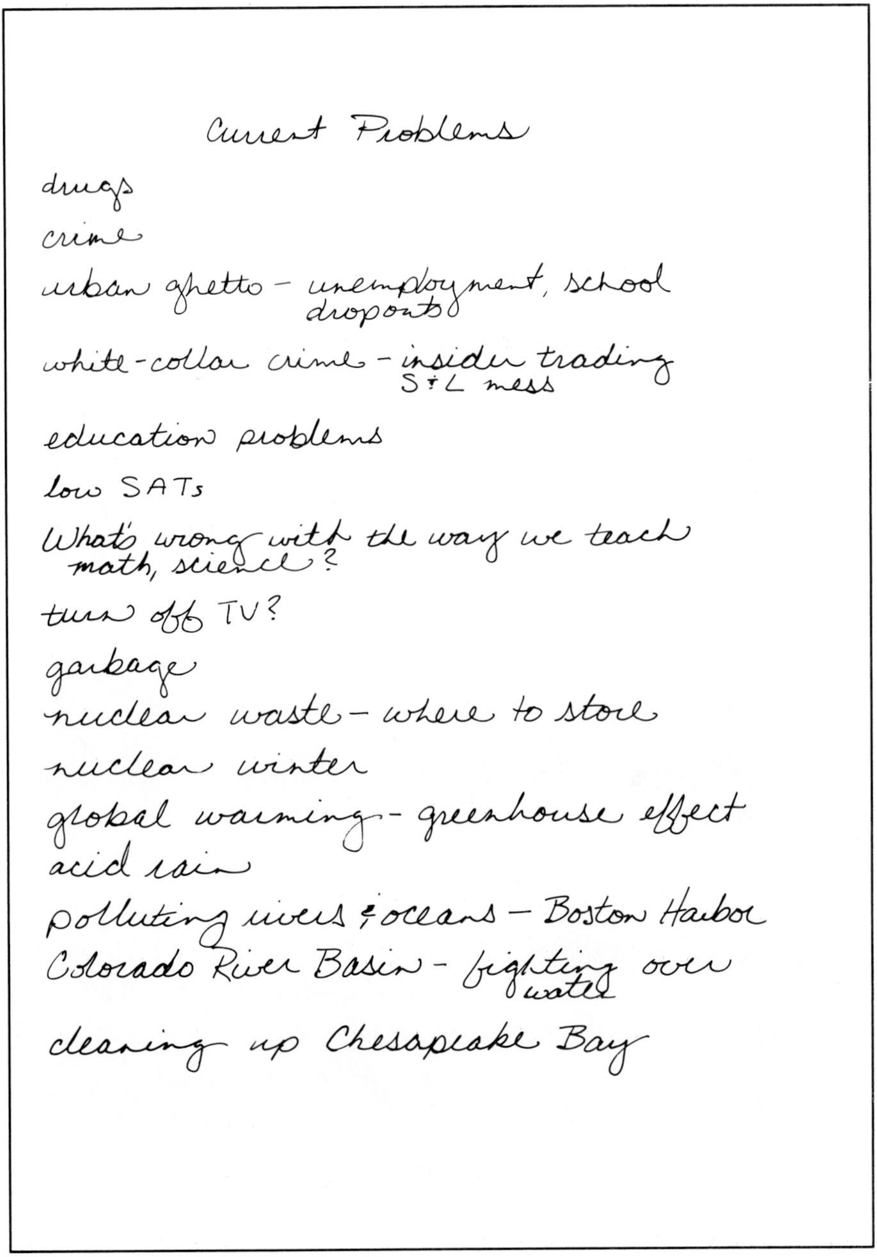

Current Problems

drugs

crime

urban ghetto – unemployment, school dropouts

white-collar crime – insider trading
S & L mess

education problems

low SATs

What's wrong with the way we teach math, science?

turn off TV?

garbage

nuclear waste – where to store

nuclear winter

global warming – greenhouse effect

acid rain

polluting rivers & oceans – Boston Harbor

Colorado River Basin – fighting over water

cleaning up Chesapeake Bay

Figure 2 Sample of Brainstorming List.

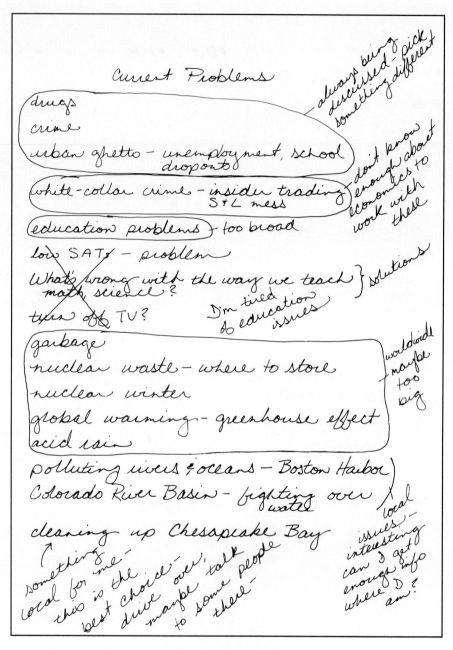

Figure 3 Interaction with Brainstorming List.

Examine Source Materials

If exploring ideas in your head or on paper doesn't lead to a workable topic, then turn to various library sources for help in generating and narrowing a topic.

Scan a Book's Table of Contents or Index. Your textbook's table of contents or index can help you find a course-related topic. Similarly, a library book may suggest a workable topic. The table of contents entries in Figure 4 and the index entries in Figure 5 suggest several topics on environmental problems. Reading the appropriate pages in the book can give you an approach to or focus on the topics of coping with radioactive wastes and the need for earthquake prediction capabilities.

Study the *Library of Congress Subject Headings* Volumes. Another work to examine for possible topics is the three-volume *Library of Congress Subject Headings* (12th ed., 1989), big red books probably found near your library's book catalog. The *LCSH* lists the subject head-

<table>
<tr><td>

5

SOIL AND WATER CONTAMINATION

6

FLOODS

</td><td>

Figure 4 Table of Contents Entries from *Environmental Geology* by Lawrence Lundgren. Prentice, 1986.

</td></tr>
</table>

Earthquake Hazard Reduction Act of 1977,
    408
Earthquake insurance, 475
Earthquake losses, 421–24, 469
Earthquakes:
    aftershocks, 427
    analysis, 427
    anomalies preceding, 464
    description, 409
    elastic rebound model, 451–52
    epicenter, 409–11
    holding time preceding, 443, 455
    information, 466
    intensity, 412, 444–47
    location, 435–40
    magnitude, 411
    policy, 466
    prediction, 431–33, 435, 440, 449, 476
    primary events, 426
    records, 411
    repeat times, 443, 455
    sources, 414
Earthquake scenarios, 468

Figure 5 Index Entries from *Environmental Geology* by Lawrence Lundgren. Prentice, 1986.

ings and subheadings used in the subject catalog—and in many periodical indexes as well. Later, in your search for sources, you may need to return to these volumes for guidance in using the subject catalog. At this step, though, you can use the *LCSH* both as a listing of possible subjects and as a guide for narrowing subjects to workable topics. The excerpt in Figure 6 illustrates the various codes used in this index. Note that *BT* and *NT* are reciprocal terms; *cocaine,* for instance, is a narrower term than *drug abuse,* whereas *drug abuse* is a broader term than *cocaine. USE* and *UF* are also reciprocals. *USE* sends you to the correct term to look up; *UF* tells you that the main heading, in dark type, is the correct term to use when you are searching the subject catalog for books on the topic. *RT* identifies another place to look for additional works. The excerpt highlights *Terrorism* as a possible subject but also makes clear that it is a broad subject that should be narrowed. You might decide to study the impact of television on terrorist activity.

Search the Computerized *Magazine Index.* If the *LCSH* volumes don't guide you to a topic, there are other search opportunities in the

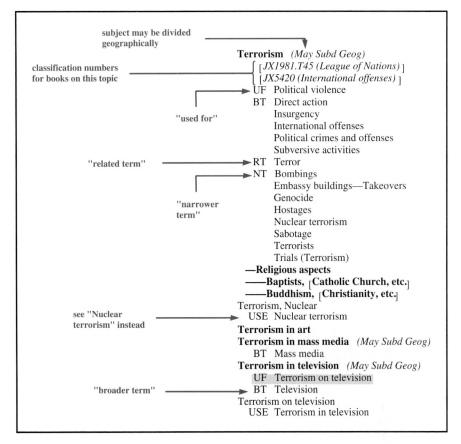

Figure 6 Excerpt from *Library of Congress Subject Headings.*

library. In addition to searching subject headings in a computerized book catalog, if your library's catalog is online, or scanning the subject entries and subheadings in *The Reader's Guide to Periodical Literature,* you can also search a computerized periodicals index such as the *Magazine Index Plus,* usually known by its trade name *InfoTrac.* If, for example, you need a controversial topic in a science or social science field and you recall an early fascination with dinosaurs, you can type in *dinosaur* to see what subheadings might suggest a paper topic. A partial list, in Figure 7, highlights two possible controversies: dinosaur behavior (were they warm-blooded, active animals?) and dinosaur extinction (what caused their demise?).

```
DINOSAURS
   see also
       Saurischia
   -anatomy
   -appreciation
   -(audio tape reviews)
   -behavior
   -bibliography
   -(book reviews)
   -books
   -classification
   -collectors and collecting
   -Colorado
   -commemorative coins, stamps, etc.
   -commemorative postage stamps
   -computer programs
   -Development
   -discovery and exploration
   -educational use
   -Eggs and nests
   -evolution
   -exhibitions
   -Extinction
   -galleries and museums
   -Migration
```

Figure 7 Excerpt from *Magazine Index/Plus (InfoTrac)*.

Explore Encyclopedia Indexes and Articles.   Your library's multi-volume general encyclopedias and specialized encyclopedias, handbooks, and dictionaries can serve as aids in topic selection and focusing and then later as places to begin learning about your topic. You should become acquainted with *The New Encyclopaedia Britannica,* considered one of the best (and probably the most sophisticated) of the general encyclopedias. This is a 32-volume work with four distinct parts. The *Micropaedia,* in Volumes 1–12, contains brief articles on topics. The *Macropaedia,* in Volumes 13–29, contains long essays on topics, each followed by a bibliography. Volume 30, called the *Propaedia,* is an outline of knowledge with suggestions for appropriate reading in the first 29 volumes. Finally, Volumes 31 and 32 contain the *Index.* If you are considering several broad subjects but need help in seeing how one might be narrowed, the volume to explore first is the *Propaedia.* If the student who needs to write on the impact of a federal law in the twentieth century had not decided on Prohibition by thinking about the course and his interests, he could have examined the outline of history. As the excerpt in Figure 8 reveals, Prohibition—as well as other possible topics—is suggested in the outline.

Section 973.

The United States and Canada Since 1920

A. The United States since 1920

  1. The post-World War I Republican administrations

    a. Politics and economics under Harding and Coolidge (1921-29): favouritism toward big business, restriction of immigration, "Coolidge prosperity"

    b. Social conditions in the 1920s: prohibition, growth of organized crime, and the jazz age

    c. Hoover's administration (1929-33) and the Great Depression: the stock market crash, domestic and international repercussions, Hoover's attempts to effect economic recovery

  2. The effects of the New Deal and World War II: the presidency of Franklin D. Roosevelt (1933-45)

    a. Comprehensive New Deal measures for economic recovery, relief, and reform

    b. Reform measures of the second New Deal and the election of 1936

Figure 8 From the *Propaedia* of *The New Encyclopaedia Britannica*, 1988 Edition.

Figure 9 From the Index of *The New Encyclopaedia Britannica*, 1988 Edition.

prohibition (alcohol suppression)
  9:722:3b
  non-uniformity of regulations
    13:222:1a
  for a list of related subjects see
    PROPAEDIA: Section 522
Prohibition (U.S. hist.)
  major ref. in prohibition **9:**723:1a
  effect on
    bootlegging **2:**376:1b
    organized crime **8:**994:3b;
      29:255:1b
    police **25:**943:2a
    Saint Valentine's Day Massacre
      10:336:1a
  popularization of
    jazz **24:**642:2b
    stock-car racing **11:**277:1a
  role of
    Capone **2:**833:2b
    Ness **8:**611:1b
  support by Anti-Saloon League
    1:448:1b
Prohibition Amendment (U.S.
    Constitution): *see* Twenty-
    first Amendment

On the other hand, the student already contemplating a study of Prohibition can begin with the Index (see Figure 9) both to locate the volume and page number for the main article on his subject and to get ideas for narrowing and focusing his topic. The main article, a part of which appears in Figure 10, provides some answers to questions the student generated about his topic and suggests a possible strategy for exploring the effects of Prohibition: examining its differing effects on rural and urban areas and on various classes in society.

Note: Because of the convenient way that encyclopedias organize in-

The drive for national prohibition emerged out of a renewed attack on the sale of liquor in many states after 1906. The underlying forces at work to support national prohibition included antipathy to the growth of cities (the presumed scene of most drinking), evangelical Protestant middle-class anti-alien and anti-Roman Catholic sentiment, and rural domination of the state legislatures, without which ratification of the Eighteenth Amendment would have been impossible. Other forces included the corruption existing in the saloons and the industrial employers' increased concern for preventing accidents and increasing the efficiency of workers.

The Anti-Saloon League, founded in 1893, led the state prohibition drives of 1906–13. During World War I a temporary Wartime Prohibition Act was passed to save grain for use as food. By January 1920 prohibition was already in effect in 33 states covering 63 percent of the total population. In 1917 the resolution for submission of the Prohibition Amendment to the states received the necessary two-thirds vote in Congress; the amendment was ratified on Jan. 29, 1919, and went into effect on Jan. 29, 1920. On Oct. 28, 1919, the National Prohibition Act, popularly known as the Volstead Act (after its promoter, Congressman Andrew J. Volstead), was enacted, providing enforcement guidelines.

Federal government support of enforcement of Prohibition varied considerably during the 1920s. Illegal manufacture and sales of liquor went on in the United States on a large scale. In general, Prohibition was enforced wherever the population was sympathetic to it. In the large cities, where sentiment was strongly opposed to Prohibition, enforcement was much weaker than in rural areas and small towns. Increased price of liquor and beer, however, meant that the working classes probably bore the restrictions of urban Prohibition to a far greater degree than the middle-class or upper class segments of the population.

Figure 10 Excerpt from "Prohibition," *The New Encyclopaedia Britannica,* 1988 Edition.

formation, they are useful to researchers seeking to limit and focus topics and needing background information. You should understand, however, that college-level research essays cannot be developed from encyclopedias and other reference books. Encyclopedias are for preliminary research only.

TALK WITH OTHERS

Some people find that they do their best thinking when testing their ideas in conversation with others. If dialogue stimulates your thinking, then find a classmate or friend who will listen to your ideas for topics and ask good questions that might help you select and focus one topic. Because of their knowledge, instructors also make good sounding boards. Most are happy to discuss possible topics with students and may provide good suggestions for narrowing and focusing a topic and locating useful sources. Instructors (and probably friends, too) will be most receptive if you have some topics to propose and are seeking help in choosing one topic or in deciding on an approach to a chosen topic. If you confess to having no ideas for a course-related topic to study, be prepared for your instructor to suggest that you try some of the search strategies discussed here first and then return to the office for conversation about several concrete possibilities.

WRITING A THESIS OR STATEMENT OF PURPOSE

Once you have selected and narrowed a topic, you should write a tentative thesis, statement of purpose, or research question to guide planning and the search for sources. Some instructors will ask to see a statement—from a sentence to a paragraph long—to be approved before you proceed with your research. Others may require a one-page proposal that will include a tentative thesis or statement of purpose, a basic organizational plan, and a description of the types of sources to be used. Even if your instructor does not require such a statement, you need to write something for *your* benefit: to direct your reading and thinking. The student who decided to study Marc Chagall as a surrealist can make this distinction between topic and thesis:

Topic: Marc Chagall as a surrealist

Thesis: Marc Chagall is a representative of the surrealist school of modern art.

Better yet, the student can take some of the ideas from her freewriting and prepare a statement of purpose:

Statement of purpose: To show that Marc Chagall is a representative of the surrealist school of modern art by defining surrealism and related terms such as expressionism, dadaism, and magic realism and by demonstrating that characteristics of these elements of modern art can be found in Chagall's painting.

Clearly, the statement of purpose is the better guide to research because it already incorporates a strategy for developing and supporting the student's thesis.

The art student was fortunate to be able to develop her thinking so fully before beginning her reading, but not all researchers start with as much understanding of their subject as she had. At times you may choose a topic that interests you but about which you know very little. When this is the case you will need a more open-ended purpose statement or a research question rather than a tentative thesis. Consider, for instance, the situation of the history student studying the effects of Prohibition. Although an encyclopedia article suggested an approach, he cannot, at this stage, write even a tentative thesis. He can write a broad research question or, better yet, a statement of purpose that suggests some possible approaches to the topic.

Topic: The effects of Prohibition

Research question: What were the effects of Prohibition on the United States?

Statement of purpose: To examine the effects of Prohibition on the United States in the 1920s (and possibly to consider some long-term effects, depending on the amount of material on the topic); specifically, to look at the varying effects on urban and rural areas and on different classes in society.

Of course, researchers generating their own data will not be able to write a tentative thesis, but they, too, will need to begin with a research question and then some decisions about a strategy or methodology for obtaining and analyzing data. Suppose you want to answer this research question: "Do the various techniques or appeals used in ads for liquor change when the audience for the ads changes?" How do you proceed? First, you need to set limits on your study and then devise your strategy. Will you study all forms of liquor advertising? Mixing forms really complicates any study, so you decide to examine print ads only, at least to begin with. "All kinds of liquor?" is perhaps the next question to answer. For the moment, you decide yes, but this decision can be reexamined after you start collecting ads. "All kinds of audiences?" Remembering that your initial interest in the project stemmed from an awareness that ads for station wagons seem to appear in women's magazines, not men's magazines, you decide to limit your study to these same two audiences. Now you will need to select representative men's and women's magazines, choose a time period (perhaps the last six months), and then collect all liquor ads from the selected magazines for those months. You will also need to find and study relevant sources on advertising strategies to enlarge your understanding of selling techniques used in print ads. Asking yourself key questions is a good way to limit and focus a research project.

As a guide to focusing a topic to generate a thesis or research question, remember that every field of study has its terms, its approaches, its ways of categorizing subject matter. Literary studies, for example, can analyze elements of a work such as *setting, plot structure, character, point of view, style,* and *symbol.* The student who wants to do a paper "on Hemingway" limits her study because of time constraints to *The Sun Also Rises* and one other novel, *A Farewell to Arms.* Having learned in class about the traits of the Hemingway hero, but fascinated by Hemingway's female characters Brett Ashley and Catherine Barkley, she decides to study these two *characters* to see if they also meet the guidelines of the Hemingway hero.

Literary studies also reveal different approaches to criticism, including *new criticism, mythic criticism, Marxist criticism,* and *reader-response criticism,* among others. In addition, literary works are classified in various ways—for example, as *comedy, tragedy, science fiction,* and *fantasy.* Both philosophical differences in approach to a field's subject matter and a field's classification system can lead to debates over definitions and the classifying of specific works. Such debates offer researchers ways of approaching a topic and establishing an interesting research question. In a modern drama course, for instance, you must do some study of Arthur Miller's *Death of a Salesman.* Remembering the instructor's early lectures on the various forms of drama, you select the topic "Tragedy and Miller's *Death of a Salesman.*" Your research question then becomes: "Is *Death of a Salesman* a tragedy?" Reviewing your class notes about tragedy, you develop the following statement of purpose:

I will answer the question "Is Miller's *Death of a Salesman* a tragedy?" I will study Aristotle's definition of tragedy in the *Poetics* and
also consider if his definition needs to be altered in any way to adjust
to the modern world. I will see if the play meets Aristotle's definition, and if it does not in some respects, I will consider if the differences can be explained by differences in time and culture. At this
point, I think that the play should be considered a tragedy.

If you begin your research with a tentative thesis, try to think of it as
a guide to research, not necessarily the exact thesis you will end up de-
fending in your paper. As you learn more about your topic, you might
change your mind—actually reverse your position—or you might change
the focus of your study and need to reflect that change in a revised thesis.
No instructor will hold you to an approved thesis if you find that logic or
the evidence points you in a different direction.

KEEPING A RESEARCH JOURNAL

The place to start work on your statement of purpose is in your *research
notebook or journal*. Some instructors teaching the research process in
composition courses will require a journal or log as part of the project;
many more will recommend that you keep a journal for your own benefit. Keeping a journal means having a place to record new ideas, vent
frustrations, prepare a work list for each week, and rejoice in steps completed. As you review what you have written, you can be encouraged by
seeing progress made—or alerted to the fact that you have not yet spent
much time thinking about your project and that you need to get going
now. Your completed journal, whether submitted to an instructor or not,
provides a detailed account of the evolution of your paper. As such, it can
be a guide to future projects, telling you much about how you think and
work, perhaps even what steps should be handled differently another
time. For example, if your journal reveals many problems in gathering
sources, the dates of your recorded frustrations may also reveal that you
did not start your search for sources promptly enough. A journal that
teaches this lesson alone is a worthwhile document.

Keep your journal in a separate spiral notebook, in a separate file in
your word processor, if you prefer, or on the blank pages provided for
this purpose at the end of the text. Prepare pages in a log format: Have
two narrow columns on the left for recording each date and the amount
of time spent and then use the rest of each page for recording your entries. Follow these guidelines for writing entries.

- **Record all work sessions,** including time spent locating sources, reading, thinking, taking notes, writing, and typing. Remember to include the time you spend reading this handbook. Make entries specific, dividing a block of time spent in the library, for example, into actual time spent searching for sources and that spent reading reference and reserve materials.

- **Record ideas on your topic.** Use your journal as a place for freewriting or brainstorming, for drafting a purpose statement, for noting ideas as they develop throughout your study.

- **Record the completion of any required steps in the process.** For example, note when you met the due dates for a statement of purpose, a working bibliography, and/or the first draft. Reward yourself for work accomplished.

- **Record problems, frustrations, distractions.** Take out your frustrations on your journal, not on the librarian or your roommate, neither one of whom is responsible for the book you need not being on the shelf. After recording problems, take time to think about solutions, and record those, too, when they are found.

- **Record plans for work.** Draw up weekly work sheets, listing specific research tasks in the library or the time you will set aside for writing.

- **Record entries on a regular, frequent basis,** preferably after each work session. Let your journal writing be a way to keep you involved in and progressing through your project.

ESTABLISHING A SCHEDULE

If the way to avoid feeling overwhelmed by a complex task is to have a plan, then you certainly need to establish a plan for completing your research project. Your instructor may help you in this by setting dates for completing some steps in the process. Instructors often require a conference with each student, at which time the student must have a tentative thesis or statement of purpose and, possibly, a partial list of sources as well. If a conference date is set as well as a due date for the project, then you need to establish two more dates for yourself: a date for completing your research and a date for completing your draft. Make sure to set a draft completion date that is several days—at least—before the project's due date so that you have time to revise your paper and prepare a final version to submit on time.

If your instructor does not expect to see a statement of purpose or partial bibliography, then you must add completion dates for these steps to your own schedule. Although "poking around" in the library can be fun as you search for ideas for topics, you must be practical, too, and set a deadline for deciding on a topic. Similarly, you can spend a lot of time reading about your topic, but at some point you must get on with the writing of the paper. Deadlines will keep you moving forward, through the steps in the process, to a completed project.

Chapter 2

Locating
Sources

A college library is a marvelous place, arguably a college's single most important facility serving both students and faculty. Perhaps this is why the college library is usually strategically—and symbolically— located near the center of the campus. You may already know your library, at least some parts of it, because you have used reserved reading materials for other courses or you have used some of the search strategies discussed in Chapter 1 to develop your research topic. But if the library is still a mystery to you, even intimidating, or if your familiarity is limited to one area of a large and complex facility, then take time to learn about your library's arrangement, hours of operation, regulations, and procedures for obtaining materials. You will save time in the long run if you take time at the beginning of your research project to learn your way around and understand how to get the sources you need from the general books and periodicals collection. Then, too, the knowledge you gain is transferable, for libraries are more alike than different; once

27

you learn how to find materials in one, you will be at home in most others.

College libraries, with their emphasis on research, have experienced many changes in techniques for retrieving and storing information. As you become acquainted with your library, you may initially feel somewhat lost among all the new procedures and equipment. You will soon find that each new application of computer technology is an advantage to research, even though changes take some getting used to. Probably the only inconvenience to the user can be found in the shifting of periodicals from paper to microform, for the readers can be a bit hard on the eyes. The advantage of microfilm and microfiche, however, is obvious, for saving storage space means saving money. Most computer applications actually make research easier and provide access to materials not previously available in many libraries. This chapter will instruct you in both the new technology and services and the standard tools of research you may not yet understand. But first you need a quick tour of the library.

KNOWING YOUR LIBRARY

Circulation Desk

Located in the center of the library or near the main entrance is the circulation desk. Here you can receive information about the library's procedures and also check out and return materials, a process probably now handled on a computer terminal. The circulation desk is also the place to learn the status of a book you cannot find on the shelf. If records show that the work is checked out, you can place a hold on it and be notified when the work is returned to the library.

Book Catalog

The chief guide to your library's book collection is the book catalog, traditionally called the card catalog because at one time book catalogs were on 3 × 5 cards in drawers. Now, however, many book catalogs are on microfiche cards read in a viewer, on microfilm already placed in a reader, or "online," that is, called up on computer terminals. The book catalog area will probably be near the circulation desk.

Stacks

A library's book collection is generally divided into three categories. First is the general collection, those books housed on long rows of shelves, usually called *stacks*. These books, making up most of the book collection, circulate for a several-week period and can sometimes be renewed for an additional period. Most but not all college library stacks are open to students; that is, you are expected to find the books you need by using their classification or "call" number and then bring them to the circulation desk for processing. If the stacks are not open, then you must complete a request slip for each book and wait for runners to bring the requested books to the circulation desk.

Reference Collection

Placed in a separate area or room is the reference collection, those books of a general nature essential to research that therefore cannot be checked out. Included in the reference collection are general encyclopedias and dictionaries, atlases, bibliographies, and many handbooks, manuals, and specialized encyclopedias arranged around the reference area by classification number. Reference books are listed in the book catalog but designated by the abbreviation *Ref* above the book's classification number. Located in the reference area are the reference desk and, behind it, the single most valuable resource in the room: the reference librarian. Although reference librarians cannot find research topics for you, they can help you find information or the right research tools for your project. The reference area is also the place to go for computer searches of databases, a new strategy for obtaining lists of sources and even full texts of articles.

Reserve Collection

In large libraries the collection of books and articles on reserve will be located in a separate reading room; in smaller libraries reserve materials will usually be found on shelves behind the circulation desk. Some reserve materials can be checked out for overnight or up to several days; others, on "closed" reserve, must be used in the library. The reserve collection consists of works that instructors consider essential aids to their courses; the checkout times have been limited so that more students have access to them.

Periodicals Collection

A library's periodicals collection consists of popular magazines, scholarly journals, and newspapers—works that are issued periodically. The collection can generally be found in a separate area or room in the library. As you tour your library, check to see if indexes to periodicals are located in the reference area or in the periodicals area. Often located with periodicals is the library's collection of pamphlets, brochures, and bulletins, useful sources of information from government and industry. These materials are collected in what is called the *vertical file,* shelves or file drawers in which pamphlets are organized alphabetically by subject.

Some libraries allow certain periodicals to circulate; most do not, so you will want to find a quiet place to "settle in" for reading and taking notes on articles relevant to your topic. (Your alternative is to feed change into the copy machines.)

Interlibrary Loans

As impressive as your library's collection may seem, it still may not have a particular work that you need. Before despairing, explore your library's interlibrary loan procedures. In many areas where several colleges are found, the schools have formed consortia, allowing students at one school to check out books at another's library. Other cooperative arrangements include statewide catalog listings in each library (indicating if there is a library in the state with the book or periodical you need that can then be requested on loan) and the International Online Computer Library Center (see page 41). Always your best choice is to go yourself to a nearby library to obtain what you need rather than to wait for interlibrary loan delivery. Still, if you start your search for sources early, you can take advantage of the interlibrary loan service.

Nonprint Collection

Your library's book and periodicals collection is enhanced by a variety of audiovisual materials. Learn the location and general content of the records, tapes, and discs, for these are designed to supplement course study, especially in languages, art, and music, and can also be valuable for some research projects.

Photocopiers

Most libraries provide several coin-operated photocopying machines and even change machines as well. These give you the alternative of studying noncirculating materials in your room. Photocopied materials must of course be fully documented in your paper, and there are restrictions on copyrighted materials beyond your personal use.

Once acquainted with your library's layout and services, you need to understand in detail how to use its major tools for locating sources. Since there are a great many sources and many tools for locating them, you will also want to think about which resources are most useful for a particular study. The following chart suggests a general plan of action for each of four different search goals. Observe that for one research project you might need to use resources in three of the four categories: the first to get started, the second to obtain background information, and then either the third or fourth category to pursue the study of your particular research subject. Use the chart as a help in organizing your understanding of the many resources explained in the following pages. Because you are likely to need books regardless of your search goal, the discussion of sources will begin with the book catalog.

USING LIBRARY REFERENCE SOURCES: A GENERAL GUIDE

To Narrow and Focus a Topic, Use:

general encyclopedias (44; 18–21)
book indexes (41–43, 47–48)
book tables of content (15–16)
periodical indexes, especially computerized indexes such as *InfoTrac* (48–51)

To Obtain Background Information on a Topic, Use:

specialized encyclopedias, handbooks, etc. (40–41)
biographical dictionaries (46–47)
other specialized dictionaries (44)
atlases, almanacs (44–46)
histories (32–41)

*To Obtain Sources on Current Topics—For Assignments in
Composition Courses—Use:*

the book catalog (32–40)
The Reader's Guide to Periodical Literature (49–50)
Magazine Index/Plus (InfoTrac) (49–50)
Newspaper Index (52)
New York Times Index (51–52)
Vertical File Index (to locate pamphlets) (56–57)
government documents ⎫
interviews   ⎪ sources outside the library;
correspondence   ⎬ use as appropriate. (66–73)
television programs   ⎭

*To Obtain Sources for Topics in a Subject Area—For Assignments in
Specific Disciplines—Use:*

the book catalog (32–40)
magazine and newspaper indexes listed above, as appropriate (49–
    52)
specialized indexes for discipline, e.g., *Art Index*, PAIS, *Social Sciences
    Index, MLA International Bibliography* (53–60)
citation indexes for discipline (61–64)
Dissertation Abstracts International (59–62)
online database search (64–67)
sources outside the library, as appropriate (66–73)

LOCATING BOOKS

Regardless of the catalog's format—card, microform, online—the information provided is essentially the same, and the access points are similar:
author, title, and subject.

The Book Catalog

The book catalog contains at least three entries for each book: the author
entry, the title entry, and one or more subject entries. Some libraries file
author, title, and subject entries together in one alphabetical listing. Others create three catalogs or combine author and title entries in one catalog and subject entries in another. Whatever method your library uses,
certain conventions for filing usually apply. Knowing which catalog to

use and how the filing system works will speed your search for the books you need.

AUTHOR CATALOG

Authors are filed alphabetically with the last name first. This catalog also includes editors, translators, illustrators, and organizations that "author" publications. Under Library of Congress filing rules, when several types of authors have the same name, the order of filing is (1) person (Raleigh, Sir Walter), (2) place or thing (Raleigh, Chamber of Commerce; Raleigh, North Carolina). Names beginning with *M'*, *Mac*, or *Mc* are filed under *Mac*, and abbreviations such as *Dr.*, *U.S.*, or *St.* are filed according to the spelling of the complete word: *Doctor*, *United States*, or *Saint*. Names beginning with *de* or *von* may be filed by ignoring these prefixes or may appear under *D* or *V*. For example, the painter de Kooning is filed as if his name were Dekooning, but the writer de Maupassant is filed under *M*. You should, therefore, check both spellings or ask a librarian for guidance. Many libraries, particularly those with computer catalogs, have adopted "file as is" rules. These rules would, for example, place names beginning with *Mc* in the *Mc*'s, not under *Mac*. Most book catalogs continue to alphabetize word by word rather than letter by letter, as in dictionaries and telephone books. The system used will make a difference in order, as this example shows.

Word by Word	Letter by Letter
San Diego	Sand, George
San Francisco	San Diego
Sand, George	San Francisco

TITLE CATALOG

Title cards contain the same information as author cards but include the title repeated across the top of the card. Title entries are filed alphabetically word by word, excluding *A, An,* and *The* at the beginning of titles. Thus *The Great Gatsby* is filed under *G*, not *T*. Titles beginning with a number are filed according to the spelling of the numeral, so *300 Minor Repairs* will be found in the *T*'s. If you know the title of a book (for example, *The Story of Art*) but not its author, use the title catalog (or an undivided catalog) and look under *S*.

SUBJECT CATALOG

This catalog contains entries filed alphabetically word by word according to the subject heading, printed at the top of the entry in capital letters. Subject headings include people (WILLIAMS, TENNESSEE; ROOSEVELT, ELEANOR), topics (GOVERNMENT AND THE PRESS; POP ART), and place names (CANADA; SAN FRANCISCO). Since academic libraries use the Library of Congress subject heading system for books, you can most efficiently use the subject catalog by first looking in the *Library of Congress Subject Headings (LCSH)*. This three-volume work (12th edition, 1989) lists subject headings used in the subject catalog, so you do not have to try to guess what headings have been used that would be relevant to your topic. Using the *LCSH* eliminates the frustration similar to looking in the Yellow Pages of the phone book under *Gas Stations* when you need instead to look in the *S*'s under *Service Stations*.

Books listed under a specific subject heading are filed alphabetically by the author's last name. When many books exist on a subject, such as BANKS AND BANKING, further subdivisions under that subject heading may be used to classify books; these subheadings are generally arranged alphabetically. But when the subject is HISTORY, subheadings are arranged both alphabetically and chronologically. For example:

Banks and Banking		History
Bank accounts		Ancient
Bank directors		Methodology
Consumer credit	Subheadings	Modern—16th century
Trust companies		Modern—18th century

The order of entries under each subheading is alphabetical by author.

UNDIVIDED CATALOG

You need to be alert to two filing customs usually followed in an undivided catalog. (1) When the same word is an author's last name, a place name used as a subject heading, and the title of a book, the entries are filed in that order:

Author (person)	Rivers, Larry
Subject heading (place)	RIVERS IN LITERATURE
Title (thing)	Rivers of Darkness (novel)

(2) Books both by and about an author are filed in this order: books by the author, books coauthored by the author, books edited by the author, books about the author (biographies), and books about the author's works (studies). Some microform catalogs, however, no longer follow this custom and use a strictly alphabetical listing.

Catalog Entries

Each catalog entry contains a wealth of helpful information in addition to a book's author, title, and classification or call number (the number by which the book is shelved in the library).

CARD OR MICROFORM CATALOGS

Figure 11 shows a sample entry for card and microform catalogs with an explanation of its details. When preparing a list of potential sources (your working bibliography) for your project, study each entry carefully and copy all needed and useful information, including:

1. *Call number.* This is necessary to locate the book in the library.
2. *Author, title, facts of publication.* This information is essential for correct documentation of all sources.

Figure 11 Annotated Catalog Entry.

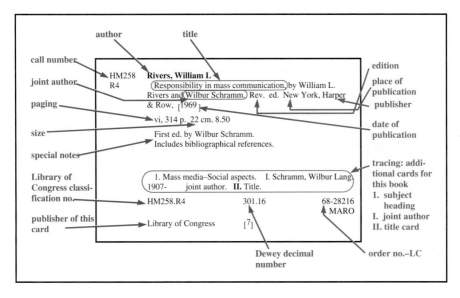

3. *Paging.* The length of the book will help you gauge the extent of coverage and help you plan your study time.

4. *Special notes.* Always check here to see if the book contains a bibliography, another list of potential sources for your research project.

5. *Tracing information.* Note the subject headings under which you will find an entry for this book and check them in the catalog for additional books on your topic.

ONLINE CATALOGS

When using a computer catalog, you will obtain the same information, but it will appear on the screen in a different format. If you begin by typing in an author's name, the screen will display all books by that author in the library's collection. Similarly, if you begin your search with a subject heading (e.g., *Mass media—Social aspects*), the screen will display all the library's books listed under that subject. In each case, you will need a second command to obtain the book's call number and location information. Figure 12 illustrates such a screen display from one online catalog. Other catalog systems will vary the format somewhat, but all will provide enough bibliographic information to identify the book and circulation information for locating the book.

Notice that the circulation-information screen does not provide complete bibliographic information, notes about the book, or tracings (subject headings). You will need another transaction to obtain all the bibliographic information necessary for documentation in your paper, or

Figure 12 Online Circulation Entry.

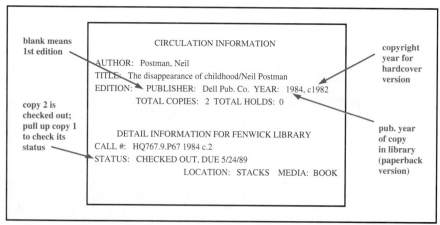

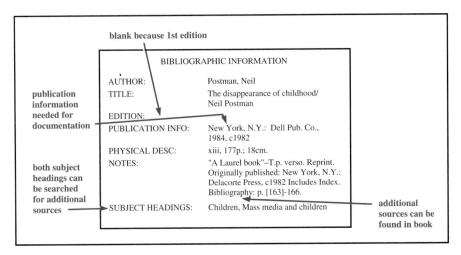

Figure 13 Online Bibliographic Entry.

you will have to remember to obtain that information from the front pages of the book when you locate it. If your online system separates circulation and bibliographic information, you would be wise to take the few seconds required to pull up the second screen of information and complete your bibliography card. (See Figure 13).

Classification Systems

Books are shelved in libraries according to either the Dewey decimal system or the Library of Congress classification system, two standardized codes combining numbers and letters that classify books by subject.

THE DEWEY DECIMAL SYSTEM

The Dewey decimal system is named for its creator (Melvil Dewey) and for the classification of subjects by divisions of 10. Figure 14 shows the system's classification of knowledge from 000 to 990 in divisions of 10. These sections are then further divided, even to the addition of a decimal number. For example, 940.56 for Helen Andrews's *New Insights on World War II*. This system can include a second number, the author number, created from the first letter of the author's last name, a code number given to that author, and the first letter of the book's title (excluding *A*, *An*, and *The*). Thus the complete call number for Andrews's

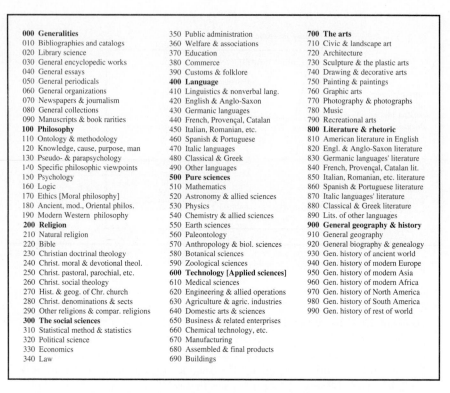

000 **Generalities**	350 Public administration	700 **The arts**
010 Bibliographies and catalogs	360 Welfare & associations	710 Civic & landscape art
020 Library science	370 Education	720 Architecture
030 General encyclopedic works	380 Commerce	730 Sculpture & the plastic arts
040 General essays	390 Customs & folklore	740 Drawing & decorative arts
050 General periodicals	400 **Language**	750 Painting & paintings
060 General organizations	410 Linguistics & nonverbal lang.	760 Graphic arts
070 Newspapers & journalism	420 English & Anglo-Saxon	770 Photography & photographs
080 General collections	430 Germanic languages	780 Music
090 Manuscripts & book rarities	440 French, Provençal, Catalan	790 Recreational arts
100 **Philosophy**	450 Italian, Romanian, etc.	800 **Literature & rhetoric**
110 Ontology & methodology	460 Spanish & Portuguese	810 American literature in English
120 Knowledge, cause, purpose, man	470 Italic languages	820 Engl. & Anglo-Saxon literature
130 Pseudo- & parapsychology	480 Classical & Greek	830 Germanic languages' literature
140 Specific philosophic viewpoints	490 Other languages	840 French, Provençal, Catalan lit.
150 Psychology	500 **Pure sciences**	850 Italian, Romanian, etc. literature
160 Logic	510 Mathematics	860 Spanish & Portuguese literature
170 Ethics [Moral philosophy]	520 Astronomy & allied sciences	870 Italic languages' literature
180 Ancient, mod., Oriental philos.	530 Physics	880 Classical & Greek literature
190 Modern Western philosophy	540 Chemistry & allied sciences	890 Lits. of other languages
200 **Religion**	550 Earth sciences	900 **General geography & history**
210 Natural religion	560 Paleontology	910 General geography
220 Bible	570 Anthropology & biol. sciences	920 General biography & genealogy
230 Christian doctrinal theology	580 Botanical sciences	930 Gen. history of ancient world
240 Christ. moral & devotional theol.	590 Zoological sciences	940 Gen. history of modern Europe
250 Christ. pastoral, parochial, etc.	600 **Technology [Applied sciences]**	950 Gen. history of modern Asia
260 Christ. social theology	610 Medical sciences	960 Gen. history of modern Africa
270 Hist. & geog. of Chr. church	620 Engineering & allied operations	970 Gen. history of North America
280 Christ. denominations & sects	630 Agriculture & agric. industries	980 Gen. history of South America
290 Other religions & compar. religions	640 Domestic arts & sciences	990 Gen. history of rest of world
300 **The social sciences**	650 Business & related enterprises	
310 Statistical method & statistics	660 Chemical technology, etc.	
320 Political science	670 Manufacturing	
330 Economics	680 Assembled & final products	
340 Law	690 Buildings	

Figure 14 Dewey Decimal Classifications (the 100 Main Divisions).

book is 940.56/A566n. A complete author number is necessary if a library needs a unique call number for each book. Many small libraries using Dewey add only the first letter of the author's last name after the primary classification number.

THE LIBRARY OF CONGRESS CLASSIFICATION SYSTEM

The Library of Congress (LC) system, now used by most college libraries, provides a more complete and logical system of classifying books and gives every book its unique call number. It begins with 21, rather than 10, broad categories, each designated by a letter. These broad categories are then divided by adding a second letter. Numbers are then used to further subdivide a subject area. Figure 15 lists the 21 initial categories, provides second-letter categories for many subject areas, and shows how numbers divide one category, the history of Great Britain. Finally, a third

A	General Works			
B	Philosophy and Religion			
BF	Psychology			
BL–BX	Religion			
C	History (General)			
D	History			
DA	Great Britain	DA	1–995	Great Britain
			20–690	England
			700–745	Wales
			750–890	Scotland
DC	France		900–995	Ireland
DD	Germany			
DE	Classical Antiquity			
DF	Greece			
DK	Russia			
DS	Asia			
DT	Africa			
E	American History			
F	U.S. History (Local); Latin American and Canadian History			
G	Geography; Anthropology; Recreation			
H	Social Science			
HA	Statistics			
HB–HD	Economics			
HF	Commerce			
HG	Finance			
HM	Sociology			
J	Political Science			
K	Law			
L	Education			
M	Music			
N	Fine Arts			
P	Language and Literature			
PN	Television, Theater, and Journalism			
PR	English Literature			
PS	American Literature			
Q	Science			
QA	Mathematics			
R	Medicine			
S	Agriculture			
T	Technology			
U	Military Science			
V	Naval Science			
Z	Library Science			

Figure 15 Library of Congress Classification System.

line is used to designate a specific book by a particular author. Thus, a specific history text—for instance, George M. Trevelyan's *The English Revolution, 1688–1689*—would have the following LC number:

DA   (history of Great Britain)

452   (history in the period of James II, 1685–1688)

.T7   (author designation combining the first letter of the last name and a code number for the second letter of the last name)

Arrangement of Books on the Shelf

Whichever system your library uses, you will need the complete call number of a book to locate it on the shelf, so be sure to copy it accurately before looking in the stacks. Each book's call number is provided in the catalog entry and on the spine of the book, where it can be seen when the book is shelved. LC call numbers arrange books on the shelves in the order illustrated in Figure 16. Note that the third line is a decimal number; thus .K214 precedes .K26.

As you proceed with your search for books, use every available opportunity to add to your working bibliography. If you use the subject catalog, make a bibliography card for every book that might prove useful. Make a special note of books described as having bibliographies and examine those pages as soon as you locate each book. When in the stacks to obtain books, take a few minutes to look at the books near those you have listed, for those nearby will be in the same subject category. If a book you want is not in its proper place on the shelf, look above and below—even behind other books—to see if the one you need is lurking in the wrong place. You might even check the carts of books awaiting reshelving before becoming convinced that the book is not available. Serious researchers need to develop a "nose for books."

USING THE REFERENCE COLLECTION

The research process often begins with the reference collection. Reference materials can be used first to suggest and narrow topics, then to provide background information and an overview of a topic, and finally to supply particular facts needed to develop the topic. In addition to dictionaries, encyclopedias, and handbooks of all kinds, the reference col-

Figure 16 Model of Shelf Order for Books.

1. alphabetical	PQ	PR	PR	PR	PR	PR
2. numerical	52	351	620	620	620	620
3. decimal	.T36	.M58	.K21	.K214	.K26	.R73

lection includes important research tools: bibliographies and indexes. No research guide can begin to explain the wealth of reference materials available to researchers, but we can examine the most important for most researchers. In addition, you will want to familiarize yourself with the key sources in your specialized field of study by examining the list of works presented, by subject field, in Appendix B; by browsing through your library's reference collection in the classification numbers appropriate to your field; and by seeking guidance from reference librarians. When approaching the librarians for help, try to ask specific questions or explain your needs clearly, take notes of titles they recommend, and listen intently to directions for using materials. And when using any reference work, take a few minutes to check the work's date (some information becomes outdated quickly), purpose, and organization. In these ways you can supplement the following discussion and develop your competence with reference materials.

The Reference Librarian's Guides and Bibliographies

Serious researchers are smart to become familiar with the reference guides relied on by librarians: the trade and general bibliographies. One of the most important, *Books in Print* (New York: Bowker, 1948 to date), lists—by author, title, and subject—all books currently in print that are available from publishers or distributors in the United States. You can check here to see if a book is still in print, to obtain bibliographic information, to obtain a publisher's address (if you want to order a book directly from the publisher), and, by using the subject listing, to locate books not in your library but perhaps available on interlibrary loan. Figure 17 shows only some of the many books on dinosaurs listed in the *Subject Guide to Books in Print* (New York: Bowker, 1957 to date). Other trade bibliographies to know include:

Cumulative Book Index. New York: Wilson, 1900 to date.
Lists all books published in the English language, not just those in print.

The National Union Catalog: A Cumulative Author List.
Ann Arbor: Edwards, 1953 to date. On microfiche since 1983.

Online Computer Library Center (OCLC).
Started regionally in the 1970s, now international in use and in contributions to the database. For many libraries, the new tool for cataloging, acquisitions, database searching, and interlibrary loans.

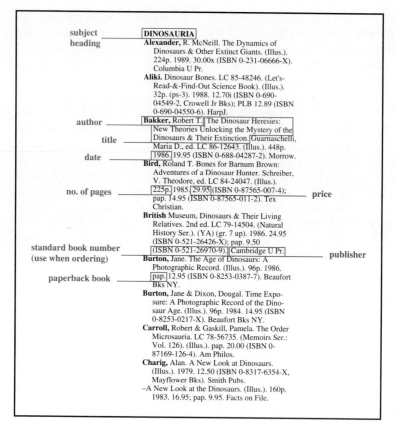

Figure 17 From *Subject Guide to Books in Print,* 1989–90.

Publishers Weekly. New York: Bowker, 1872 to date.

A good source of information on new books.

Ulrich's International Periodicals Directory. Ed. Merle Rohinsky. 15th ed. New York: Bowker, 1973.

Here you will find information needed for ordering reprints of articles and locating foreign periodicals.

Union List of Serials in Libraries of the United States and Canada. 3rd ed. New York: Wilson, 1965. Supplements: *New Serials Titles,* Washington, DC: Library of Congress, 1953 to date.

Use this work to find a library subscribing to a needed periodical not held by your library.

General bibliographies and guides to reference works can be useful to researchers as well as to librarians. These bibliographies and guides direct you to reference works, bibliographies, or indexes in various subject areas. In other words, they initiate a two-step process of guiding researchers to particular books on specific subjects by providing a list of works that contain bibliographic listings. One example is the *Bibliographic Index: A Cumulative Bibliography of Bibliographies* (New York: Wilson, 1938 to date). Originally covering 1937 to 1942 but updated with yearly supplements, *Bibliographic Index* indexes, by both author and subject, books and articles that contain bibliographies. The excerpt from 1984 shown in Figure 18 lists a book and an article on television and young viewers containing bibliographies on the topic. Here are additional reference guides worth knowing:

Besterman, Theodore. *A World Bibliography of Bibliographies.* 4th ed. 5 vols. 1963.

Gates, Jean Key. *Guide to the Use of Books and Libraries.* 4th ed. 1974.

Hillard, James. *Where to Find What: A Handbook to Reference Service.* Rev. ed. 1984.

Sheehy, Eugene P., ed. *Guide to Reference Books.* 10th ed. 1986.

Figure 18 From *Bibliographic Index,* 1984.

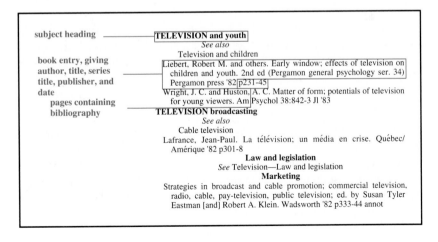

Basic Reference Works

When most researchers think of the reference collection, they envision the many dictionaries, handbooks, and encyclopedias providing information and factual details in a condensed format. The following discussion reviews the basic reference works that support learning in many subject fields.

DICTIONARIES

If you need the spelling or current definitions of a word, use a good desk dictionary. For specialized words, consult the appropriate subject dictionary; for foreign words, the appropriate foreign language dictionary. If you want to learn about a word's origin or definitions at an earlier time, the place to go is one of the unabridged or specialized dictionaries in your library. Here are four you should know about:

The Oxford English Dictionary. 20 vols. 2d ed. 1989.
> Known as the *OED*. A storehouse of information on English language use and word origins.

The Random House Dictionary of the English Language. 1987.

Webster's Third New International Dictionary of the English Language. 1986.

Craigie, William A., and James R. Hulbert. *Dictionary of American English on Historical Principles.* 4 vols. 1936–1944.

GENERAL ENCYCLOPEDIAS

Two multivolume encyclopedias found in most college libraries are the *Encyclopedia Americana* and the *Encyclopaedia Britannica*. Both are 30 volumes and revised annually. See pages 18–20 for a detailed discussion of the *Encyclopaedia Britannica*'s format.

ATLASES

Atlases should not be overlooked, for they provide much more than simple maps showing capital cities and the names of rivers. Historical atlases show, through maps and other graphics, changes in political geography and economic and cultural changes as well. Topographical atlases support studies in the earth sciences and provide information essential to many contemporary environmental issues. Just a few of the many good atlases are listed here.

Historical Atlas of the United States. National Geographic Society, 1988.

National Geographic Atlas of the World. 5th ed. National Geographic Society, 1981.

The Times Atlas of the World. 7th comprehensive ed. 1988.

The Times Atlas of World History. Ed. Geoffrey Barraclough. 1979.

QUOTATIONS, MYTHOLOGY, AND FOLKLORE

The following works are useful for understanding references or allusions unfamiliar to you in your reading. "To err is human; to forgive divine" may seem too well known to warrant identification by the author of a book you are reading, but if you do not recognize it, then you must look it up. Similarly, if you do not know who Apollo or Orpheus was, you need to refer to a book on mythology. Standard works include:

Bartlett, John. *Familiar Quotations.* 1983.

Frazer, Sir James G. *The Golden Bough.* 12 vols. 1907–1915.
Supplements. An exhaustive study of myths. A one-volume condensed version is available.

Funk and Wagnall's Standard Dictionary of Folklore, Mythology, and Legend. 1984.

Hamilton, Edith. *Mythology.* 1942 (paperback, 1971).
A brief but useful guide to Greek, Roman, and Norse myths.

Stevenson, Burton. *The Home Book of Quotations.* 1984.

ALMANACS AND YEARBOOKS

The following works will answer all kinds of questions about current events and provide statistical information on just about anything: how your congressional representative voted on a key bill, the number of people in college in a given year, income distribution in the United States, the size of the largest watermelon.

Congressional Record. 1873 to date.
Detailed information about activities of Congress. Issued daily during sessions.

Facts on File. 1940 to date.
Digest of important news events. Issued weekly.

Guinness Book of World Records. 1955 to date.

Information Please Almanac. 1947 to date.

Statesman's Year Book. 1864 to date.
>   Political and economic information of international scope. Issued every two years.

Statistical Abstract of the United States. 1878 to date.
>   Annual publication of the Bureau of the Census, providing information on American institutions and demographics.

World Almanac and Book of Facts. 1868 to date.

INDEXES TO BIOGRAPHICAL DICTIONARIES

Indexes tell researchers where to look for needed information. Biographical indexes direct you to appropriate biographical dictionaries. Here are two standard indexes:

Author Biography Master Index. 2d ed. 1984.
>   This index, arranged alphabetically by author, will tell you in which biographical dictionaries to look up entries for both living and deceased authors.

Biography and Genealogy Master Index. 8 vols. 1980.
>   This work indexes entries in 350 contemporary biographical reference sources. It is a good place to begin if you need to locate a biographical source for a person whose occupation or reason for fame is unknown to you.

BIOGRAPHICAL DICTIONARIES

Most libraries have an array of biographical dictionaries, some providing brief entries, others specializing by country or profession, still others offering full essays analyzing the life and contributions of famous people. The following are important research tools:

Universal

Contemporary Authors. 1962 to date.
>   Provides a biographical and bibliographic guide to current fiction and nonfiction writers and their books.

Current Biography. 1940 to date.
>   Provides articles on living persons of significance in a variety of fields throughout the world. Each volume contains a list of persons included, classified by profession.

International Who's Who. 1935 to date.
  Contains brief biographies of important persons from almost every country. Each new edition updates existing biographies and adds new ones.

Webster's New Biographical Dictionary. 1983.
  A one-volume biographical reference work, worldwide in scope, this dictionary has been enlarged with each new edition since its beginnings in 1943.

American

American Men and Women of Science (formerly *American Men of Science*). 17th ed. 1989.
  Provides brief sketches of more than 150,000 scientists. Lists degrees held and fields of specialization.

Dictionary of American Biography. 20 vols. 1928–1937. Supplementary volumes issued in 1944 and 1958.
  Offers reliable biographical and critical essays on important Americans no longer living.

Who Was Who in America. 60 vols. 1951–1973.
  Contains brief biographical sketches of Americans no longer living.

Who's Who in America. 1899 to date.
  Offers brief biographical sketches on living Americans. Continually updated.

Who's Who in American Women. 1958 to date.
  Contains brief articles on more than 24,000 women.

British

Dictionary of National Biography. 63 vols. 1885–1901. Reprinted in 22 vols., 1908–1909. Supplements to 1960.
  Supplies authoritative biographies of important English men and women no longer living.

Who's Who. 1849 to date.
  Offers biographical information on living English men and women.

ESSAY AND GENERAL LITERATURE INDEX

Begun in 1900, this index to a broad range of subject areas is published twice a year; a hardcover, permanent cumulation is then issued every five years. In this author and subject index, you will be directed to essays that

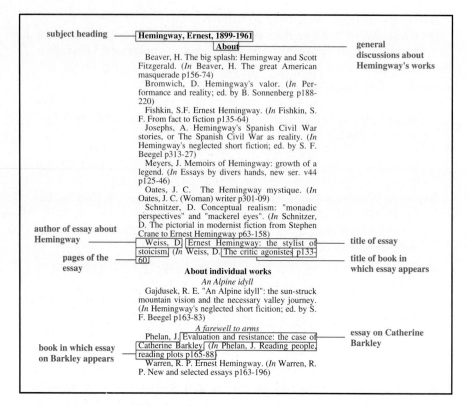

Figure 19 From *Essay and General Literature Index.*

appeared in books. Without checking the *Essay and General Literature Index,* you might otherwise overlook the book as a possible source of information on your topic. As Figure 19 reveals, several essays that might prove useful to the student's exploration of Brett Ashley and Catherine Barkley as Hemingway heroes can be located by using *Essay and General Literature Index.*

USING INDEXES TO PERIODICALS

Periodicals (popular magazines, newspapers, and scholarly journals) provide good source materials for research projects. Some of the most important, certainly the most up-to-date, studies of specialized topics are found in journal articles, and recent issues of newspapers and magazines

offer information and opinions on current events. Periodicals, usually located in a separate area of your library, are generally shelved alphabetically by title. Back issues of journals are bound in hardcover volumes or
placed on microform; current issues may be shelved with the bound volumes or on a separate rack. Current issues of newspapers are often stored
on rollers. Back issues of newspapers are usually on microfilm. Lists of a
library's periodicals collection (alphabetical by title and occasionally by
subject heading) are usually located at the circulation desk, at the reference desk, and in the periodicals area.

The most efficient way to discover articles on a particular subject is
to use one or more of the periodicals indexes. The most popular indexes
are described and illustrated below.

Indexes to Magazines

The Reader's Guide to Periodical Literature (1900 to date), probably the
most used index, combines author and subject headings that guide the
reader to about 200 popular magazines. Many of those indexed here, including *American Scholar, Psychology Today,* and *Science,* have articles of
value to undergraduate research. The *Reader's Guide* is a cumulative index, issued twice monthly (except monthly in July and August) and
bound in hardcover volumes annually. When a person is both author and
subject, articles *by* the person are given first, followed by articles *about*
him or her. Note in the sample entries in Figure 20 that information is
heavily abbreviated. Study the explanation provided and, when using the
index, check the list of periodicals found in the front of each volume for
the complete title of each magazine.

As with book catalogs, indexes to magazines are now also available in
microform and computer formats. Many students find *Magazine Index*
(microfilm) and *Magazine Index/Plus* (*Magazine Index* on CD-ROM)
convenient alternatives to the *Reader's Guide.* Both index over 400 magazines for the most current four years, and *Magazine Index/Plus* also includes the *New York Times* for the most current 60 days. *Magazine
Index/Plus,* referred to as *InfoTrac,* is a user-friendly computerized index
that guides you through your search, responding to your author or subject entries. (You may already have used *InfoTrac* in your search for a research topic; see pages 16–18.) The attached printer provides a list of the
citations you want copied. Although using the printer seems more convenient than preparing separate bibliography cards, if your instructor requires that you submit a partial bibliography during a conference on
your project, you will have to copy the citations onto cards—in the cor-

subject heading ———	**DINOSAURS**
	See also
	Dinamation International Corporation
	Birth of the dinosaurs [Petrified Forest National Park; cover story] S. Nash. il *National Parks* 63:16-23 N/D '89
	Could a cold heart stand a cold winter? [Australian dinosaurs; research by Thomas H. Rich and Patricia V. Rich] R. Monastersky. *Science News* 136:38 Jl 15 '89
title of article ———	The cycle of fate. J. S. Trefil. bibl il por *Modern Maturity* 32:60-4 D '89/Ja '90
volume number ———	The Dinosaur Discovery Kit. J. Zornberg. il *Home Office Computing* 7:96 N '89
page number ———	Dinosaur Discovery Kit [computer program] L. Eiser. il *Compute!* 11:118+ D '89
title of periodical ———	The dinosaur rip-off. S. J. Gould. *Natural History* p14+ Ag '89
	Dinosaur tracks found, on exhibit in Virginia [Culpeper quarry: research by Robert Weems] il *Earth Science* 42:8 Fall '89
	Dinosaur tragedy yields birth clues [research by Karl F. Hirsch] *Science News* 135:220 Ap 8 '89
	Dinosaurs galore! [educational software] C. S. Holzberg. il *Home Office Computing* 7:86+ Je '89
date: November 11, 1989 ———	Dinosaurs used their heads to beat the heat [work of J. Keith Rigby] R. Monastersky. il *Science News* 136:309 N 11 '89
article contains illustrations	Dragons and dinosaurs [Dinosaur Project findings in China and Alberta] P. J. Currie. il *Earth Science* 42:10-13 Summ '89
explanation of article ———	'Earth-shaker' found: seeing is believing this 50-ton monster [Seismosaurus] N. Hickey. il *TV Guide* 36:27-8 F 4-10 '89
	A fleet-footed Montana monster [Tyrannosaurus skeleton uncovered] il *U.S. News & World Report* 107:18 N 13 '89
article contains bibliography	Giant meteor impacts and great eruptions: dinosaur killers? G. S. Paul. bibl f il *BioScience* 39:162-72 Mr '89

Figure 20 From *Reader's Guide to Periodical Literature.*

rect format—before your conference. Note: *All entries in the various periodicals indexes must be rearranged into the correct documentation format for citation in your paper.* Keep in mind as well that these indexes cover only the most current four years; if you need articles on a less recent subject, you will have to use the *Reader's Guide* or another appropriate reference source.

Illustrating the speed with which updated technology is coming into the library is the newer CD-ROM index *General Periodicals Ondisc,* usually called *ProQuest.* Like *InfoTrac, ProQuest* is an index to articles in general interest magazines. But *ProQuest's* over 500 journals provide a greater range than those covered by *InfoTrac,* including more scholarly journals. Further, for each article indexed a brief abstract is included, and articles in over 200 of the journals indexed are available in full text that can be reproduced on the accompanying laser printer. *ProQuest* can often eliminate the frustration that comes from locating potentially useful articles only to learn that your library does not subscribe to the needed journal. The brief explanation of each article is also very helpful in judging the work's usefulness. On the other hand, *ProQuest* is more difficult to access than *InfoTrac* because it does not provide the list of suggested subtopics offered by *InfoTrac*. Instead, you need to find the right terms that will narrow the list of articles to those directly related to your topic. Note: Be sure to print a copy of the record for each article before printing the complete article. The index record will contain the information needed for your bibliography; the facsimile pages of the article may not provide all needed bibliographic information.

Indexes to Newspapers

Newspapers are a good source of information about contemporary topics. Since it is one of the most thorough and respected newspapers, the *New York Times* is available in most libraries; back issues are on microfilm. Become familiar with the *New York Times Index,* for it can guide you to articles as far back as the mid-nineteenth century. It is a subject index, issued twice each month and cumulated annually, with articles arranged chronologically under each subject heading. The *Index* provides a brief summary of each article. Figure 21 explains sample entries.

Newer and on microfilm and CD-ROM is the *National Newspaper Index.* This is a combined index, covering the most current three years, of five major newspapers: *New York Times, Wall Street Journal, Christian Science Monitor, Washington Post,* and *Los Angeles Times.* Like *Magazine*

Figure 21 Excerpt from *New York Times Index.*

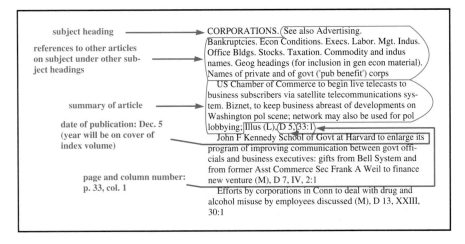

Index, National Newspaper Index indexes more sources, but covers only the last three years. It is your best choice *if* you are researching a current topic and *if* your library has back issues of some of these newspapers. If your library has only the *New York Times* on microfilm, then the *New York Times Index* is the best index to use because it will be faster. Additionally, the summaries of articles are longer, giving you a better idea of an article's usefulness to your project. An excerpt from *National Newspaper Index* is shown in Figure 22.

The newest newspaper index is the CD-ROM *NewsBank*, a selective index of articles from many (often small-town) newspapers that comes

Figure 22 Excerpt from *National Newspaper Index.*

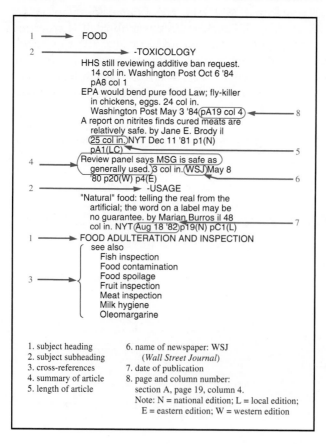

1. subject heading
2. subject subheading
3. cross-references
4. summary of article
5. length of article

6. name of newspaper: WSJ
   (*Wall Street Journal*)
7. date of publication
8. page and column number:
   section A, page 19, column 4.
   Note: N = national edition; L = local edition;
   E = eastern edition; W = western edition

with the articles themselves reproduced on microfiche. The advantage of this service is that if your library has the index, it will also have the articles and a microfiche reader-printer for using them. The disadvantage is that the index is by no means complete and relies, perhaps too heavily, on articles drawn from newspapers other than the "big" (reliable and detailed) papers. If you use *NewsBank,* special care must be exercised in citing your source; proper documentation of *NewsBank* articles is illustrated on page 101.

Indexes to Academic Journals

Although popular magazines and newspapers can provide many good articles for some undergraduate research topics, others will require the use of at least some academic journals. And as you progress into upper-level courses, you will be expected to rely primarily on the work of scholars. You can begin your work with scholarly articles by becoming acquainted with two useful general indexes to scholarly journals: *Social Sciences Index* and *Humanities Index.* Initially one index first called the *International Index* and then the *Social Sciences and Humanities Index,* these indexes have been divided since 1974. The *Social Sciences Index* covers articles on political science, psychology, sociology, economics, law, medical science, and related subjects. The student interested in studying terrorism on television can add sources from this index to enrich a bibliography of books and of articles from newspapers and popular magazines. The entries shown in Figure 23 are from the 1987 volume of *Social Sciences Index.*

Similarly, the student investigating Marc Chagall as a surrealist painter can use *Humanities Index,* for it covers articles on art, literature,

Figure 23 Excerpt from *Social Sciences Index.*

Terrorism in mass media
Format and symbols in TV coverage of terrorism in the United States and Great Britain. D. L. Altheide. bibl *Int Stud Q* 31:161-76 Je '87
Softly, softly. J. Baudrillard. *New Statesman* 113:44 Mr 6 '87
Television and terrorism: patterns of presentation and occurrence, 1969 to 1980. M. X. Delli Carpini and B. A. Williams. bibl *West Polit Q* 40:45-64 Mr '87
Why we need more but better coverage of terrorism. P. Clawson. *Orbis* 30:701-10 Wint '87

philosophy, folklore, history (since 1974), and related subjects. When she looks under the subject heading in the 1989 volume, she will find several articles of a general nature that might increase her understanding of surrealism, and a list of additional subject headings to check (see Figure 24). She can also check *Marc Chagall* as a subject heading.

Like the *Reader's Guide,* these two indexes are combined author and subject indexes. Also, the order of information in each entry and the abbreviations used are similar to those in the *Reader's Guide.* Note, though, that the journals indexed are quite different. Journals such as *International Studies Quarterly* and *Artforum* will not be found in the *Reader's Guide* or *Magazine Index.* There is one CD-ROM index, called *Academic Index,* that includes some scholarly journals. It looks just like *InfoTrac,* and it is probably located in the same reference area. Although it will broaden the range of your sources, *Academic Index* does not include nearly the number of scholarly journals indexed in the *Social Sciences* and *Humanities* indexes. But even these two research tools cannot include all the articles printed each year in the many hundreds of academic journals. Thus almost every major field of study has its own periodicals index (or annual bibliography) that lists articles (or both articles and books) published in that field. Some of these specialized reference tools are discussed later in this chapter; others can be found in the list of reference works organized by discipline in Appendix B.

Figure 24 Excerpt from *Humanities Index.*

Surrealism
> *See also*
Dadaism
Fantasy in art
Magic realism (Literature)
Pop art
The antipodes of surrealism: Salvador Dalí and Remedios Varo. G. Duran. il *Symposium* 42:297-311 Wint '89
A cinema of cruelty: Antonin Artaud. S. Barber. *Artforum* 28:163-6 O '89
Enrico Donati: Manhattan transfer. C. Ratcliff. il *Art Am* 77:175-80 My '89
A land of myth and dreams. N. Barrett. il *Aperture* no115:50-5 Summ '89
Memory palaces. W. Christenberry. il *Aperture* no115:46-9 Summ '89
The methodology of the marvelous. G. F. Orenstein. il *Symposium* 42:329-39 Wint '89
Purity. D. Cotton. *Crit Inq* 16:173-98 Aut '89
Toyen: toward a revolutionary art in Prague and Paris. W. Chadwick. *Symposium* 42:277-95 Wint '89

USING INDEXES TO GOVERNMENT
DOCUMENTS AND RELATED PUBLICATIONS

The federal government is, among other things, one of the country's largest publishing houses, each year printing tens of thousands of documents ranging from pamphlets to maps to monographs to multivolume reports. Some government documents are available without charge; others are for sale. Most libraries subscribe to two kinds of indexes to government documents:

Monthly Catalog of U.S. Government Publications.

Each monthly issue lists between 1500 and 3000 new entries, organized into four indexes: author, title, subject, and series report. For each document, the catalog provides sales information and complete bibliographic information.

The GPO Publications Reference File (PRF).

Issued bimonthly on microfiche, this is a total sales catalog organized into three sections in which the documents are arranged (1) by GPO stock number, (2) by Superintendent of Documents classification number, and (3) in a combined author, title, subject, agency series, and key words alphabetical list.

Documents can be obtained by calling (202) 783–3238 to place an order charged to a Visa or MasterCard account. Alternatively, order documents by mail, with payment enclosed, to:

Superintendent of Documents
U.S. Government Printing Office
Washington, DC 20402

Two other reference sources index government documents in addition to other works. Researchers in many fields should become acquainted with *PAIS*. The *Public Affairs Information Service Bulletin* indexes materials on public affairs and public policy. The bulletin includes articles, books, and public documents from the social sciences, economics, political science, public administration, international law, business, finance, and education. Issued four times a year and cumulated yearly in hardbound volumes, *PAIS* is international in scope, indexing works in six languages and emphasizing works that are strong on facts and statistics. The index includes a directory of publishers and organizations, providing

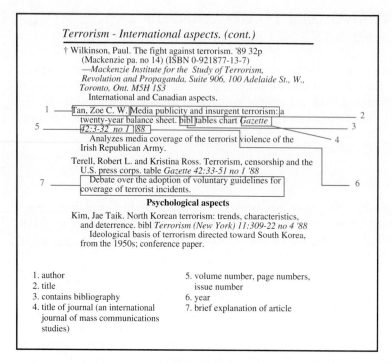

Figure 25 Excerpt from *Public Affairs Information Service Bulletin (PAIS).*

complete addresses. You can, then, write to such organizations as Urban Land Institute or Worldwatch Institute to obtain sources not available in your library. As Figure 25 illustrates, the researcher into terrorism on television will find useful materials indexed in *PAIS*.

You should also know the *Vertical File Index,* your reference guide to pamphlets. Published quarterly and cumulated semiannually, this is a subject and title index to pamphlets in English published in the United States and Canada. Like *PAIS,* the *Vertical File Index* covers both government and private-sector sources, briefly annotates each source, and includes information for ordering materials. (See Figure 26.)

USING SPECIALIZED REFERENCE WORKS

Although specialized indexes to materials in particular disciplines are most often used by graduate students and faculty members, undergradu-

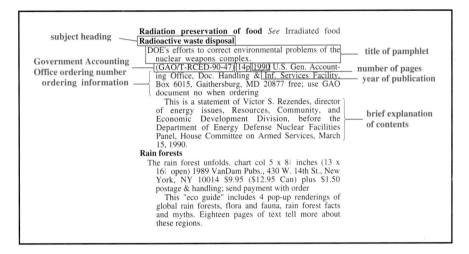

Figure 26 Excerpt from *Vertical File Index.*

ates should become aware of some of these tools and use them when appropriate to their research projects. Specialized indexes teach about the discipline in addition to adding scholarly sources to one's working bibliography.

MLA International Bibliography

Students in literature and language courses will want to use the *MLA International Bibliography,* an annual listing by the Modern Language Association of books, articles, and dissertations in the field. Entries are organized first geographically (French literature; American literature), next by period (1800–1899; 1900–1999), and then by individual author (Gustave Flaubert; Ernest Hemingway). Since 1981, items under each author are subdivided into general studies of the author, bibliographies, and then studies of particular works by the author.

Thus, the student interested in Hemingway would find, in 1986 alone, more than a page of entries under "Hemingway, Ernest": a dozen general works, a bibliographic article, works on his fiction in general, and many items on individual works, including 14 items under *The Sun Also Rises.* As Figure 27 reveals, there are some articles on the character Brett Ashley, articles that might prove helpful to the student's study of Brett and Catherine Barkley. The student will also learn from this index that

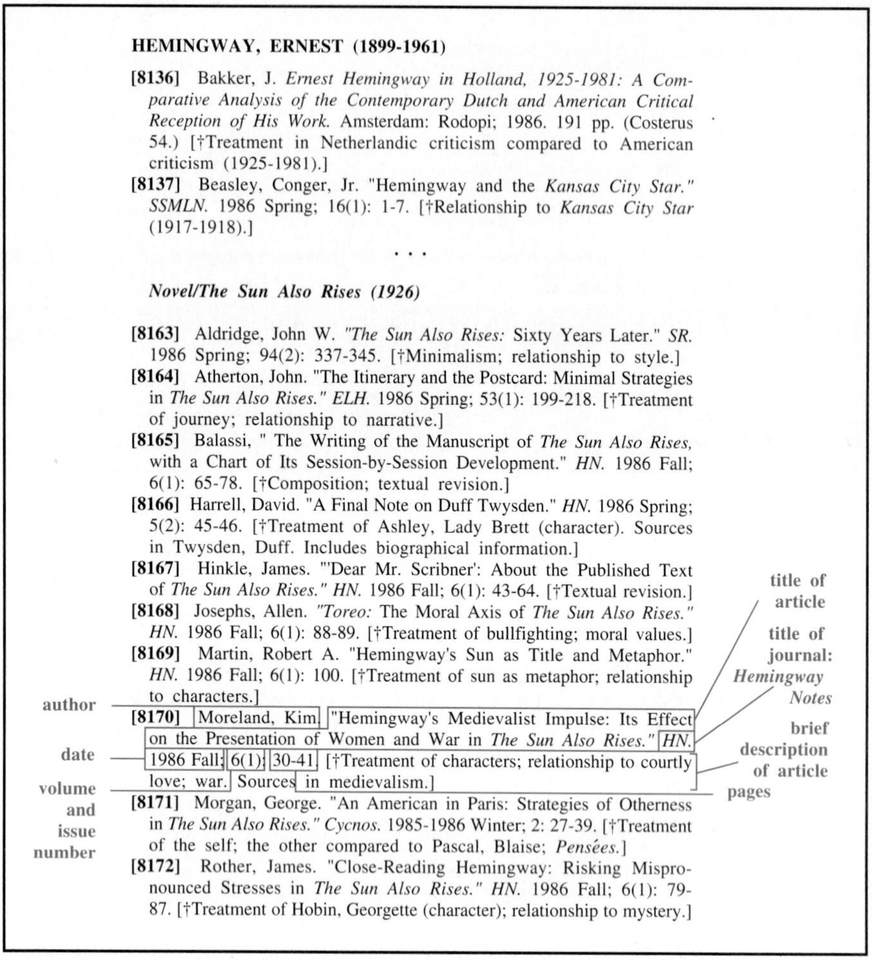

HEMINGWAY, ERNEST (1899-1961)

[8136] Bakker, J. *Ernest Hemingway in Holland, 1925-1981: A Comparative Analysis of the Contemporary Dutch and American Critical Reception of His Work.* Amsterdam: Rodopi; 1986. 191 pp. (Costerus 54.) [†Treatment in Netherlandic criticism compared to American criticism (1925-1981).]

[8137] Beasley, Conger, Jr. "Hemingway and the *Kansas City Star.*" *SSMLN.* 1986 Spring; 16(1): 1-7. [†Relationship to *Kansas City Star* (1917-1918).]

. . .

Novel/The Sun Also Rises (1926)

[8163] Aldridge, John W. *"The Sun Also Rises:* Sixty Years Later." *SR.* 1986 Spring; 94(2): 337-345. [†Minimalism; relationship to style.]

[8164] Atherton, John. "The Itinerary and the Postcard: Minimal Strategies in *The Sun Also Rises." ELH.* 1986 Spring; 53(1): 199-218. [†Treatment of journey; relationship to narrative.]

[8165] Balassi, " The Writing of the Manuscript of *The Sun Also Rises,* with a Chart of Its Session-by-Session Development." *HN.* 1986 Fall; 6(1): 65-78. [†Composition; textual revision.]

[8166] Harrell, David. "A Final Note on Duff Twysden." *HN.* 1986 Spring; 5(2): 45-46. [†Treatment of Ashley, Lady Brett (character). Sources in Twysden, Duff. Includes biographical information.]

[8167] Hinkle, James. "'Dear Mr. Scribner': About the Published Text of *The Sun Also Rises." HN.* 1986 Fall; 6(1): 43-64. [†Textual revision.]

[8168] Josephs, Allen. *"Toreo:* The Moral Axis of *The Sun Also Rises." HN.* 1986 Fall; 6(1): 88-89. [†Treatment of bullfighting; moral values.]

[8169] Martin, Robert A. "Hemingway's Sun as Title and Metaphor." *HN.* 1986 Fall; 6(1): 100. [†Treatment of sun as metaphor; relationship to characters.]

[8170] Moreland, Kim. "Hemingway's Medievalist Impulse: Its Effect on the Presentation of Women and War in *The Sun Also Rises." HN.* 1986 Fall; 6(1): 30-41. [†Treatment of characters; relationship to courtly love; war. Sources in medievalism.]

[8171] Morgan, George. "An American in Paris: Strategies of Otherness in *The Sun Also Rises." Cycnos.* 1985-1986 Winter; 2: 27-39. [†Treatment of the self; the other compared to Pascal, Blaise; *Pensées.*]

[8172] Rother, James. "Close-Reading Hemingway: Risking Mispronounced Stresses in *The Sun Also Rises." HN.* 1986 Fall; 6(1): 79-87. [†Treatment of Hobin, Georgette (character); relationship to mystery.]

author
date
volume and issue number
title of article
title of journal: Hemingway Notes
brief description of article
pages

Figure 27 Excerpt from *MLA International Bibliography.*

there is a journal devoted entirely to Hemingway: *Hemingway Notes.* The student would be wise to scan the most recent issues of *HN* not yet covered in the bibliography.

ERIC Indexes

The Educational Resources Information Center (ERIC), a federally funded organization, provides two indexes to sources on educational issues. Many undergraduate researchers can find useful materials here for a wide range of topics.

CURRENT INDEX TO JOURNALS IN EDUCATION

CIJE indexes articles from 780 education and education-related journals. The index, issued monthly and cumulated in hardcover semiannually, contains two sections: (1) a main-entry section listing articles under such broad headings as "Rural Education" and "Higher Education," but ordered by a number assigned to each article and (2) a subject listing giving each article's title and its accession number, which will guide a user to the main entry. Each accession number begins with *EJ* to distinguish an article published in a journal from an educational document (ED) indexed in *Resources in Education*. Thus, if you wanted to explore the problem of cheating on the college campus, you could first use the subject index to locate, as shown in Figure 28, a half dozen articles on the topic. You would then use the accession number to locate each article's main entry. In the example of a main entry that is shown in Figure 28, observe that it includes a brief summary of the article and a list of "descriptors"—related subject headings.

RESOURCES IN EDUCATION

RIE is a collection of reports, unpublished documents, on educational issues that can be accessed through monthly indexes. Each monthly booklet has two parts: (1) an index section with separate subject, author, institution, and document type listings and (2) the résumé (main entry) section organized by accession number (the ED number), which includes a paragraph abstract of each document. Note (see Figure 29) that the abstract has not been written by the author of the report. In most cases, you will want to read the report. However, if you do use anything from the abstract in your paper, you must cite the abstract just as you would give credit to any other source used in your paper. Many libraries have the reports available on microfiche; they can also be obtained, in paper form, from the ERIC Document Reproduction Service.

Dissertation Abstracts International

Although most of the indexes discussed in this chapter follow the fairly standard format of a combined author and subject alphabetical listing, the two ERIC indexes described above differ somewhat in organization and, for *RIE,* in format as well. There are, actually, many indexes that provide abstracts of articles; most of these, serving a particular discipline (e.g., *Psychological Abstracts, Chemical Abstracts*), are cited in Appendix B.

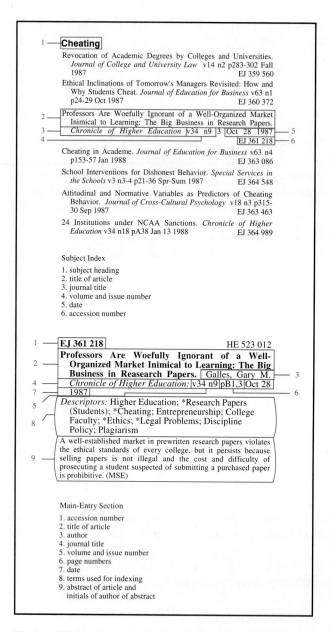

Figure 28 Excerpts from Subject Index and Main-Entry Section of *CIJE*.

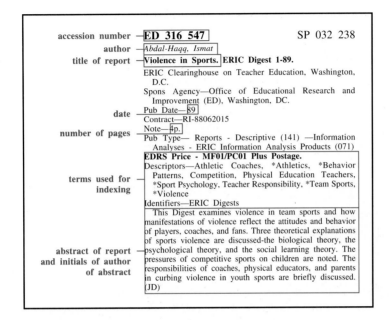

Figure 29 Excerpt from *Resources in Education.*

One important abstracts collection serves all researchers: *Dissertation Abstracts International (DAI)*. A monthly publication of University Microfilms International, *DAI* has both an author and a key-word index to direct you to the main volumes of abstracts, prepared by each student, of graduate dissertations. The main volumes, divided into Humanities and Social Sciences (A), Sciences and Engineering (B), and Worldwide (C), organize the abstracts alphabetically by author under subheadings of these main divisions. Each complete dissertation is available from University Microfilms in paper and on microform. If the fairly detailed abstract (see Figure 30) is referred to in a research essay, it must, as with *RIE* abstracts, be documented. See page 103 for the proper form of citation; note that the university is given as part of the bibliographic citation, so be certain to include that information on your bibliography card.

Citation Indexes

The citation indexes *(Arts and Humanities Citation Index, Science Citation Index,* and *Social Sciences Citation Index)* have still another look—

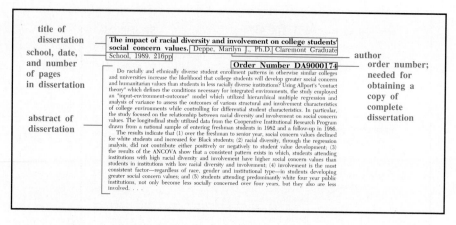

title of
dissertation

school, date,
and number
of pages
in dissertation

abstract of
dissertation

**The impact of racial diversity and involvement on college students'
social concern values.** Deppe, Marilyn J., Ph.D. Claremont Graduate
School, 1989. 216pp

Order Number DA9000174

Do racially and ethnically diverse student enrollment patterns in otherwise similar colleges
and universities increase the likelihood that college students will develop greater social concern
and humanitarian values than students in less racially diverse institutions? Using Allport's "contact
theory" which defines the conditions necessary for integrated environments, the study employed
an "input-environment-outcome" model which utilized hierarchical multiple regression and
analysis of variance to assess the outcomes of various structural and involvement characteristics
of college environments while controlling for differential student characteristics. In particular,
the study focused on the relationship between racial diversity and involvement on social concern
values. The longitudinal study utilized data from the Cooperative Institutional Research Program
drawn from a national sample of entering freshman students in 1982 and a follow-up in 1986.

The results indicate that (1) over the freshman to senior year, social concern values declined
for white students and increased for Black students; (2) racial diversity, through the regression
analysis, did not contribute either positively or negatively to student value development; (3)
the results of the ANCOVA show that a consistent pattern exists in which, students attending
institutions with high racial diversity and involvement have higher social concern values than
students in institutions with low racial diversity and involvement; (4) involvement is the most
consistent factor—regardless of race, gender and institutional type—in students developing
greater social concern values; and (5) students attending predominantly white four year public
institutions, not only become less socially concerned over four years, but they also are less
involved. . . .

author

order number;
needed for
obtaining a
copy of
complete
dissertation

Figure 30 Excerpt from *Dissertation Abstracts International.*

quite literally—but their rather complex coding and a print so small you
might wonder about the need for glasses are not good enough reasons to
avoid these research tools when they would be helpful to your project.
The name—using *Science Citation Index* as our example—highlights one
of four interrelated parts found in each yearly cumulation. The *Citation
Index* leads you to recent journal articles (over 3000, worldwide) that
have cited (referred to) an earlier work on your topic. Thus if you know
one work on your subject, you can look it up under the author's name to
find other authors who have cited it. The idea is that articles referring to
a source for your study will probably also be relevant to your study.

Another part of *Science Citation Index* is the *Corporate Index,* a list
of members of specific organizations and institutions who have published
in a given year. Scientists with the U.S. Geological Survey can be expected to publish studies on, for example, earthquake prediction problems. Undergraduate researchers are more likely to begin, though, with
the *Permuterm Subject Index,* a list of key terms that becomes a subject
index. Thus, as Figure 31 demonstrates, you can look up "Dinosaurs"
and find a long list, organized by subtopics, of authors who have published on this topic in 1988.

These three parts of *Science Citation Index* all provide access to the
fourth part, the *Source Index,* the volumes that supply a full bibliographic
listing of specific articles. The *Source Index* is an alphabetic-by-author
listing, so for researchers who do not already know authors on their subject, checking one of the other three parts is a necessary first step to locating articles.

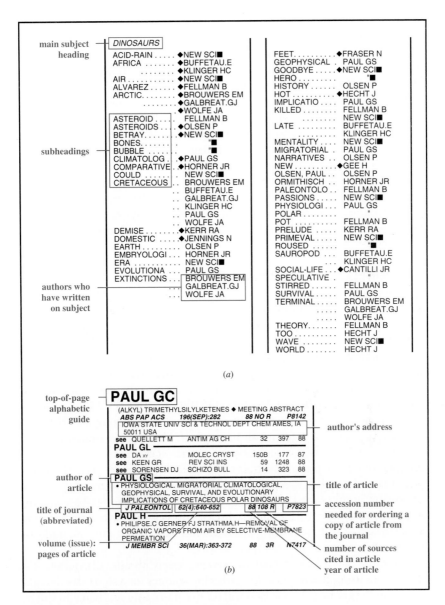

Figure 31 Excerpts from Science Citation Index. *(a)* From *Permuterm Subject Index; (b)* from *Source Index.*

After finding writers on the subject of dinosaur extinction, the researcher can find needed bibliographic information on each article written by those writers. The *Source Index*'s listing of G. S. Paul's article is illustrated in Figure 31. After studying the explanation, look again at the *Permuterm Subject Index* excerpt. Notice that "G. S. Paul" appears several times—in one year; there are also other names appearing more than once. These heavily published scholars are likely to be experts on your topic; their works must be read and considered seriously. Further, when you locate the first two writers on dinosaur extinction, you will learn that their articles are letters, responses to a previous article, in one issue of *Science* magazine. These letters, and the original article, might offer good insight into the debate over dinosaur extinction. In sum, specialized indexes do more than help you prepare a bibliography on your topic; they help you understand the field of research you are exploring.

SEARCHING DATABASES

This chapter began by mentioning the impact of computer technology on the modern college library. If your search of the library's book catalog and indexes to periodicals (whether in paper or CD-ROM format) has resulted in either too few or too many sources, you might want to try another marvel of the computer age: the database search.

Most college libraries today subscribe to one or more information retrieval systems, such as DIALOG, ORBIT, or BRS. DIALOG, for example, provides access to over 320 databases. Using a computer terminal with the appropriate software and a modem, libraries can obtain directories of companies and associations, financial statements of a company, bibliographies for topics, abstracts of some sources, and even the complete texts of articles. Researchers needing particular information or a list of possible sources for a project can benefit from online database searching. This approach to building a list of sources can save time, provide access to current materials not yet indexed in the paper indexes, and isolate sources that pertain to a specific topic.

Because of the cost of database searches, many libraries discourage students from using this method for gathering sources for a short (six to eight pages) undergraduate paper. You will receive more sources than you will be expected or have time to use but which you will (in most cases) have to pay for. Other disadvantages of this search technique include:

1. The sources listed are not necessarily in your library.

2. The coverage is often limited to only the most recent 5 to 10 years.

3. The range or completeness of databases is uneven.

In spite of these limitations, database searching has many advantages as one strategy for obtaining sources, especially for long, complex projects on narrow topics. To conduct a search, you will need to list the key terms—*descriptors*—that pertain to your topic. (Usually you will supply this information to a trained librarian who will conduct the online search for you.) If, for example, you wanted to study *cheating* among *students* in *higher education,* the librarian would select one or more appropriate files (certainly ERIC for educational sources and one or more databases in the social sciences) and then command a search of those files for sources that include the three descriptors you have provided, that is, for books and articles that fit into the shaded area of the following chart.

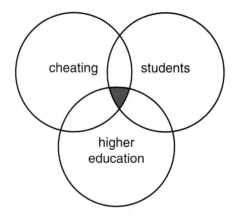

If you were to use these three descriptors to conduct a search in *Sociological Abstracts,* for example, you would learn that whereas there are 26 sources that combine *students* and *cheating,* there are only two sources when *higher education* is added as a third descriptor. Should you conclude that only a few sources on your topic exist in this database? Not yet, for the problem might be with the term you have used. You would be wise to try a different term before going to another database. If you substitute *college* for *higher education,* the search will lead to 21 sources.

Many databases come with a thesaurus of descriptors to help researchers around the problem just illustrated. If there is no thesaurus, you will have to count on the librarian conducting your search to use some serendipity and, in experimenting with various synonyms, to find sources on the topic. The more information about your project that you can give the librarian, the better able she or he will be to search successfully for you. Note that the partial list of sources on cheating and college students presented in Figure 32 includes the descriptors, identifiers, and section headings for each source. Asking for this additional information in the printout from your first search can help you select terms to use in subsequent searches.

Increasingly, the databases available through DIALOG, for example, are being placed on CD-ROM disks for scanning at a terminal not requiring a modem hookup. The disks, updated regularly, are purchased by the library and are then available without cost to students conducting their own searches. The *MLA International Bibliography* and PSYC-INFO are two specialized databases now available on CD-ROM. When conducting your own search, take a few minutes to read the directions for searching, try different combinations of descriptors, and then, if you are not getting the results you expected, ask a librarian for help.

LOCATING SOURCES OUTSIDE THE LIBRARY

Although books and articles found in libraries are essential tools for most research projects, other sources can enrich many topics and should not be overlooked. Students developing experiments or doing fieldwork in science disciplines will rely on library sources as background for their unique projects. To turn this idea around, many research topics in humanities and social science courses that usually rely on library sources primarily can often be turned into unique projects with the use of sources outside the library. Here are some suggestions.

Federal Government Documents

As already noted, the *PAIS Bulletin,* the *Vertical File Index,* the *Monthly Catalog of U.S. Government Publications,* and other indexes will lead you to many studies and reports published by government agencies. (See page 55 for guidelines for obtaining federal government publications.) In addition, you can examine materials in the National Archives Building in Washington, DC, or use one of the regional branches located in Atlanta, Boston, Chicago, Denver, Fort Worth, Kansas City, Los Angeles, New York, Philadelphia, and Seattle. Two guides can help you discover materials that might be useful to your research: *Guide to the National Archives of the United States* and *Select List of Publications of the National Archives and Records Service.* Some documents may be borrowed on microfilm.

2093970   89V0869
An Empirical Investigation of Actual Cheating in a Large Sample of
    Undergraduates
Karlins, Marvin; Michaels, Charles; Podlogar, Susan
Dept Management U South Florida, Tampa 33620-5500
Research in Higher Education 1988, 29, 4, Dec, 359-364.
    CODEN:RHEDAT
PUB. YEAR: 1988
COUNTRY OF PUBLICATION: United States
LANGUAGE: English
DOCUMENT TYPE: Abstract of Journal Article (aja)
AVAILABILITY: Hardcopy reproduction available from UMI, Ann
    Arbor, MI
DESCRIPTORS: College Students (D147600); Cheating (D120000)
IDENTIFIERS: cheating behavior, business course students; text
    analysis; library logs;
SECTION HEADINGS: social problems and social welfare- sociology
    of crime & victimology (2147) sociology of education-
    sociology of education (1432)

16/2/2
2087649   89U6999
How College Freshmen View Plagiarism
Kroll, Barry M.
Indiana U, Bloomington 47405
Written Communication 1988, 5, 2, Apr. 203-221. CODEN:WRCOEB
PUB. YEAR: 1988
COUNTRY OF PUBLICATION: United States
LANGUAGE: English
DOCUMENT TYPE: Abstract of Journal Article (aja)
DESCRIPTORS: Deception (D200800); College Students (D147600);
    Cheating (D120000)
IDENTIFIERS: plagiarism, college freshmen's reasoning/attitudes;
    questionnaire;
SECTION HEADINGS: sociology: history and theory- of professional
    interest (teaching sociology) (0202)

16/2/3
2070394   86Q8917
Student Cheating and Perceived Social Control by College Students
Haines, Valerie J.; LaBeff, Emily E.; Clark, Robert E.; Diekhoff,
    George M.
Midwestern State U, Wichita Falls TX 76308
Free Inquiry in Creative Sociology 1986, 14, 1, May, 13-16.
    CODEN:FICSDA
PUB. YEAR: 1986
COUNTRY OF PUBLICATION: United States
LANGUAGE: English
DOCUMENT TYPE: Abstract of Journal Article (aja)
AVAILABILITY: Hardcopy reproduction available from UMI, Ann
    Arbor, MI
DESCRIPTORS: Student Attitudes   (D837600); College Students
    (D147600); Cheating (D120000)
IDENTIFIERS: anticheating measures, college students'
    perceptions; questionnaire;
SECTION HEADINGS: social problems and social welfare- sociology
    of crime & victimology (2147) sociology of education-
    sociology of education (1432)

Figure 32 From *Sociological Abstracts Database*—DIALOG Search.

Further, you can write to government agencies to request copies of specified documents. Many documents are available to you under the Freedom of Information Act. Your requests will be responded to either with copies of the requested documents (50 pages are sent at no cost; subsequent pages cost 10 cents each) or with an explanation for the denial of your request. (There are some restrictions under the FOIA.)

State and Local Government Sources

Do not overlook additional government sources: your state and county archives, maps, and other published materials. Your school library or a nearby public library may have a "state room," an area devoted entirely to materials relevant to state history and government. Instead of selecting a global topic for a history or government course, consider examining the debates over a controversial bill introduced in your state legislature. Use periodicals from the period preserved in the state room and interview legislators and journalists who participated in or covered the debates or served on committees that the bill passed through.

You can also request specific documents on a topic from appropriate state or county agencies and nonprofit organizations. One student, given the assignment of examining solutions to any ecological problem, decided to study the local problem of preserving the Chesapeake Bay. She obtained issues of the Chesapeake Bay Foundation newsletter and brochures prepared by the CBF advising homeowners about hazardous household waste materials that end up in the Bay. Reading these sources led to a decision to focus on ways that northern Virginia homeowners and builders can preserve the land and the local streams that feed into the Bay. Added to her sources were U.S. Department of Agriculture bulletins on soil conservation, Virginia Department of Conservation brochures on soil and water conservation, and Fairfax County bulletins on landscaping tips for improving the area's water quality. (Local telephone directories, available in your library, will give you the addresses and phone numbers of state and local government agencies and local organizations interested in the topic you are researching.) Local problems can lead to interesting research topics because they are current and relevant to you and because they involve uncovering different kinds of source materials.

Correspondence

Business and government officials are usually willing to respond to written requests for information. Make your letter brief and well written, and include a self-addressed, stamped envelope for the person's convenience and as a measure of your seriousness. To be further obliging, you might also invite the person to call you, but only if you have an answering machine or can specify times that you are usually available. If you have to rely on a written response, write as soon as you discover the need for information and be prepared to wait several weeks. It is appropriate to indicate your deadline and ask for a timely response. Three guidelines you should keep in mind include:

1. Explain precisely what information you need. Avoid writing a general "please send me anything you have on this topic" kind of letter. Busy professionals are more likely to respond to requests that are specific and reveal a control of the topic.

2. Do not request information that can be found in your library's reference collection. See Appendix B under "Business and Economics" for sources that provide information about companies.

3. Explain how you plan to use the information you are requesting. Businesses are understandably concerned with their public images and will be disinclined to provide information that you intend to use as a means of attacking them. (For example, a chemical company is not likely to tell you how many times the EPA has cited it for dumping toxic waste into a nearby stream. You will have to uncover this information from other sources: the EPA and local newspapers, perhaps.)

Use reference guides to companies and government agencies to obtain the complete address and to determine the person to whom your letter should be addressed. For companies, address your request to the public information officer.

Interviews

Some officials may be available for personal interviews. Call or write for an appointment as soon as you recognize the value of an interview so that you can get scheduled in time for the results to be useful. Remember that interviews are more likely to be scheduled with state and local officials—both elected and in government agencies—than with the president of General Motors. If you are studying a local issue, also consider leaders of the civic associations that would have a particular interest in the issue. In many communities, the local historian or a librarian will be a storehouse of information about the community's customs or past or its famous citizens. Professors or former teachers and principals can be interviewed for papers on a current problem in education. Interviews with doctors or nurses can add a special dimension to papers on various contemporary medical issues—on passive euthanasia for severely deformed newborns, for example. If an interview is appropriate for your topic, follow these guidelines:

1. Prepare specific questions in advance.

2. Arrive on time, properly dressed, and behave in a polite, professional manner throughout the interview.

3. Take notes, asking the interviewee to repeat key statements so that your notes are accurate.

4. Take a tape recorder with you but ask for permission to use it before beginning to tape the conversation.

5. If you quote any statements in your paper, quote accurately, eliminating only such minor speech habits as *you know*'s and *uhm*'s. Make certain that the interviewee knows that you may quote or paraphrase portions of the interview. (See page 104 for the proper documentation pattern for interviews.)

6. Direct the interview with your prepared questions but also give the interviewee the opportunity to approach the topic in his or her own way. You may obtain information or views that had not occurred to you.

7. Do not get into a debate with the interviewee. You are there to obtain information and ideas, not to do all the talking or to convince the interviewee to change some opinions.

Lectures

Check the appropriate information sources at your school to keep informed of visiting speakers. On most college campuses speakers appear frequently, lecturing on a wide range of topics. If you are fortunate enough to attend a lecture relevant to a current research project, take careful, detailed notes during the lecture. Since a lecture is a source, just like a book or article, use of information or ideas from it must be presented accurately and then documented. (See page 104 for documentation format.)

Films, Tapes, and Television

Your library will have audiovisual materials that provide good sources for some kinds of topics; in the collection will also be professors' lectures. Many videotapes, films, and television programs are also valuable resources. If you are studying *Death of a Salesman,* view the videotaped version of the play starring Dustin Hoffman. Mel Gibson's version of *Hamlet* can be contrasted with earlier film versions. The film version of the musical comedy *My Fair Lady* makes an interesting comparison to Shaw's *Pygmalion,* the play upon which the musical comedy and its film version were based.

Also pay attention to documentaries on public television and to the many news and political "talk shows" on both public and commercial TV. In many cases transcripts of documentaries and filmed or taped interviews of officials can be obtained from the television station. Usually a transcript is free but must be requested in writing. You are wise to take thorough notes when watching a program and then request a transcript if you want to quote from the program. Alternatively, if you have access to a VCR, tape the program while watching so that you can view it several times. The documentation format for nonprint sources is illustrated on pages 104–106.

Surveys, Questionnaires, and Original Research

Depending on your project, you might want to take a simple survey or write and administer a questionnaire. Surveys can be used for many campus and local issues, for topics on the behavior and attitudes of college students and/or faculty, and for topics on consumer habits. You could, for example, enrich a study of voter apathy in the United States by conducting a survey of voting habits among students and faculty. Prepare a brief list of questions (Are you registered to vote? If so, did you vote in the 1990 congressional election?) with space for answers. You may want to ask for each respondent's age and sex (if you want to compare voting habits by these factors), even party affiliation or preference—whatever variables you think might make for interesting comparisons. You can reach faculty members through their campus mailboxes; include a cover letter with your survey questions that explains your project and requests return by a specific date. You can reach students by polling personally in several dorms or by asking your instructors for a few minutes of class time to poll students in your classes. Observe in the second student research essay in Chapter 6 that Joan incorporated a brief survey of consumer habits in her study of car advertisements. You can use her essay and the discussion of preparing tables (see Chapter 5) as guidelines for presenting the results of your survey.

Complicated questionnaires that require control for bias and random sampling need skillful preparation. Instructors in upper-level courses in the social sciences approving projects based on questionnaires will advise you on appropriate wording and sampling strategies. Without reaching for those standards of statistical validity, however, you can effectively engage in simple but useful surveys and questionnaires, and your efforts will be rewarded with original evidence to analyze and present along with your reading on a topic. If, to give another example, you are studying the Depression, see if you can question several people who lived during the 1930s and incorporate their experiences into your paper. When writing questions, keep these guidelines in mind:

1. Use simple, clear language.

2. Devise a series of short questions rather than only a few questions that have several parts to them. (You want to separate information for better analysis.)

3. Phrase questions to avoid bias—wording that seeks to control the answer. For example, do *not* ask: How did you survive the *horrors* of the Depression? Do *not* write: Did you perform your civic duty by voting in the last election? These are loaded questions that prejudge the respondent's answers.

In addition to adding the results of surveys and questionnaires to your research essay, you can incorporate some original research. As you read sources on your topic, be alert to reports of studies that you could redo and update in part or on a smaller scale. Many topics on advertising and television provide opportunities for your own analysis. Joan's research essay on auto advertising (see Chapter 6) is a good example of repeating an earlier study to see, in her case, if car ads have changed in their approach in the last 10 years. Joan collected and analyzed current auto ads and compared her results with the previous study. Her reading on advertising helped guide her analysis, but her paper is developed primarily from her original research, not from library sources.

Local-issue topics may also provide opportunities for you to gather information on your own, not just from your reading. One student, examining the controversy over the proposed building of a new mall on part of the Manassas Battlefield, made the argument that the shopping

mall served no practical need in the community. He supported his assertion by describing the existing malls in the area, including the number
and types of stores each contained and the number of miles each was
from the proposed new mall. How did he obtain this information? He
drove around the area, counting miles and stores. Sometimes a seemingly
prosaic approach to a topic turns out to be an imaginative one.

Chapter 3

Preparing a Bibliography

*A*fter you have selected and focused a research topic and become familiar with your library's resources, your next step will be to identify specific sources that may help you develop your topic. As you learned in Chapter 2, the place to begin is with the library's reference guides: subject indexes, bibliographic indexes, periodicals indexes, reference works, and the book catalog. Some of these reference sources may have been used as part of your topic selection process, but now you need to return to them and the other reference guides that are appropriate to your particular topic to conduct a systematic and thorough search for sources. As you find works whose titles suggest that they will be useful to you, you need to take down the bibliographic information about each work, again in a systematic and thorough fashion, to prepare a preliminary or *working bibliography*.

GUIDELINES FOR PREPARING
A WORKING BIBLIOGRAPHY

A working bibliography is a list of sources—books, articles, government documents, whatever is relevant—on your topic. You will use this list in three important ways:

1. To survey your proposed topic to determine that sources are available to complete a research project
2. To find the specific works on the list for study and note-taking
3. To prepare the proper documentation of the sources used in your research

There are several guidelines for preparing a list of sources, procedures that researchers have found successful. Whether or not an instructor requires these procedures you are wise to adhere to them for the best reason of all: they work.

- Use 3 × 5 index cards.
  (Do *not* use a legal pad, notebook paper, or the backs of envelopes!)
- Put only *one* source on a card.
  (Never write on the back of a card; you might overlook the information on the back.)
- Check *all* reasonable catalogs and indexes for possible sources.
  (Do *not* use only one reference source—*InfoTrac*, for example—even if that reference source provides enough titles to meet your assignment's guidelines.)
- Complete a card for *every* relevant source listed in catalogs, indexes, and other reference sources.
- Copy *all* information needed to complete a bibliographic citation and locate the source.
  (When using an index that does not provide all needed information, leave space on the card to be filled in when you read the work itself.)
- Put bibliographic information in the *correct format* on every card.

Over time, these guidelines acquired the force of rules for several reasons. First, cards provide flexibility. You can easily add to your list while keeping the cards alphabetized, or organized in the sequence in which you plan to read the sources, or arranged by location if you are using more than one library. Eventually, cards for sources not used can be eliminated, and the remaining cards can be alphabetized in preparation for typing your final list of works cited. Obviously the flexibility of cards is lost if you put more than one source on a card.

The third guideline is a reminder that the idea of research is to learn about a topic, not to meet minimum requirements for an assignment. Although undergraduate researchers will not be expected to compile an exhaustive list of sources on a topic, still the goal must be to find an adequate number of reliable sources—indeed, the most important sources—on the subject. Use your course texts, your instructor, and reference works as guides to determining who the experts are on the topic and to locating the key sources. Remember that the research of college students cannot be based on encyclopedias or exclusively on articles from popular magazines. The study of a social problem, for example, should send you to the scholarly journals indexed in *Social Sciences Index,* of a foreign policy issue to the key journal *Foreign Affairs,* of a business topic to the *Harvard Business Review.*

The final three guidelines focus on using time efficiently, on looking ahead to subsequent steps in the research process. It is faster to prepare cards for all potential sources and to copy all needed information the first time around than to return to the library to find additional sources or complete a citation. Remember that one purpose of preparing a working bibliography is to survey sources on a topic to make certain that the topic is a workable one. You want to compile a list of more sources than you can reasonably study in the time you have. If all of them turn out to be available and useful, you will have to narrow your topic. If your search for sources results in only four or five cards, you will probably have to enlarge or change your topic.

If you copy all needed bibliographic information in the correct format initially, you will save time and avoid frustration when preparing your completed paper. It is unwise to think that you can write first and then "put in" the documentation later or worry about preparing an accurate list of works cited the night before the paper is due. In addition, many instructors, for freshman composition to graduate courses, require conferences with each student during which they will examine the working bibliography to see how the student is coming in the search for sources, to discuss the student's approach, and perhaps to offer advice. At such a conference, do not expect half-completed citations in a notebook or a printout from *InfoTrac* to be acceptable. You will be rewarded at each step in the research process if you take time to compile a set of cards that will work for you.

Finally, keep your cards safely banded together and always have blank cards with you when you are working in the library or reading sources containing notes and reference lists. You can use the pocket on the inside back cover of this text as a good place to keep your cards.

WRITING BIBLIOGRAPHY CARDS
FOR YOUR FIELD OF STUDY

Citations of books and articles and any other sources used in a research project are presented to readers at the end of a research paper in an alphabetic list of Works Cited. These bibliographic citations include, regardless of the type of source or the style manual followed, the work's *author, title,* and *publication information.* Since these are the facts you will need to complete your paper, these are the facts you want to record on each bibliography card. All researchers, regardless of field, will need these basic facts about a source, but not all fields of research follow the same conventions for presenting the information. Many researchers in the humanities follow the style established by the Modern Language Association (MLA), and this is the style usually expected in college composition courses. Researchers in the social sciences follow, for the most part, the style established by the American Psychological Association (APA). Researchers in the sciences follow a greater variety of styles depending on the specific discipline.

Illustrated below are models of MLA, APA, and (to represent the sciences) American Chemical Society styles. Observe that these patterns for books, although similar, are sufficiently varied to demand careful attention to each style's guidelines. (Citations of articles vary even more among the three styles.)

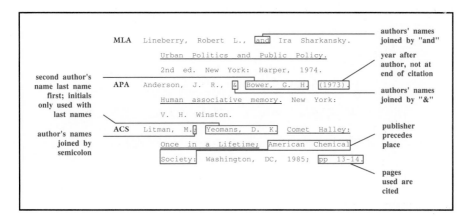

The sample bibliography cards and detailed patterns of citations in this chapter display the correct patterns of citation according to the Modern Language Association. If you are using a citation pattern other than MLA, turn to Chapter 7 for the order of information and pattern of punctuation required for citations in your field of study. Do *not* try to mix or blend styles; select the style used in your field or requested by your instructor and follow it exactly.

WRITING BIBLIOGRAPHY CARDS: MLA STYLE

Basic Form for Books

As Figure 33 illustrates, the basic bibliographic form for books requires the following information, in this pattern:

1. The author's full name, last name first
2. The title (and subtitle, if there is one) of the book, underlined
3. The facts of publication: the place of publication (followed by a colon), the publisher (followed by a comma), and the date of publication

Figure 33 Sample Bibliography Card for Books.

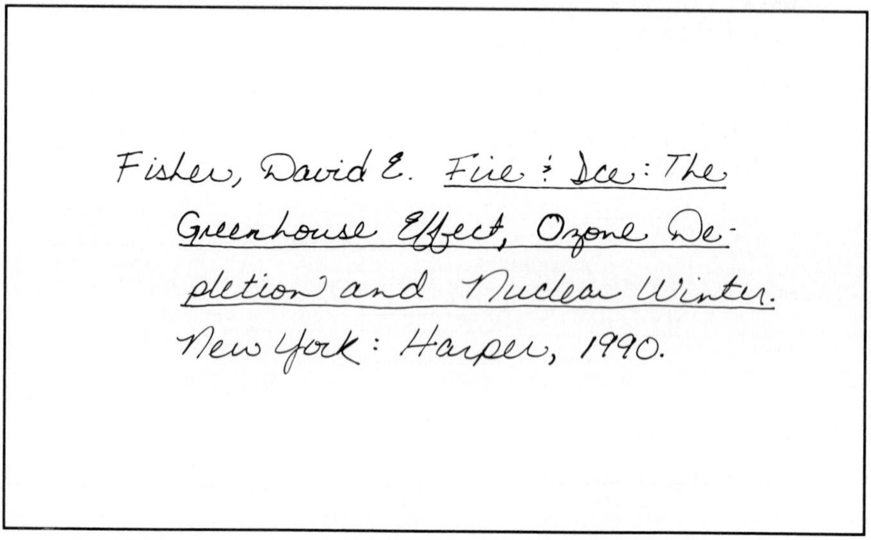

Fisher, David E. Fire & Ice: The Greenhouse Effect, Ozone Depletion and Nuclear Winter. New York: Harper, 1990.

Notice that periods are placed after the author's name, after the title, and at the end of the citation. Other information appropriate to some books (e.g., the name of an editor, the number of volumes) is added in appropriate places to the basic pattern. These variations are illustrated in the many sample citations that follow at the end of the chapter.

Basic Form for Periodicals

Figure 34 illustrates the simplest form for journal, magazine, and newspaper articles. Periodicals citations require the following information, in this order:

1. The author's full name, last name first
2. The title of the article, in quotation marks
3. The facts of publication: the title of the periodical (underlined), the volume number (if the article is in a scholarly journal), the date (followed by a colon), and inclusive page numbers

Notice again that periods are placed after the author's name, after the article's title, and at the end of the citation.

Figure 34 Sample Bibliography Card for Articles.

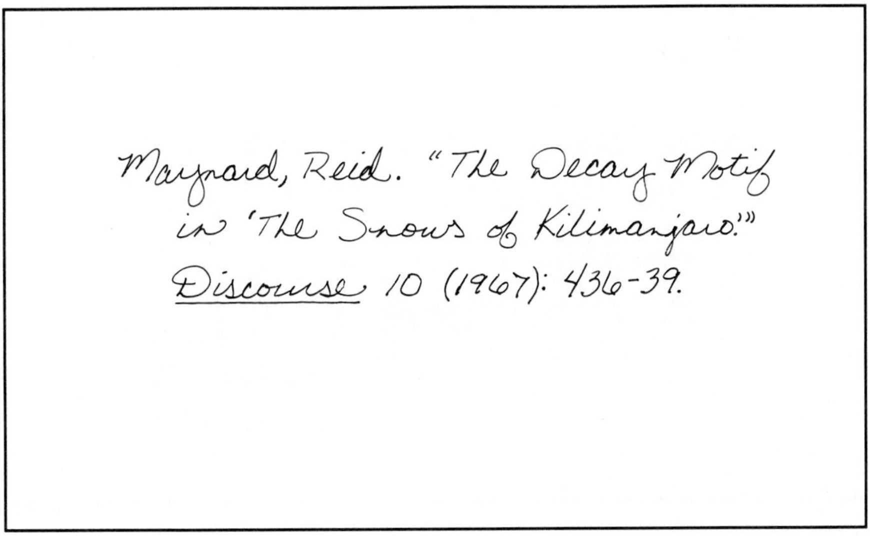

Maynard, Reid. "The Decay Motif in 'The Snows of Kilimanjaro.'" _Discourse_ 10 (1967): 436-39.

Turning Information into Citations

In your search for sources, you will discover that bibliographic information does not usually come in the required MLA format. Information given in most periodicals indexes, for example, will have to be rearranged on your card into the format needed for documenting your paper. Here, for example, is a source on dinosaurs found in *InfoTrac:*

> Stop to consider the stones that fall from the sky. (comets and aster-oids) by James Trefil il v20 Smithsonian Sept '89 p80(12)

To turn this information into a correct bibliographic citation, rearrange the information, place the article title in quotation marks, underline the magazine title, and eliminate such information as the volume number, the total number of pages, the indication of illustrations in the article, and the explanation of the article's content. A correct card for this source is shown in Figure 35. Since you do not know if the 12-page article is paged continuously, write *80+* for the pages, but circle this information as a reminder to determine the correct citation of pages when you obtain and read the article. (If paging is continuous, then inclusive pages are cited; thus: *80–91*).

Figure 35 Bibliography Card for an Article Cited in *InfoTrac.*

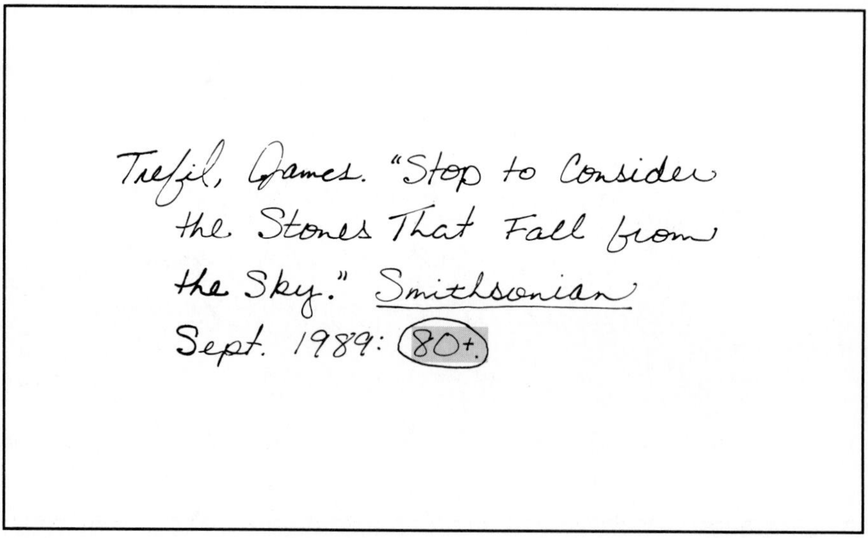

Trefil, James. "Stop to Consider
the Stones That Fall from
the Sky." <u>Smithsonian</u>
Sept. 1989: (80+.)

The same procedure will be needed with the following source, obtained from a list of references in a geology text:

KENNEDY, V. S., ed., 1980, Estuarine Perspectives. Academic Press, Inc., New York. 533 pp.

On your card, put the facts of publication in the right order and format, underline the book's title, and circle the author's first initial as a reminder to obtain the full name from the title page when you read the book. (See Figure 36.)

Once you get used to the order of information presented in the major periodicals indexes and the fact that titles are not indicated by underlining or quotation marks, you will find that getting bibliography cards completed accurately for periodicals is not too difficult. Books, however, have more variations and require careful reading of the title and copyright pages if you want to be certain to prepare complete and accurate citations. Examine, for example, the title and copyright pages annotated in Figure 37. Your bibliography card, illustrated in Figure 38, must include the original publication date, the publisher's imprint (Harper

Figure 36 Bibliography Card for a Book Listed in a Textbook's List of References.

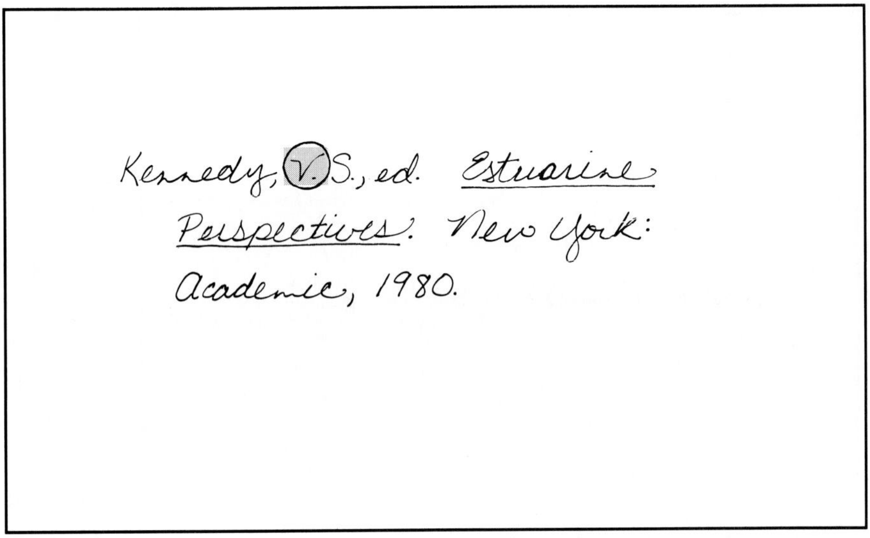

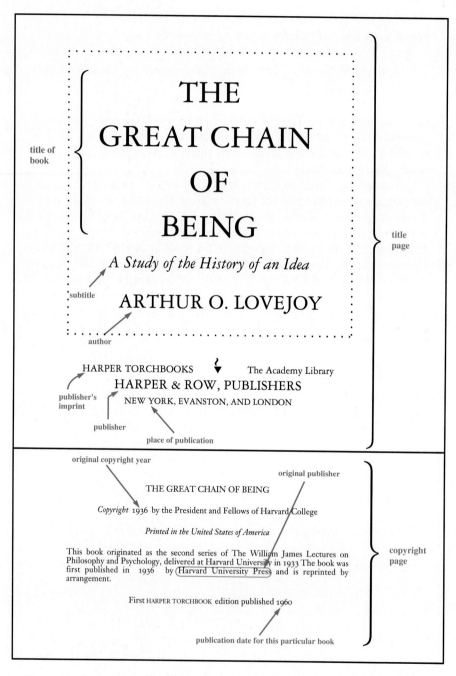

Figure 37 Annotated Title and Copyright Pages of a Book.

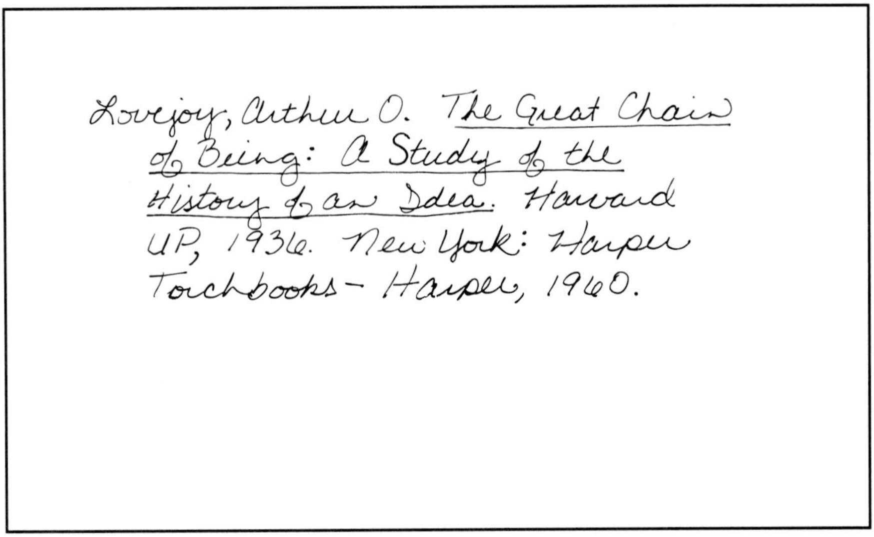

Lovejoy, Arthur O. *The Great Chain
of Being: A Study of the
History of an Idea.* Harvard
UP, 1936. New York: Harper
Torchbooks — Harper, 1960.

Figure 38 Bibliography Card for a Book Shown in Figure 37.

Torchbooks), and the publication date of the Torchbook edition, the one used for your research.

These and other key variations of the basic citation forms are illustrated and explained in the latter part of this chapter. Study the general conventions of citation on pages 84–89 and then take this handbook with you as a reference when you gather your list of sources.

Working with Bibliography Cards

In addition to writing all bibliographic information in the correct order and format on your cards, you should include additional information that will help you locate and use the sources you have listed. If you are using more than one library, for instance, indicate on each index card the location of the source. When checking the catalog for books, copy onto your cards the full call number for each book you cite. Make a note of all books that contain a bibliography, a good place to look for additional sources on your topic. Finally, when you begin skimming sources, note the contents of the work or how you expect to use it. Figure 39 shows a sample card that is part of a working bibliography.

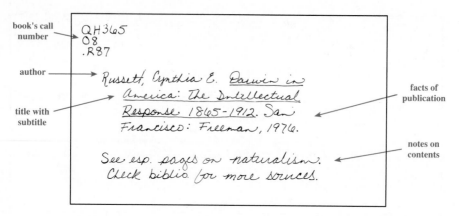

Figure 39 Bibliography Card with Student's Notes.

CONVENTIONS OF BIBLIOGRAPHIC FORM

You have reviewed the basic parts of a bibliographic citation for both
books and articles. You have also been alerted to some of the variations
found in citations. The following summary of the conventions of citation
will guide you in preparing a working bibliography and, later, your
Works Cited page. After the rules come many pages of examples to serve
you as models. Strive to write each citation correctly on your cards so
that you learn the proper form and so that you do not introduce errors
that may be transferred, later, to your final paper.

Bibliographic Citations—General

1. **Present each citation with hanging indentation.** The first line of
   each citation begins at the left margin; second and subsequent lines
   of each citation are indented five spaces from the left margin. The
   appearance is the reverse of paragraphing.

2. **Place a period after each of the three main parts of a citation:
   author, title, facts of publication.** Allow two spaces after each period, just as you space between sentences. However, if the author's
   name ends with a middle initial, the one period after the initial is sufficient. If the title ends in a question mark or exclamation point, do
   not add a period after it.

3. **Supply information about books, as appropriate, in the following order:**
author*
chapter or part of book
title of book*
editor or translator
number or type of edition
number of volumes
name of the series
place of publication*
publisher*
date of publication*
Items marked with an asterisk are required; others may be needed for some books.

4. **Supply information about periodicals, as appropriate, in the following order:**
author*
title of the article*
name of the periodical*
volume, issue
date*
page numbers*
Items marked with an asterisk are required. Volume and issue numbers are needed for scholarly journals. (Section letter or number and edition may be needed for newspapers.)

5. **Do *not* number citations in a Works Cited list.**

Conventions for Authors

1. **Give the author's full name as it appears with the work.** If you use an index that gives only initials, complete the author's name when you obtain the work.
   Example: J. A. Lee (from Reader's Guide) becomes Lee, John A.

2. **For a work by two or three authors, cite all names but give only the first author's name with the last name first.** The second and third authors' names should be given in signature order.
   Example: Gove, Walter R., Michael Hughes, and Michael R. Geerken.

3. If a work has four or more authors, give only the first name listed, followed by a comma and the Latin abbreviation *et al.* or the expression *and others.*
   Example: Baugh, Albert C., et al.

Conventions for Titles

1. **Underline titles of books, magazines, newspapers, plays, movies, works of art, and computer software.** Long poems, published in book form, are underlined. Pamphlet titles are underlined because, regardless of length, pamphlets are separate publications.

2. **The Bible and the books of the Bible are not underlined.** Unless you specify a particular version, readers assume that you have cited the King James Version of the Bible.

3. **Place quotation marks around titles of articles, essays, newspaper articles, lectures, poems, short stories, chapter titles, TV or radio episodes in a series, songs, and speeches.** Place the period ending the title part of the citation before the final quotation mark.
   Example: "The Palestinian Tug-of-War."

4. **Capitalize the first and last words of a title and all the other words except articles** *(a, an, the),* **conjunctions** *(and, or, but, for, nor, yet, so),* **and prepositions of fewer than six letters** (e.g., *for, to, with,* but *Between*). Follow this rule even if the title is not capitalized in the periodicals index or other source used.

5. **Include a work's subtitle as part of the title, also underlined and preceded by a colon, even if there is no colon on the title page or in the reference source used.** The first word of the subtitle is capitalized.
   Example: The American Landscape: A Critical View

6. **Indicate a work in its second or later edition, or in a revised edition, by adding the appropriate information after the title.**
   Example: The Growth of American Thought. 3rd ed.

Conventions for Publication Information—Books

1. **Give the city of publication (followed by a colon), the publisher's name (followed by a comma), and the date of publication**

(followed by a period). Confirm information taken from a reference source by checking the book's title and copyright pages.
Example: New York: Morrow, 1977.

2. **Cite only the city of publication, not the state.** Add the country, abbreviated, for books published abroad, *if* the city may be unfamiliar to readers.
Example: Manchester, Eng. *But not:* London, Eng.

3. **Give only the first city listed on the book's title page,** even if several cities are listed.

4. **If no place or no date appears in a book, write *n.p.* or *n.d.* in the appropriate place in the citation.**

5. **Give the most recent copyright date provided on the copyright page.** Do *not* cite a printing date for the copyright date.

6. **Use the shortened forms of publishers' names. Follow these guidelines:**

- Omit business abbreviations *(Co., Inc.)* and descriptive terms *(Press, House, Publishers).*

Full Name	Citation Form
Macmillan Publishing Co., Inc.	Macmillan
The Free Press	Free
Basic Books	Basic

- If the publisher's name includes several surnames, cite only the first name.

Farrar, Straus, and Giroux, Inc.	Farrar
Appleton-Century-Crofts	Appleton
Prentice-Hall	Prentice

- If the publisher's name is one person's name, cite only the surname.

Harry N. Abrams, Inc.	Abrams
George Allen and Unwin Publishers, Inc.	Allen
Alfred A. Knopf, Inc.	Knopf

- Shorten university press names thus:

Harvard University Press	Harvard UP
The Johns Hopkins University Press	Johns Hopkins UP
University of Chicago Press	U of Chicago P

- Use standard abbreviations of publishing organizations that will be known to your readers.

The National Education Association	NEA
The Modern Language Association of America	MLA
Government Printing Office	GPO

Conventions for Publication Information—Periodicals

1. **For popular magazines, cite the following publication information: title of the magazine (underlined), date of publication (followed by a colon), and the page numbers of the article. Do *not* put any punctuation after the magazine title.**
   Examples: Psychology Today Mar. 1975: 43–47.
   Newsweek 4 Nov. 1974: 36–38.

2. **Most scholarly journals are paged consecutively throughout all the issues in one year. For journals paged annually, cite the following publication information: title of the journal, volume number (an arabic numeral), the year of publication in parentheses (followed by a colon), and the page numbers of the article.** In some cases, an issue number or the month and year in parentheses will be necessary; see pages 97–98.
   Example: Modern Drama 8 (1966): 347–61.

3. **Abbreviate months of the year except May, June, and July.** Put a period at the end of the abbreviation.

4. **For magazines published weekly, cite the full date in the order of day, month, year.**

5. **Provide inclusive page numbers for articles printed on successive pages. For articles that are interrupted with other material, provide the first page number followed, without spacing, by a "+."**
   Examples: Psychology Today Mar. 1975: 43–46.
   BUT
   New Republic 13 Jan. 1979: 12+.

6. **For articles appearing on page 100 or higher, cite inclusive page numbers without repeating the first digit of the three-digit number.**
   Example: 347–61 or 122–34. BUT 397–412.

7. **For newspapers, cite the following publication information: name of the paper (underlined); the day, month, and year of publication (followed by a colon); and the page(s) on which the article appeared.**
   Example: Christian Science Monitor 15 Jan. 1991: 18.

8. **If the newspaper has lettered sections, add the appropriate letter before the page number, without a space.**
   Example: Washington Post 14 Mar. 1975: D5.

9. **If the newspaper has numbered sections, provide the section number, with the abbreviation "sec.," after the date.**
   Example: Los Angeles Times 1 Apr. 1989, sec. 2: 8.

10. **If the newspaper appears in more than one edition each day, include the edition name after the date.**
    Example: Wall Street Journal 10 Feb. 1988, eastern ed.: 23.

11. **When citing the name of the newspaper, omit the initial article, even though it is on the paper's masthead.** Thus, *The New York Times* is cited as *New York Times.*

12. **If the city is not part of the newspaper's name as it appears on the masthead, give it in square brackets.** Exception: nationally published papers such as the *Wall Street Journal.*
    Example: Plain Dealer [Cleveland]

PREPARING MLA CITATIONS FOR THE "WORKS CITED" PAGE

If you have prepared complete and accurate bibliography cards during your search for sources, then when you prepare your final paper, the documenting of sources should not be difficult. One part of that documentation—the in-text citing of author and page—is explained and illustrated in Chapter 5. These in-text citations are supported, or completed, by the final page of your paper: the "Works Cited" page (or pages). To prepare your Works Cited, all you need to do is alphabetize, by the author's last name, the cards for all the sources you actually cite and then type each source's citation accurately, according to the forms illustrated in the following pages. [Guidelines for formatting the entire Works Cited page(s) are found on pages 230–32.]

Forms for Books: Citing the Complete Book

✳ A Book by a Single Author

Fisher, David E. Fire & Ice: The Greenhouse Effect, Ozone
     Depletion and Nuclear Winter. New York: Harper,
     1990.

The subtitle is included, preceded by a colon, even if there is no colon on the book's title page.

✳ A Book by Two or Three Authors

Beard, Charles A., and Mary R. Beard. The American Spirit:
     A Study in the Idea of Civilization in the United
     States. New York: Macmillan, 1942.

Second (and third) authors' names appear in signature form.

✳ A Book with More Than Three Authors

Baugh, Albert C., et al. A Literary History of England. New
     York: Appleton, 1948.

Use the name of the first author listed on the title page. The English "and others" may be used instead of "et al."

✳ Two or More Works by the Same Author

Allen, Frederick Lewis. The Big Change. New York: Harper,
     1952.

---. Only Yesterday: An Informal History of the Nineteen-
     Twenties. New York: Harper, 1931.

In a list of works cited, give the author's name only once. Alphabetize the entries by the books' titles. For the second (and additional) works, begin the citation with three hyphens followed by a period.

A Book Written under a Pseudonym with Name Supplied

Wrighter, Carl P. [Paul Stevens]. I Can Sell You Anything.

New York: Ballantine, 1972.

Supply the author's name in square brackets.

An Anonymous Book

Beowulf. Trans. E. Talbot Donaldson. New York: Norton,

1966.

Do not use *"anon."* Alphabetize by the book's title.

✳An Edited Book

Franklin, Benjamin. The Autobiography of Benjamin Frank-

lin. Ed. Max Farrand. Berkeley: U of California P,

1949. *editor*

Lynn, Kenneth S., ed. Huckleberry Finn: Text, Sources, and

Criticism. New York: Harcourt, 1961.

If you cite the author's work, put the author's name first and the editor's
name after the title, preceded by "Ed." If you cite the editor's work, perhaps an introduction or notes, then place the editor's name first, followed by a comma and "ed."

A Translation

Solzhenitsyn, Alexander. August,1914. Trans. Michael

Glenny. New York: Farrar, 1972.

Homer. The Odyssey. Trans. E. V. Rieu. Baltimore: Penguin,

1946.

If the author's work is being cited, place the author's name first and
the translator's name after the title, preceded by "Trans." If the translator's work is the important element, place the translator's name first,
thus:

Cornford, Francis MacDonald, trans. The Republic of Plato.

New York: Oxford UP, 1945.

If the author's name does not appear in the title, provide it after the title; for example: By Plato.

A BOOK IN TWO OR MORE VOLUMES

Sewall, Richard B. <u>The Life of Emily Dickinson</u>. 2 vols. New

York: Farrar, 1974.

A BOOK IN ITS SECOND OR SUBSEQUENT EDITION

Curti, Merle. <u>The Growth of American Thought</u>. 3rd ed. New

York: Harper, 1964.

Always include the number of the edition you have used, abbreviated as shown, if it is not the first edition.

A BOOK IN A SERIES

Waggoner, Hyatt H. <u>Nathaniel Hawthorne</u>. University of Min-

nesota Pamphlets on American Writers, No. 23. Minne-

apolis: U of Minnesota P, 1962.

Maclean, Hugh, ed. <u>Edmund Spenser's Poetry</u>. A Norton Crit-

ical Edition. New York: Norton, 1968.

The series title—and number, if there is one—follows the book's title but is not underlined.

A REPRINT OF AN EARLIER WORK

Marlowe, Christopher. <u>The Works of Christopher Marlowe</u>.

Ed. C. F. Tucker Brooke. 1910. Oxford: Clarendon,

1966.

Faulkner, William. <u>As I Lay Dying</u>. 1930. New York: Vintage-

Random, 1964.

Twain, Mark. <u>Adventures of Huckleberry Finn</u>. 1885. Centen-

nial Facsimile Edition. Intro. Hamlin Hill. New York:

Harper, 1962.

Since the date of a work is often important, cite the original date of publication as well as the facts of publication for the reprinted version. The second example illustrates the form for a book reprinted, by the same publisher, in a paperback version. (Vintage is a paperback imprint of the publisher Random House.) Indicate any new material that is part of the reprinted book, as in the third example.

A BOOK WITH TWO OR MORE PUBLISHERS

Green, Mark J., James M. Fallows, and David R. Zwick. <u>Who Runs Congress?</u> Ralph Nader Congress Project. New York: Bantam; New York: Grossman, 1972.

If the title page lists two or more publishers, give all as part of the facts of publication, placing a semicolon between them, as illustrated above.

A CORPORATE AUTHOR

Brown University Library. <u>Dictionary Catalogue of the Harris Collection of American Poetry and Plays</u>. 12 vols. Boston: Hall, 1972.

New York State Office of Planning Coordination. <u>Local Planning and Zoning, 1969: A Manual of Powers and Procedures for Citizens and Governmental Officials</u>. Albany: Office of Planning Coordination, 1969.

List the institution as the author even when it is also the publisher.

A BOOK IN A FOREIGN LANGUAGE

Blanchard, Gerard. <u>Images de la musique au cinéma</u>. Paris: Edilig, 1984.

Gnüg, Hiltrud, ed. <u>Literarische Utopie-Entwürfe</u>. Frankfurt: Suhrkamp, 1982.

Capitalize only the first word of titles and subtitles and words normally capitalized in that language, e.g., proper nouns in French, all nouns in German. A translation in square brackets may be provided. Check your work carefully for spelling and accent marks.

✳ THE BIBLE

The Bible. [Always refers to the King James Version.]

The Bible. Revised Standard Version.

The Reader's Bible: A Narrative. Ed. with Intro.

    Roland Mushat Frye. Princeton: Princeton UP, 1965.

Do not underline the title. Indicate the version if it is not the King James Version. Provide facts of publication for versions not well known.

A BOOK WITH A TITLE IN ITS TITLE

Piper, Henry Dan, ed. Fitzgerald's The Great Gatsby: The

    Novel, the Critics, the Background. Scribner Research

    Anthologies. Gen. Ed. Martin Steinmann, Jr. New York:

    Scribner's, 1970.

If a book's title contains a title normally placed in quotation marks, retain the quotation marks, but if it contains a title normally underlined, do not underline that title, as illustrated above.

Forms for Books: Citing Part of a Book

A PREFACE, INTRODUCTION, FOREWORD, OR AFTERWORD

Sagan, Carl. Introduction. The Red Limit: The Search for

    the Edge of the Universe. By Timothy Ferris. New York:

    Morrow, 1977. 13-16.

Use the appropriate identifying word after the author's name and give inclusive page numbers for the introduction, the part of the book that is by Sagan, at the end of the citation.

AN ENCYCLOPEDIA ARTICLE

Ostrom, John H. "Dinosaurs." McGraw-Hill Encyclopedia of

    Science and Technology. 1987 ed.

"Prohibition." New Encyclopaedia Britannica: Micropaedia.

    1988 ed.

When articles are signed or initialed, provide the author's name. Complete the name of the author of an initialed article thus: K[enney], E[dward] J. Although well-known encyclopedias and dictionaries can be identified by the year of the edition only, the complete facts of publication should be given for less well known works or those in only one edition:

"Benjamin Franklin." Concise Dictionary of American Biog-

raphy. Mgr. Ed. Joseph G. E. Hopkins. New York: Scrib-

ner's, 1964.

ONE OR MORE VOLUMES OF A MULTIVOLUME WORK

James, Henry. The Portrait of a Lady. Vols. 3 and 4. The

Novels and Tales of Henry James. 26 vols. New York:

Scribner's, 1908.

When using a complete work that makes up one or more volumes of a multivolume work, cite the title and volume number(s) of that work followed by the title, editor (if appropriate), number of volumes, and facts of publication for the multivolume work.

A WORK WITHIN ONE VOLUME OF A MULTIVOLUME WORK

Shaw, Bernard. Pygmalion. The Complete Plays with Pref-

aces. 6 vols. New York: Dodd, 1963. 1:197-281.

Cite the author and title of the single work used, followed by the title and facts of publication for the multivolume work. Then give the volume and inclusive page numbers for the specific work. The volume number is an arabic numeral; a colon separates volume and page numbers.

A WORK IN AN ANTHOLOGY OR COLLECTION

Hurston, Zora Neale. The First One. Black Female Play-

wrights: An Anthology of Plays before 1950. Ed. Kathy

A. Perkins. Bloomington: Indiana, 1989. 80-88.

Provide inclusive page numbers, at the end of the citation, for the specific work used. Better yet, include as well the specific work's original date of publication; thus:

Jackson, Shirley. "The Lottery." 1948. The Story and Its

    Writer: An Introduction to Short Fiction. Ed. Ann

    Charters. New York: Bedford-St. Martin's, 1983. 943-

    49.

An Article in a Collection, Casebook, or Sourcebook

Welsch, Roger. "The Cornstalk Fiddle." Journal of American

    Folklore 77 (1964): 262-63. Rpt. in Readings in Amer-

    ican Folklore. Ed. Jan Harold Brunvand. New York:

    Norton, 1979. 106-07.

Spitzer, Leo. "A Reinterpretation of 'The Fall of the House

    of Usher.'" Comparative Literature 4 (1952): 351-63.

    Rpt. in Twentieth Century Interpretations of "The

    Fall of the House of Usher": A Collection of Critical

    Essays. Ed. Thomas Woodson. New York: Prentice, 1969.

    56-70.

MacKenzie, James J. "The Decline of Nuclear Power." engage/

    social April 1986. Rpt. as "America Does Not Need

    More Nuclear Power Plants" in The Environmental Cri-

    sis: Opposing Viewpoints. Eds. Julie S. Bach and Lynn

    Hall. Opposing Viewpoints Series. Ser. Eds. David L.

    Bender and Bruno Leone. St. Paul: Greenhaven, 1986.

    136-41.

Most articles in collections have been previously published, so a complete citation should include the original facts of publication as well as the facts of publication for the collection. The original facts of publication, sometimes excluding page numbers, can be found at the bottom of the first page of the article or on an acknowledgments page in the front or the back of the casebook. Include page numbers for the article in the casebook.

CROSS-REFERENCES

If you are citing several articles from one collection, you can cite the collection and then provide only the author and title of specific articles used, with a cross-reference to the editor(s) of the collection:

```
Bloom, Harold, ed. Ernest Hemingway's The Sun Also Rises.

    Modern Critical Interpretations. New York: Chelsea,

    1987.

Spilka, Mark. "The Death of Love in The Sun Also Rises."

    Bloom 25-37.

Vopat, Carole Gottlieb. "The End of The Sun Also Rises: A

    New Beginning." Bloom 91-101.
```

Forms for Periodicals: Articles in Journals

ARTICLE IN JOURNAL WITH CONTINUOUS PAGING THROUGHOUT THE ISSUES OF EACH YEAR

```
Maynard, Reid. "The Decay Motif in 'The Snows of Kiliman-

    jaro.'" Discourse 10 (1967): 436-39.
```

Give the volume number first, then the year only, in parentheses, followed by a colon and inclusive page numbers. The short story's title, within the article title, is indicated with single quotation marks.

ARTICLE IN JOURNAL WITH SEPARATE PAGING FOR EACH ISSUE

```
Lewis, Kevin. "Superstardom and Transcendence." Arete: The

    Journal of Sport Literature 2.2 (1985): 47-54.
```

When each issue begins with new paging, volume and year are not sufficient to locate the article, so provide issue number, immediately following the volume number, separated by a period. Alternatively, provide the month or season with the year to locate the article:

```
Lewis, Kevin. "Superstardom and Transcendence." Arete: The

    Journal of Sport Literature 2 (Spring 1985): 47-54.
```

Article in Journal That Uses Issue, Not Volume, Numbers

Keen, Ralph. "Thomas More and Geometry." <u>Moreana</u> 86 (1985):

    151-66.

If the journal uses only issue numbers, treat the issue number as a volume number.

Article in a Journal with More than One Series

Chacko, David, and Alexander Kulcsar. "Israel Potter: Gen-

    esis of a Legend." <u>William and Mary Quarterly</u> 3rd ser.

    41 (1984): 365-89.

Provide the series number and the abbreviation "ser." immediately after the journal title, again without using any punctuation. To indicate a new or original series of a journal, use the abbreviation "ns" or "os" immediately after the journal title, without any punctuation.

Forms for Periodicals: Articles in Magazines

Article in a Monthly Magazine

Ostrom, John H. "A New Look at Dinosaurs." <u>National Geo-</u>

    <u>graphic</u> Aug. 1978: 152-85.

Blankenship, Jane, and Janette Kenner. "Images of Tomor-

    row: How Advertisers Sell the Future." <u>Futurist</u> May-

    June 1986: 19-20.

Comer, James P. "Educating Poor Minority Children." <u>Scien-</u>

    <u>tific American</u> Nov. 1988: 42-48.

Articles in popular magazines are best identified by date, not volume number, so do not use volume or issue number, even if the magazine gives them. Instead, cite the month(s) and year after the title, followed by a colon and inclusive page numbers. Abbreviate all months except May, June, and July.

Article in a Weekly Magazine

Greenwald, John. "The Twilight of Apartheid." <u>Time</u> 11 Feb.

    1991: 56-57.

Watson, James D. "DNA Folly Continues." <u>New Republic</u> 13

Jan. 1979: 12+.

Provide the complete date, after the magazine title, using the order of day, month, and year, followed by a colon and inclusive page numbers. If the article begins on one page and then skips several pages before continuing, give the first page number followed, without spacing, by a plus sign, as the second example shows.

An Anonymous Article

"Death of Perestroika." <u>Economist</u> 2 Feb. 1991: 12-13.

The order is the same for any article. Thus the missing name is sufficient indication that the article is anonymous. This citation would be alphabetized under *D*.

A Published Interview

Wanning, Esther. "Allan Lindh." Interview. <u>Omni</u> Mar. 1991:

68+.

Follow the pattern for a published article, but add the identifying word "Interview" (followed by a period) after the article's title.

A Review

Waldron, Arthur. "The Longer March." Rev. of <u>China's Cri-</u>

<u>sis: Dilemmas of Reform and Prospects for Democracy</u>

by Andrew J. Nathan. <u>New Republic</u> 25 Feb. 1991: 39-

41.

Elson, John. "And Now, a R-r-really Big Shew." Rev. of "The

Very Best of the Ed Sullivan Show" CBS 17 Feb. 1991.

<u>Time</u> 18 Feb. 1991: 60.

"Brave New World." Rev. of <u>Perestroika and Soviet National</u>

<u>Security</u> by Michael McGwire. <u>Economist</u> 2 Feb. 1991:

87.

If the review is signed, begin with the author's name, then the title of the review article. Since review titles rarely make clear the work being reviewed, give the title of the work being reviewed and its author, preceded by "Rev of." For reviews of art shows, videos, or computer software, provide place and date or descriptive label to make the citation clear.

AN ARTICLE WITH A QUOTATION IN THE TITLE

```
Greenfield, Meg. "'Colorizing' the News." Newsweek 18 Feb.
     1991: 76.
```

Use single quotation marks around quoted words or phrases, or a quoted title, in the title of the article you are citing.

Forms for Periodicals: Newspapers

✳ AN ARTICLE FROM A NEWSPAPER

```
Sperling, Godfrey. "Sizing Up the Reagan Presidency."
     Christian Science Monitor 15 Jan. 1991: 18.
```

Newspapers are cited much the same as articles in weekly magazines, except for some additional information illustrated in the examples below. A newspaper's title should be cited as it appears on the masthead, excluding any initial article; thus, New York Times, not The New York Times. If the city is not part of the newspaper's title, it should be added in square brackets (not underlined) after the title; thus, Plain Dealer [Cleveland]. Do not add the city for nationally published newspapers such as Wall Street Journal.

AN ARTICLE FROM A NEWSPAPER WITH LETTERED SECTIONS

```
Samuelson, Robert J. "The Deceptive Decade." Washington
     Post 7 Mar. 1990: A27.
```

Place the section letter immediately before the page number, without any spacing.

AN ARTICLE FROM A NEWSPAPER WITH NUMBERED SECTIONS

```
Rosener, Judy B. "Confiscate the Gender Advantage." Los An-
     geles Times 1 Apr. 1989, sec. 2: 8.
```

Place the section number after the date, preceded by a comma and the abbreviation "sec."

An Article from a Newspaper with a Designated Edition

Pereira, Joseph. "Women Allege Sexist Atmosphere in Of-

    fices Constitutes Harassment." Wall Street Journal 10

    Feb. 1988, eastern ed.: 23.

If the newspaper is published in more than one edition each day, the edition used is cited after the date.

An Editorial

"Rights and Remedies." Editorial. New York Times 25 Jan.

    1976, sec. 4: 16.

Add the descriptive label "Editorial" after the article title. Alphabetize by the title.

A Letter to the Editor

Kitching, Beverly. "So You Want to Live in France, Do You?"

    Letter. New York Times 12 Feb. 1991: A18.

If the letter is titled, add the descriptive word "Letter" after the title; if it is untitled, place "Letter" after the author's name.

An Article from NewsBank

Birch, Doug. "Congress Acts to Save More Land for Historic

    Antietam." Sun [Baltimore] 25 Sept. 1988. NewsBank,

    Housing and Land Development, 1988, fiche 89, grid E9.

Give the facts of publication for the article and then the facts needed to locate the article in the computer retrieval service.

Other Sources

The materials in this section, though often important to research projects, do not always lend themselves to documentation by the forms illustrated above. Follow the basic order of author, title, facts of publication as much as possible and add whatever information is necessary, such as a descriptive label, to make the citation clear and useful to a reader.

Bulletin

Krasnowiecki, Jan, and others. Legal Aspects of Planned
   Unit Residential Development, with Suggested Legisla-
   tion. Technical Bulletin No. 52. Washington: Urban
   Land Institute, 1965.

Cartoons and Advertisements

Schulz, Charles M. "Peanuts." Cartoon. Washington Post 10
   Dec. 1985: D8.

Give the cartoon title, if there is one; add the descriptive label "Cartoon"; and then give the facts of publication. The pattern is similar for advertisements:

Halleyscope. "Halleyscopes Are for Night Owls." Advertise-
   ment. Natural History Dec. 1985: 15.

Computer Software

Eysenck, H. J. Know Your Own I.Q. Computer software. Bantam
   Software, 1985. Commodore 64, disk.

Give author, title, descriptive label, distributor, and year of issue. The computer the software is designed for and the form can also be given.

Database Sources

Henderson, Bruce D. "The Origin of Strategy." Harvard Business Review Nov./Dec. 1989: 139+. DIALOG file 122,
   item 125935 896050.

"Marc Chagal." Academic American Encyclopedia. BRS file
   AAED, 1990, item 0057250 9012.

Cite sources obtained from a computer service—such as DIALOG or BRS—like other printed material, but add this information about the source: the name of the service, the file number or letters, and the accession or identifying number for the particular item.

Dissertation—Unpublished

Deppe, Marilyn J. "The Impact of Racial Diversity and In-
     volvement on College Students' Social Concern Val-
     ues." Diss. Claremont Grad. Sch.

Dissertation—Abstract from *Dissertation Abstracts*

Deppe, Marilyn J. "The Impact of Racial Diversity and In-
     volvement on College Students' Social Concern Val-
     ues." <u>DAI</u> 50 (1990): 2397A. Claremont Grad. Sch.

Note that *Dissertation Abstracts (DA)* became *Dissertation Abstracts
International (DAI)* with volume 30 (1969). Since each volume (A—
Humanities and Social Sciences, B—Sciences and Engineering,
C—Worldwide dissertations) is paged separately, include the appropriate
letter following the page number. Use this citation form when you cite
only the abstract, not the dissertation itself.

Government Documents

U.S. President. <u>Public Papers of the Presidents of the
     United States</u>. Washington: Office of the Federal Reg-
     ister, 1961.

United States. Senate. Committee on Energy and Natural Re-
     sources. Subcommittee on Energy Research and Develop-
     ment. <u>Advanced Reactor Development Program: Hearing,
     May 24, 1988</u>. Washington: GPO, 1988.

---. Environmental Protection Agency. <u>The Challenge of the
     Environment: A Primer on EPA's Statutory Authority</u>.
     Washington: GPO, 1972.

Observe the pattern illustrated here. If the author of the document
is not given, cite the name of the government first followed by the name
of the department or agency. If you cite more than one document published by the United States government, do not repeat the name but use
the standard three hyphens followed by a period instead. If you were to

cite a second document prepared by the Environmental Protection Agency, you would then have the following pattern in your list of works cited:

```
United States. Senate. . .

---. Environmental Protection Agency . . . .

---. ---. [second source from EPA]
```

If the author is known, follow this pattern:

```
Geller, William. Deadly Force. U.S. Dept. of Justice Na-
    tional Institute of Justice Crime File Study Guide.
    Washington: U.S. Dept. of Justice, n.d.
```

If the document contains no date, use the abbreviation "n.d."

```
Hays, W. W., ed. Facing Geologic and Hydrologic Hazards.
    Geological Survey Professional Paper 1240-B. Washing-
    ton: GPO, 1981.
```

The U.S. Government Printing Office should be abbreviated *GPO*.

INTERVIEW

```
Plum, Kenneth. Personal interview. 5 Mar. 1982.
```

Alternative descriptive labels include "Interview" and "Telephone interview."

LECTURE

```
Fowler, William. "Henry VIII." Lecture delivered at the
    College of William and Mary, 3 Dec. 1956.
```

LEGAL DOCUMENTS

```
U.S. Const. Art. 1, sec. 3.
```

The Constitution is referred to by article and section. Abbreviations are used; do not underline.

```
Turner v. Arkansas. 407 U.S. 366. 1972.
```

In citing a court case, give the name of the case (the plaintiff and defendant); the volume, name, and page of the report cited; and the date. The name of a court case is underlined (italicized) in the text but not in the Works Cited.

Federal Highway Act, as amended. 23 U.S. Code 109. 1970.

Labor Management Relations Act (Taft-Hartley Act). Stat-
       utes at Large. 61. 1947. 34 U.S. Code. 1952.

Citing laws is complicated, and lawyers use many abbreviations that may not be clear to nonexperts. Bills that become law are published annually in *Statutes at Large* and later in the *U.S. Code*. Provide the title of the bill and the source, volume, and year. References to both *Statutes at Large* and the *U.S. Code* can be given as a convenience to readers.

Letter

McCulley, Cecil M. Letter to the author. 5 June 1968.

Treat a published letter as a work in a collection.

Maps and Charts

Hampshire and Dorset. Map. Kent, Eng.: Geographers' A-Z
       Map, n.d.

The format is similar to that for an anonymous book, but add the appropriate descriptive label.

Mimeographed or Photocopied Material

Burns, Gerald. "How to Say Some Interesting Things about
       Poems." Dittoed essay. 1972.

Pamphlet

So You'd Like to Do Something about Water Pollution. Pub-
       lication 344. Washington: League of Women Voters of
       the U.S., 1969.

Plays or Concerts

A Seagull. By Anton Chekhov. American National Theater.
       Kennedy Center Eisenhower Theater. Washington, D.C.
       21 Dec. 1985.

Include title, author, theater, city, and date of performance. Principal actors, singers, musicians, and/or the director can be added as appropriate.

RECORDINGS

Stein, Joseph. Fiddler on the Roof. Jerry Bock, composer.
Original-Cast Recording with Zero Mostel. RCA, LSO-1093, 1964.

The conductor and/or performers help identify a specific recording. Also include manufacturer, catalog number, and date of issue.

REPORTS

Environment and Development: Breaking the Ideological Deadlock. Report of the Twenty-first United Nations Issues Conference, 23-25 Feb. 1990. Muscatine, Iowa: Stanley Foundation, n.d.

TELEVISION OR RADIO PROGRAMS

"The Making of a Foreign Policy." PBS telecast produced by the National Public Affairs Center for Television. 26 Mar. 1975.

Understanding
Sources and Taking
Notes

*N*ow that you have selected and focused a topic and have gathered sources on that topic in a systematic way, preparing an accurate working bibliography, you are finally ready to "dig in" to your sources: to read, to learn about your subject, and to take notes on the material you need.

THE RESEARCHER'S RELATIONSHIP TO SOURCES

At this stage of your project, you will surely experience the recursive nature of research. To select a topic you may have done some reading, *exploring* reference sources for topic ideas. To prepare a working bibliography, you may have done additional reading, *skimming* articles and the prefaces and tables of contents of books to decide if sources are likely to be useful. Now you need to read again, *studying* in depth this time to learn about the subject, while continually *rethinking* your purpose and

107

approach to the subject. Of all the steps in the research process, this fourth step is the longest, most complex, and probably most important one in determining the quality of your project. The following chart suggests both the complexity of Step 4 and the researcher's relationship to sources throughout the first four steps in research.

Steps in Research	Using Sources
1. Select and limit topic.	**Explore** reference sources to find topic ideas.
2. Focus and plan.	**Explore** reference sources to focus topic.
3. Gather sources, preparing a working bibliography.	**Use** reference works to find potential sources. **Skim** sources to find additional sources.
4. Begin study of sources: Read primary sources first. Read general works before specific ones for background.	**Flip** and **skim** to judge reliability and usefulness; take summary notes.
Expand purpose statement into preliminary outline.	Begin preliminary **reading** of sources.
Study sources in depth.	**Take detailed notes.**

The chart reveals that using sources is an *interactive process,* not a mechanical copying activity. Observe that the guidelines for taking notes are placed near the end of this chapter.

Reasons for Using Sources

Your work with sources will be more profitable if you keep in mind why you need sources and what different sources have to offer the researcher. The way you work with sources will vary somewhat depending on your writing purpose, the knowledge you bring to the project, and the expectations for the research assignment.

Let's consider four research projects:

1. A current problem and possible solutions: Terrorism on television.

2. The effects of a law on a particular period: The effects of Prohibition on the 1920s.

3. A literary analysis: Are Catherine Barkley and Brett Ashley Hemingway heroes?

4. An examination of an unresolved debate: The cause(s) of the dinosaurs' extinction.

1. If you have already decided that terrorism reported on television is a problem and have given some thought to solutions, you may approach your sources primarily to obtain evidence to support your position. You need facts and expert opinion to demonstrate that terrorism on TV is a problem and that your proposed solutions are sound. Should you scan sources quickly, looking just for the evidence to support your argumentative position? That approach is probably too hasty. Remember that good arguments are built on a knowledge of counterarguments; you would be wise to study sources offering a variety of positions on this issue so that you will know what the opposition thinks and be able to develop a challenge to their views. Furthermore, solutions are not simple, for there are issues of freedom of the press and the public's need to know that must be considered.

2. Remember that the Prohibition topic, as presented in Chapter 1 and 2, was selected by a student because of his interest in the 1920s, not because he already possessed knowledge and a position to develop. This student will be turning to sources to learn about a relatively new subject. He will need to read widely, beginning with sources presenting an overview before moving on to more specialized works. As he reads, he will be looking not just for information but for ways to focus his topic, for discussions that will develop or challenge the idea of differing effects on different classes and parts of the country.

3. The student selecting the Hemingway study has been introduced to the concept of the Hemingway hero in class and decides to explore two of Hemingway's novels, *The Sun Also Rises* (read for class) and *A Farewell to Arms,* to see if the lead female characters also fit the hero concept. What sources will she need? First, she will need to read *A Farewell to Arms* and to reexamine key passages in *The Sun Also Rises* that feature Brett Ashley. Second, the student will need to read the chief studies that explain and debate the concept of the Hemingway hero. Third, she may want to read some analyses of the two novels, especially those that focus on Brett and Catherine. The first two steps are essential to developing the topic. The third type of source will be studied briefly or in depth depending on the expectations of the assignment. For a short pa-

per in a 200- or 300-level course, few sources in the third category will be expected. The emphasis should be on the student's application of the concept to her understanding of the characters. In advanced courses, especially in a seminar course requiring a lengthy study, the student will be expected to know the major studies of the novels.

4. This assignment calls for a review of the literature, of the critical debate, on an unresolved issue. The student will need to read widely on the issue of the dinosaurs' extinction, study the theories of the key scientists, and then frame a clear and organized account of the debate. In response to this assignment, students are expected to show an understanding of the issue but not to argue for one theory, even though students learn so much about their topic that they frequently become strong supporters of a particular position. The report of such a study usually takes the form of either an annotated bibliography (a summary of each source studied) or an essay that explains the various theories, in our example, of dinosaur extinction. (Both the annotated bibliography and the review-of-the-literature essay are illustrated in this chapter; see pages 138–50.)

These four research assignments differ in purpose and thus in the researcher's use of sources. Still, each *research* task shares a special relationship to what has already been written on the given topic. Remember that doing research is a way of participating in the scholarly community, in the ongoing examination of the body of knowledge and issues that concern people in a given field. Individual scholars do not operate entirely independently of previous work but rather build on existing knowledge, ideas, and strategies for examining the material (models). Indeed, it is the responsibility of scholars to know what work has already been done, to acknowledge that work, and then to qualify, challenge, or build on that work. Undergraduate researchers are also expected to do more than "write something" on a topic. They are expected to learn this process of surveying the information and ideas already presented and to place their contribution in the context of an ongoing discussion and debate among experts. These expectations apply to the argumentative research essay as well as to the review of literature.

Because scholars share their work with others through conferences, classes, and publishing, others can participate in the ongoing debate by attending lectures and reading sources and then presenting their own work. Whatever your primary purpose in reading sources may be—to review the current literature on a topic, to demonstrate limitations in previous studies, to obtain evidence to support a position—you need to read broadly and in depth, to understand how your work fits into the ongoing discussion of the topic, and to acknowledge your indebtedness to those sources that have given you an approach or model, ideas, and information.

Documenting Sources to Avoid Plagiarism

Your relationship to sources is made clear to readers by the formal pattern of documentation you use. The pattern of documentation you select depends on your field of study, but the need to document accurately and fully applies to all, regardless of the researcher's field. Proper documentation shows readers the breadth of your research and distinguishes between the work of others and your contribution to the understanding of a topic.

Improper documentation of sources—plagiarism—is both unethical and illegal. To fail to make clear your relationship to sources used is to lose your credibility and reputation in the scholarly community. Ideas, new information, and wording belong to their author; to borrow them without acknowledgment is against the law and has led to many celebrated lawsuits. Clearly, paying for a paper from a service and submitting a friend's paper are examples of plagiarism. More often, though, student researchers plagiarize unintentionally because they do not understand the researcher's relationship to sources and the requirements of documentation. Be certain that you know what constitutes appropriate documentation.

MLA documentation requires that precise page references be given for all ideas, opinions, and information taken from sources—except for common knowledge. Author and page references provided in the text are supported by complete bibliographic citations on the Works Cited page. In sum, you are required to document the following:

- Direct quotations from sources
- Paraphrased ideas and opinions from sources
- Summaries of ideas from sources
- Factual information, except common knowledge, from sources

Understand that putting an author's ideas in your own words in a paraphrase or summary does *not* eliminate the requirement of documentation. To illustrate, consider the following excerpt from Thomas R. Schueler's report *Controlling Urban Runoff* (Washington Metropolitan Water Resources Planning Board, 1987: 3–4) and a student paragraph based on the report.

Source

The aquatic ecosystems in urban headwater streams are particularly susceptible to the impacts of urbanization. . . . Dietemann (1975),

Ragan and Dietemann (1976), Klein (1979) and WMCOG (1982) have all tracked trends in fish diversity and abundance over time in local urbanizing streams. Each of the studies has shown that fish communities become less diverse and are composed of more tolerant species after the surrounding watershed is developed. Sensitive fish species either disappear or occur very rarely. In most cases, the total number of fish in urbanizing streams may also decline.

Similar trends have been noted among aquatic insects which are the major food resource for fish. . . . Higher post-development sediment and trace metals can interfere in their efforts to gather food. Changes in water temperature, oxygen levels, and substrate composition can further reduce the species diversity and abundance of the aquatic insect community.

Student paragraph

Studies have shown that fish communities become less diverse as the amount of runoff increases. Sensitive fish species either disappear or occur very rarely and, in most cases, the total number of fish declines. Aquatic insects, a major source of food for fish, also decline because sediment and trace metals interfere with their food-gathering efforts. Increased water temperature and lower oxygen levels can further reduce the species diversity and abundance of the aquatic insect community.

The student's opening words establish a reader's expectation that the student has taken information from a source, as indeed the student has. But where is the documentation? The student's paraphrase is a good example of plagiarism: an unacknowledged paraphrase of borrowed information that even collapses at the end into copying the source's exact wording. For MLA style, the author's name and the precise page numbers are needed (as illustrated in Chapter 5). Additionally, the final phrase must be put into the student's own words or be placed within quotation marks.

Students are often uncertain about what is considered common knowledge and wonder if most of their sentences will need documentation. In general, common knowledge includes:

- Undisputed dates
- Well-known facts
- Generally known facts, terms, and concepts in a field of study

Thus, even if you had to check a reference source for the exact dates of the Battle of Waterloo or read in several biographies that Benjamin Franklin experimented with electricity, you would not document the sources used because such information is readily available in many reference texts.

You also do not cite sources for the concepts of character conflict in literature or the superego in psychology. But you should acknowledge a historian who analyzes the causes for Napoleon's defeat at Waterloo, a scientist who evaluates Franklin's contribution to the study of electricity, or a critic who explains Hemingway's concept of a hero. *Opinions* about well-known facts must be documented; *discussions* of debatable dates, terms, or concepts must be documented. The more you learn about a field of study the more comfortable you will become deciding when to document. If, after studying your sources to judge what most writers accept as common knowledge, using common sense, and checking with your instructor, you are still uncertain, defend your integrity by documenting the information. Understanding your proper relationship to sources will guide you to accurate note-taking. In Chapter 5, additional guidelines will help you turn notes into passages in your paper that are free from unintentional plagiarizing.

EVALUATING SOURCES

Establishing an appropriate relationship to sources requires (1) understanding when primary sources are needed in addition to secondary sources and (2) finding sources that are both reliable and useful for your topic. To pursue a study successfully, you must ask yourself what information you need and what sources you must review. Keep in mind that the first six sources you locate may not be the best six for your research task. Develop a healthy skepticism about everything you read; check more than one source to verify information and judge the credibility of potential sources. What sources you select and how you use them will do much to determine the quality of your study.

Distinguishing Between Primary and Secondary Sources

Although particular research assignments vary in the relative weight given to primary and secondary sources, researchers need to be able to distinguish between the two and to know, if both are required, what the balance should be between them. *Primary sources* have the most immediate or direct relationship to the subject; they are firsthand works. *Secondary sources* are studies and interpretations of primary sources; they are secondhand. The following partial list, by subject area, will help you distinguish between the two.

Subject Area	Primary Sources	Secondary Sources
History and government	State papers Legislation Letters, diaries	Histories Biographies
Literary studies	Novels, plays, short stories, poems, letters, early drafts	Analyses and interpretations Biographies
Social sciences	Findings from questionnaires, interviews, case studies, tests, experiments	Evaluations in books and articles of data found in primary sources
Sciences	Experiments, discoveries, testing methods	Discussions in books and articles of test results, discoveries, and experiments
Business	Market research, computer data, technical reports, designs	Articles and books on business and management

Rarely are research projects based solely on primary sources. Reports of experiments or discoveries in the sciences and social sciences are usually accompanied by both analyses and interpretation of the results *and* reference to previous relevant research. Some kinds of research topics, such as the study of terrorism on television, can be developed from secondary sources only, although the student selecting this topic would be expected to have observed television news coverage of terrorist events. A review of the theories of dinosaur extinction would be one kind of study based on secondary sources.

Research topics frequently call for a combination of primary and secondary sources. This balance is valuable because primary sources provide a check against inaccuracies that may be found in secondary sources. Also, secondary sources present the opinions, the biases, of their authors, just as your research essay will present your viewpoints. Your study of the appropriate primary sources will allow you to develop your own ideas and analyses. You should never, for example, attempt an analysis of Hemingway's Catherine Barkley based entirely on critical studies; you must read *A Farewell to Arms* and examine the character yourself. If your paper is an argument in support of U.S.-Russian disarmament treaties, you must read the treaties, not just articles about them. If you want to study the effect of television advertising on children, you must be prepared to spend several mornings in front of the television watching and taking notes during children's programs. There are important differences between the entire text of a president's speech, a news story about the speech (even "straight" news has a particular point of view), and a *Wall Street Journal* editorial reacting to the speech. If the speech is a vital part of your project, you must know it thoroughly. Every other source you may choose to read is of secondary importance.

Judging Reliability and Usefulness of Sources

When you use facts and opinions from sources, you are saying to readers that those facts are accurate and that those ideas are credible. Thus you cannot risk losing your credibility by taking information from any source. Just because they are in print does not mean that a writer's "facts" are reliable or ideas worthwhile. As you examine potential sources for reliability, examine them for usefulness as well. Credible sources that are only marginally related to your topic are not useful. As already established, for some types of research projects, primary sources are not just useful but essential. Use the following strategies to judge reliability and usefulness.

USE THE BEST AUTHORS AND WORKS

Selecting the best scholars and the key studies of a topic will show your instructor that you are learning about the field, not just about a specific topic. You will also build the most effective study if you draw on the topic's most substantial works. How do you judge the credibility of writers and works?

Locate an Author's Credentials.   A writer's degrees, current position, and other publications are often provided with an article or at the back of a book. If not, try to find an article on the writer in a biographical dictionary such as *Contemporary Authors* or *American Men and Women of Science*. If these strategies fail, ask your instructor if she or he has heard of the writer.

Find Reviews of the Work.   Examine the *Book Review Digest* volume for a book's publication year to learn how reviewers received the book. Several thousand books are covered in each yearly volume. As Figure 40 illustrates, the *Book Review Digest* includes a summary and one or more reviews of each book. *The Booklist,* a source primarily for librarians that researchers can also use, reviews new books in a monthly magazine format. There are also indexes to reviews in periodicals. Indexes, of course, do not include the reviews but tell researchers where to find them. Here are four: *Book Review Index, Current Book Review Citations, Index to Book Reviews in the Humanities,* and *Index to Book Reviews in the Social Sciences.*

Use the Appropriate *Citation Index* to Locate the Books and Articles Most Frequently Cited in Other Works.   The various parts of the *Citation Indexes* (for the arts and humanities, the social sciences, and the sciences) and the methods for using them are explained in Chapter 2. Remember that the *Citation Index* lists sources that are cited by other writers. We can conclude that works frequently cited by others writing on the subject are the key works on that subject. Another part of each *Citation Index,* the *Permuterm Subject Index,* lists authors who have written on a given subject. Writers who are listed several times, who have published frequently on a subject, are probably experts whose works should be included in your study.

Note Authors Whose Works are Included in Your Text's References and Who Appear Frequently in the Bibliographies Found in the Sources You Have Already Located.   The concept here is the same as with *Citation Index*. Writers who have written several works on

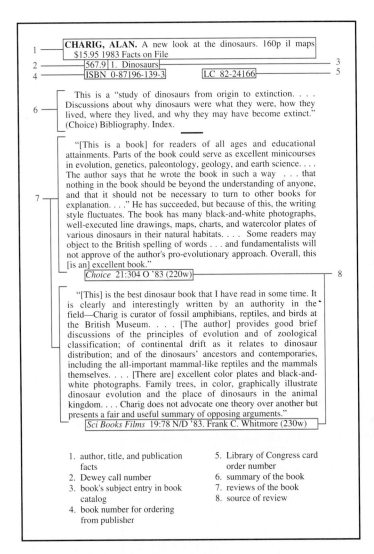

Figure 40 From *Book Review Digest.*

your topic and have been acknowledged by other writers are among the experts you need to study. Consider, for example, the partial list of references, shown in Figure 41, from an article on television and children. Clearly, Rubinstein is an important researcher on this topic; so are Comstock and Gerbner.

REFERENCES

McCombs, and D. Roberts. 1978. *Television and Human Behavior.* Columbia University Press.

Comstock, G., and M. Fisher. 1975. *Television and Human Behavior: A Guide to the Pertinent Scientific Literature.* Santa Monica, CA: Rand Corporation.

Comstock, G., and G. Lindsey. 1975. *Television and Human Behavior: The Research Horizon, Future and Present.* Santa Monica, CA: Rand Corporation.

Consumers Union. 1976. *The Six Billion Dollar Sell.* Mount Vernon, NY.

Cook, T. D., H. Appleton, R. F. Conner, A. Shaffer, G. Tomkin, and S. J. Weber. 1975. *Sesame Street Revisited.* New York: Russell Sage Foundation.

Dienstbier, R. A. 1977. Sex and violence: Can research have it both ways? *J. Communication* 27:176-88.

Fernandez-Collado, C., and B. S. Greenberg. 1977. *Substance Use and Sexual Intimacy on Commercial Television.* Report #5, Mich. State Univ.

Feshbach, S. 1961. The stimulating versus cathartic effects of a vicarious aggressive activity. *J. Abnormal and Soc. Psych.* 63:381-85.

Ford Foundation. 1976. *Television and Children: Priorities for Research.* New York.

Franzblau, S., J. N. Sprafkin, and E. A. Rubinstein. 1977. Sex on TV: A content analysis. *J. Communication* 27:164-70.

Frueh, T., and P. E. McGhee. 1975. Traditional sex-role development and amount of time spent watching television. *Devel. Psych.* 11:109.

Gerbner, G. 1972. Violence in television drama: Trends and symbolic functions. In *Television and Social Behavior,* vol. 1. *Media Content and Control,* ed. G. A. Comstock and E. A. Rubinstein. U. S. Government Printing Office.

Gerbner, G., L. Gross, M. Jackson-Beeck, A. Jeffries-Fox, and N. Signorielli. 1978. *Violence Profile No. 9.* Univ. of Pennsylvania Press.*

Kochnower, J. M., J. F. Fracchia, E. A. Rubinstein, and J. N. Sprafkin. 1978. *Television Viewing Behaviors of Emotionally Disturbed Children: An Interview Study.* New York: Brookdale International Institute.

Lefkowitz, M. M., L. D. Eron, L. O. Walder, and L. R. Huesmann. 1972. Television violence and child agression: A follow-up study. In *Television and Social Behavior,* vol. 3. *Television and Adolescent Aggressiveness,* ed. G. A. Comstock and E. A. Rubinstein. U. S. Gov. Printing Office.

Lesser, G. S. 1974. *Children and Television: Lessons from "Sesame Street."* Random House.

Liebert, D. E., R. M. Liebert, J. N. Sprafkin, and E. A. Rubinstein. 1977. Effects of television commercial disclaimers on the product expectations of children. *J. Communication* 27:118-24.

Lyle, J., and H. Hoffman. 1972. Children's use of television and other media. In *Television and Social Behavior,* vol. 5. *Television in Day-to-Day Life: Patterns of Use,* ed. E. A. Rubinstein, G. A. Comstock, and J. P. Murray. U. S. Government Printing Office.

Ratner, E. M., et al. 1978. FTC *Staff Report on Television Advertising to Children.* Washington, DC: Federal Trade Commission.

Robertson, T. S., and J. R. Rossiter. 1974. Children and commercial persuasion: An attribution theory analysis. *J. Consumer Research* 1:13-20.

Rubinstein, E. A. 1975. Social science and media policy. *J. Communication* 25:194-200.

____. 1976. Warning: The Surgeon General's research program may be dangerous to preconceived notions. *J. Soc. Issues* 32:18-34.

Rubinstein, E. A., J. F. Fracchia, J. M. Kochnower, and J. N. Sprafkin. 1977. *Television Viewing Behaviors of Mental Patients: A survey of Psychiatric Centers in New York State.* New York: Brookdale International Institute.

Rubinstein, E. A., R. M. Liebert, J. M. Neale, and R. W. Poulos. 1974. *Assessing Television's Influence on Children's Prosocial Behavior.* New York: Brookdale International Institute.

Figure 41 Partial List of References from "Television and the Young Viewer."

118

SELECT RECENT SECONDARY SOURCES

Some studies published years ago remain classic works in their field, but many older works become outdated because new information is available to today's scholars. In scientific and technical fields, the "information revolution" has outdated works of only five or ten years ago. For example, many studies based on information obtained in the 1980 Census will no longer be reliable. And studies of Saturn that fail to take into account the new knowledge obtained from Voyager II are no longer up-to-date. The classic studies in any field have acquired the status of "primary" sources; read them to learn about your field of study. But pass over old, undistinguished secondary sources in favor of current studies. Studies of the dinosaurs, for instance, that describe them all as slow and dim-witted are themselves fossils.

SELECT PROPERLY DOCUMENTED SOURCES

Consider a work's use of documentation when judging its reliability. Scholarly works will cite sources. Well-researched and reliable pieces intended for a less specialized audience will also make clear the source of any statistics used or the credentials of any authority who is quoted. One good rule: Never use undocumented statistical information presented in a secondary source.

USE CREDIBLE SOURCES AT THE APPROPRIATE LEVEL

Consider a writer's intended audience and purpose in writing as part of your evaluation. Is the source intended for a specialized or general audience? You can estimate the degree of specialized knowledge in an article by considering the writer's intended audience. *Psychological Bulletin* is written by specialists for specialists; *Psychology Today* is a popular magazine for a general audience. Considering the location of articles, and hence their intended audience, will help you choose among potential sources those that are not too general or too specialized, too elementary or too sophisticated for your needs. In books, study the language as a guide to their intended audiences. If skimming reveals short sentences and a simple vocabulary, the book may be too elementary for your project.

A writer's purpose needs consideration too. Often articles in popular magazines, although easier to read, may lack the balanced, objective approach of a scholarly work. The goal of the popular article may be to persuade rather than to analyze and inform. Be especially cautious with works designed to reinforce biases already shared by the intended audience. Such works are helpful to a researcher who needs to know the views of opposing sides on an issue, but the "evidence" contained in these works must be weighed carefully. The *Nation* contains articles on political and social issues that reflect a liberal slant; *National Review* presents the views of conservative thinkers.

EXAMINE SOURCES FOR RELEVANCE

Judging the usefulness of sources can be a problem for beginning researchers. When evaluating articles, consider the context of the intended audience and purpose of the periodical. How much information can you expect the article to provide? When the article is accompanied by an abstract, read that first. Then skim the first few paragraphs or flip through the article to note its subheadings. You can save time (and money) if you check articles for usefulness before reading or photocopying many pages that turn out to be useless.

Judging books may take a little longer, except for those essential primary sources for some projects. For other potential books, explore their various parts:

1. The *title* and *subtitle*. Sometimes titles that might be misleading are clarified by their subtitles. Cynthia Russett's title *Darwin in America* is clarified by the subtitle *The Intellectual Response 1865–1912*.

2. The *preface* or *introduction*. Here the author sets forth the book's focus and scope, and perhaps some key ideas that underlie his or her approach to the subject.

3. The *table of contents* provides chapter titles that will give you an idea of specific topics covered in the book.

4. *Appendices*, when included, often contain statistical information or other specifics that support the text's discussion.

5. *The reference notes and bibliography* guide you to other sources, an important contribution even if the book is not used in any other way. They also mark the scholarly nature of the source.

6. The *index* provides the most detailed list of topics covered in the book.

The student studying Prohibition applied these guidelines to judge a book he found while browsing through the American history section of the library stacks. The book, published by a university press, was written by a college professor. The title—*Into the Twenties: The United States from Armistice to Normalcy*—suggests that the book will examine the years during which the Eighteenth Amendment was passed by Congress and ratified by the states, so it could well have a section on Prohibition. Flipping through the book, the student saw that the text was heavily documented with footnotes and concluded with a 10-page bibliographical essay. The book certainly appeared to have credibility, and if it treated the student's topic at all, it should yield additional sources on the topic. Neither the Preface nor the Table of Contents mentioned Prohibition specifically, but one chapter, "American Society, 1920," showed promise, so the student examined the Index and found the following entry:

> Prohibition, 165, 166; and fundamentalism, 166; and rural-urban conflict, 166–67; and progressivism, 166–67

Although the book gives only three pages to the student's subject, they turned out to be three important pages containing references to a dozen sources and a debate on the extent to which Prohibition represented an "urban-rural, Catholic-Protestant, and immigrant-nativist" dichotomy. In only a few minutes, the student was able to evaluate the source and find the portion of it that was relevant to his research.

SELECTING A PRELIMINARY OUTLINE

Reflecting on what kinds of sources your topic needs and skimming sources as you evaluate their potential should combine to help you shape a preliminary outline to guide reading and note-taking. A preliminary outline does not need to be in finished form, because it is designed only for you. Still, make it as detailed as you can so that it is the best guide to your reading. Most important: Make it reflect your research purpose.

Review Your Research Purpose

You have used your research purpose as a guide to selecting sources. You also want to start here to develop a preliminary outline. Let's consider the sample topics once again.

TERRORISM ON TELEVISION

The student exploring this issue began by stating a position and then listing elements to be covered.

```
    Thesis:  Extensive coverage of terrorism by the
media, giving terrorists the forum they want, may be
contributing to additional terrorist acts.
    Items to cover: examples of terrorist acts
                    treatment by press, TV attitudes
                    toward issue expressed by
                    journalists, political leaders
                    ways to limit/control coverage
```

This student has done some thinking about the development of the thesis but still has much to do to frame an approach to the problem.

The Effects of Prohibition on the 1920s

From his preliminary reading, the student took the idea of examining the effects on urban and rural areas and on different classes of society. After gathering sources and doing some preliminary reading, the student decided to focus his study on this research question: Why was Prohibition more acceptable to rural areas than to the urban Northeast? He then developed this preliminary guide:

```
social/cultural demographics
        country
        city
economics of Prohibition
        country
        city
religious values
        country
        city
conc.: Look past the 1920s to long-range effects of
        Prohibition.
```

Catherine Barkley and Brett Ashley as Hemingway Heroes

After determining the kinds of sources needed, reading *A Farewell to Arms,* and preparing a bibliography on the Hemingway hero concept, the student decided to limit her topic to better fit the guidelines of a six-page paper. She decided to concentrate on Catherine in *A Farewell to Arms.* She prepared the following research question and preliminary outline:

```
Does Catherine Barkley show the dominant traits

of Hemingway's male heroes?

Intro.: Establish critical concept of Hemingway hero.

Body:   Describe dominant traits of Hemingway hero;

        taking traits one by one, analyze Catherine to

        determine if she demonstrates each trait.

Conc.:  Answer research question.
```

The Dinosaurs' Extinction: A Literature Review

Because the assignment calls for an essay reviewing the literature, the student is expected to produce an organized paper, not a series of summaries of sources loosely "glued" together. When Aaron (whose essay appears on pages 142–50) first started reading, he thought that using chronological order would be the best approach; he would explain the older theories first and then move to the current ones. After further reading, however, Aaron decided that the more useful distinction for his particular topic was between the theories based on extraterrestrial causes and those based on terrestrial causes. Here is his preliminary outline:

```
Intro.: The critical debate—-What led to dinosaur

        extinction?

Body:   Extraterrestrial theories

            asteroids, comets, supernova (key is

            iridium)

        Terrestrial theories

            continental drift, global warming,

            excessive size, others?

Conc.:  Is one theory decisive?
```

Although an annotated bibliography is organized by the sources studied, a literature review needs to be organized primarily by ideas. Aaron's outline reflects that understanding of his research purpose.

Review Basic Organizational Strategies

Researchers should be aware of several basic organizational strategies that are used repeatedly because they correspond to the kinds of questions that we ask and approaches that we take to studying issues. Knowing these patterns, instructors often frame research assignments that will generate one of the following strategies.

THE "JOURNAL" REPORT STRUCTURE

The expected organization for journal articles reporting findings in the sciences and social sciences will be appropriate for student primary investigations and experiments. This structure is firmly established and should be adhered to with little variation.

> Introduction: states hypothesis or research question
>
> Review of literature: examines previous studies and discussions of issue
>
> Methods: explains research procedures
>
> Results: presents data obtained from experiment, case studies, interviews, questionnaires, etc.
>
> Discussion: presents an analysis and interpretation of data; implications of results

COMPARISON/CONTRAST STRUCTURE

Research projects frequently call for a comparison or contrast: of two philosophies, two psychological models, two management strategies, two literary works, two educational theories, and so on. At times you may be expected to give full and equal treatment to both similarities and differences. More often, you will need a thesis that dictates either a comparative study or a contrasting study. If your thesis is "In spite of some obvious similarities, 'A' and 'B' differ in significant ways," then you can begin by noting some similarities, but the body of your paper will be organized by differences. If your thesis notes similarities, then the body of your paper will be organized to show similarities. Whether your project is predominantly a comparative or contrasting study, organize your paper by using either the "whole-by-whole" or the "part-by-part" structure.

Whole-by-Whole	Part-by-Part
Theory A	Difference 1
difference 1	Theory A
difference 2	Theory B
difference 3	Difference 2
Theory B	Theory A
difference 1	Theory B
difference 2	Difference 3
difference 3	Theory A
	Theory B

Usually, the "part-by-part" structure is the better choice because it is a stronger comparison/contrast pattern, focusing the reader's attention on the similarities or differences. Unless handled carefully, the "whole-by-whole" structure can collapse into two loosely connected summaries.

TEST OR APPLY A THEORY, CONCEPT, OR MODEL

A common assignment in many fields is the testing of a theory, concept, or model or the application of a theory, concept, or model to a new situation. In foreign policy analyses, one can test the concept of nation-states acting autonomously. In his psychology paper presented in Chapter 7, Adam Wilhite tests the view that adolescent ego identity formation is "a transition from one polar alternative . . . to another." In the sample study of Catherine as a Hemingway hero, the student is applying a concept about several male Hemingway characters to a female character. Exactly how such a paper should be developed will depend on the specific topic and the student's field of study, but in general, follow this pattern:

Intro.:   Establish theory, concept, or model.
           Review literature on theory, concept, or model.
           Present test or application to be developed.

Body: Develop test or application of theory, concept, or model.

Conc.:   Draw conclusion about theory, concept, or model, namely that it is (or is not) sound, that it can (or cannot) be applied to the situation studied.

PROBLEM/SOLUTION STRUCTURE

Many argumentative research essays examining public policy issues can be understood as arguments over solutions to problems. There are a number of elements to include in such arguments, depending on the problem you are writing about and your purpose in writing. Some arguments need to concentrate on the nature of the problem, because how a problem is defined has much to do with finding appropriate solutions. (For example, is world hunger an agricultural or political problem?) Other arguments need to convince readers that some situation is a problem, or convince readers of the causes of the problem. Possibly as many as seven steps may be needed to develop and support a solution to a problem. When planning, consider each of the following steps and decide which are relevant to your issue. Then discuss each of the relevant steps in the following order.

1. Demonstrate that a situation exists.
   (Cite low test scores in math and science by American students.)

2. Demonstrate that the situation is a problem.
   (Weaker skills in math and science can reduce American scientific and technical competitiveness, and many American citizens are scientifically illiterate.)

3. Explain causes of the problem. If your proposed solution calls for removing the causes of the problem, then you must establish the causes.
   (One cause: teenagers' negative attitudes about academic performance.)

4. Present your solution(s).
   (One solution: change students' attitudes; get students to believe that it is cool to learn.)

5. Explain the process for achieving your solution(s).
   (Start a media blitz.)

6. Support the feasibility of your solution(s).
   (TV "ads" can change attitudes over time.)

7. Show that your solution is better than others.
   (If attitudes don't change, then adding courses or extending the school year will not make much difference.)

Consider how these steps can be used by the student studying terrorism on television to develop a preliminary outline that will be more helpful than what he has to date (see page 122). Since most people are aware of terrorist acts and their television coverage, Step 1 need not be addressed. Observe, though, that the student's tentative thesis, as currently worded, is a defense of the second step, namely that covering terrorism in the media creates the problem of encouraging further terrorism. Can this thesis be convincingly supported? Covering terrorism on television seems to be giving terrorists exactly what they want: recognition and a public forum for their demands. But can we demonstrate that the coverage actually increases terrorist acts? Probably not. What the student really wants to discuss are the best solutions to the problem (Steps 4–7), given the possibility that media coverage may be adding to the problem of terrorism.

The student can begin by narrowing his topic to television only, because solutions might need to be quite different for the different forms of media coverage. Next he can revise his tentative thesis to focus on solutions, *even though he may not be certain of the precise solutions he wants to support.* Finally, he can develop a better preliminary outline based on the seven steps:

```
Thesis: Because extensive coverage of terrorism
by television news may contribute to additional
terrorist acts, we should establish ways to control
the type and extent of television coverage to avoid
contributing to the problem.
        Intro.: Examples of terrorist acts to remind
                readers of the situation--focus on use of
                media to make demands.
        Body:   1. Explanation of ways that television
                   distorts reality; how this aids
                   terrorists and adds to the problem.
                2. Discussion of most frequently proposed
                   solutions.
                3. Argument against those solutions not
                   considered good or feasible. E.g.,
```

```
                   complete banning of coverage of a

                   newsworthy event incompatible with

                   freedom of the press.

              4.   Argument for preferred solutions.

                   Explain why they are best.

        Conc.:     Explain how to implement proposed

                   solutions to show that they are workable

                   and can satisfy both the news reporters

                   and the need to avoid contributing to

                   terrorism.
```

TAKING NOTES

Finally, with sources in hand and a preliminary outline to guide your reading and thinking, you are ready to study those sources in depth and to take notes. The following guidelines offer advice for preparing accurate, complete, and useful notes.

Guidelines for Taking Notes

1. **Use cards,** preferably 4 × 6 cards. This size gives you more space for writing and allows you to distinguish between note cards and the 3 × 5 bibliography cards.

2. **Write in ink.** Penciled notes will blur with shuffling and rearranging.

3. **Write only one item on each card.** Each card should contain only one idea, piece of information, or group of related facts. The flexibility gained by using cards is lost if you do not follow this principle. You need the flexibility of shuffling and grouping note cards to adhere to the organization you develop.

4. **Use only one side of each card.** Material on the back of a card may be forgotten when you start drafting your paper. If you must go to the back to finish a long note, write "OVER" at the bottom of the card as a reminder.

5. **Study first; write notes later.** Avoid rushing into note-taking. First, do background reading. Second, skim what appear to be your chief

sources and write summary notes. Read to obtain a general familiarity with your topic and to develop a preliminary outline. Learn what the experts consider to be important details and concepts. In this way, you will avoid writing many useless notes, which wastes time and is frustrating.

6. **Identify the source for each note.** *Before writing the note,* place the author's name, a shortened title if necessary to identify the source, and the precise number of the page from which the note is taken on the card's upper right-hand corner. *Remember that all borrowed information and ideas must be documented in your paper with precise page numbers.*

7. **Identify the type of information contained in the note.** Place a word or phrase at the top of each card to identify the note. This will simplify the sorting of cards into the major parts of your paper when you are ready to start the draft. The identifying words or phrases should be selected carefully to correspond to the subsections of your paper according to your preliminary outline.

8. **Write the information itself—legibly and accurately—on the note card.** Record the information in summary or paraphrase form or as a direct quotation, as illustrated below.

9. **Distinguish carefully between fact and opinion.** A note that records facts does not need labeling, but a note that records opinion should be introduced with a statement such as "Smith believes that," "Smith asserts that," or "Smith concludes that." Alternatively, label the note "opinion."

10. **Distinguish clearly between ideas or opinions taken from sources and your own opinions, questions, or reactions to the information recorded.** Write your reactions so that you do not forget good ideas that come to you as you are reading. Just be certain to avoid confusion either by placing your ideas on separate note cards— marked "my notes"—or by drawing a line between information from a source and your response.

Figure 42 shows a sample note card written according to these guidelines.

Methods of Note-Taking

Writing notes should be mechanical only insofar as you develop the habit of recording all necessary information in a consistent pattern on each

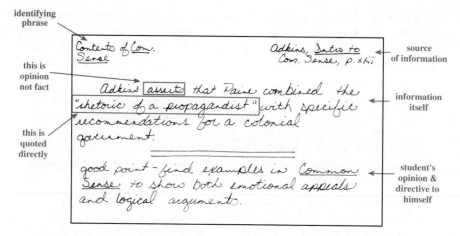

Figure 42 Sample Note Card.

card. Notes are actually brief letters to yourself; they need to make sense and serve the researcher weeks after they are first written. As you review the conventions of note-taking, think not only about format but also about when each type of note will best serve your research purpose.

SUMMARY NOTES

Summary notes, as mentioned previously in this chapter, are especially useful during the preliminary or background reading stage. When prepared at this stage, they will help you decide which sources to return to later for more specific note-taking. Further, when you write about what you are reading, you will retain more of the background information you are reviewing.

Summary notes also provide a condensed version, in your own words, of a longer passage of information or ideas. When written for this purpose, summary notes must contain the precise page numbers for the passage that has been condensed, for you will need to document the information if it is used in your paper. Figure 43 shows a summary note of an article on television news programs. Observe that "shows" is in quotation marks to capture Postman's use of the term as a criticism of network news programs.

PARAPHRASE NOTES

A paraphrase is a restatement in your own words of a passage. A paraphrase note differs from a summary note because it is not a condensed

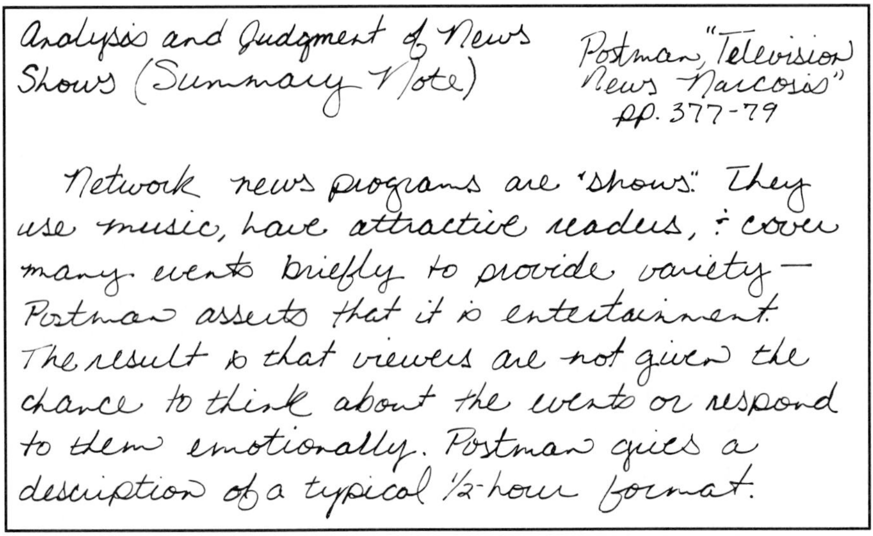

Analysis and Judgment of News
Shows (Summary Note)

Postman, "Television
News Narcosis"
pp. 377-79

Network news programs are "shows." They use music, have attractive readers, + cover many events briefly to provide variety — Postman asserts that it is entertainment. The result is that viewers are not given the chance to think about the events or respond to them emotionally. Postman gives a description of a typical ½-hour format.

Figure 43 Summary Note Card.

version; paraphrasing can produce about the same number of words as in the original—just different ones. A paraphrase note differs from a direct-quotation note because it uses *your* words. Read and understand the material; then completely rewrite the passage. *If you change or rearrange a few words only, you will be plagiarizing.*

For example, the student working with Postman's article wants to take a note on the following passage:

> It is also believed that audiences are captivated by variety and re-pelled by complexity, which is why, during a typical thirty-minute show, there will be between fifteen and twenty "stories." Discount-ing time for commercials, promos for stories to come, and news readers' banter, this works out to an average of sixty seconds a story.

Suppose she were to prepare the following note:

> Because it is believed that audiences like variety and
> dislike complexity, a typical thirty-minute show has
> between fifteen and twenty "stories." When you

```
discount time for commercials, promos, and banter,

this works out to about sixty seconds a story.
```

Is this an acceptable paraphrase of the source? No; it relies too heavily on Postman's words and ordering of ideas. Figure 44 presents an acceptable paraphrase of Postman's material.

Some instructors advise that you take time at the note-taking stage to write fairly polished paraphrases so that you can insert the material into your draft with little revision. Others advise writing rough paraphrases—using fragments, listing points—on the argument that you may have to reword each note anyway, once you see where and how it will be used. Also, rough notes are less likely to pick up the words and style of the original passage; hence, you will avoid the risk of plagiarism. *A reminder:* Paraphrased material, just like direct quotations, must be documented, so make certain to include a precise page number on each paraphrase note card. Figure 45 provides a good example of a paraphrase note that is simply written, or "rough." The note also makes clear that the statements represent Postman's opinion.

Figure 44 Paraphrase Note Card.

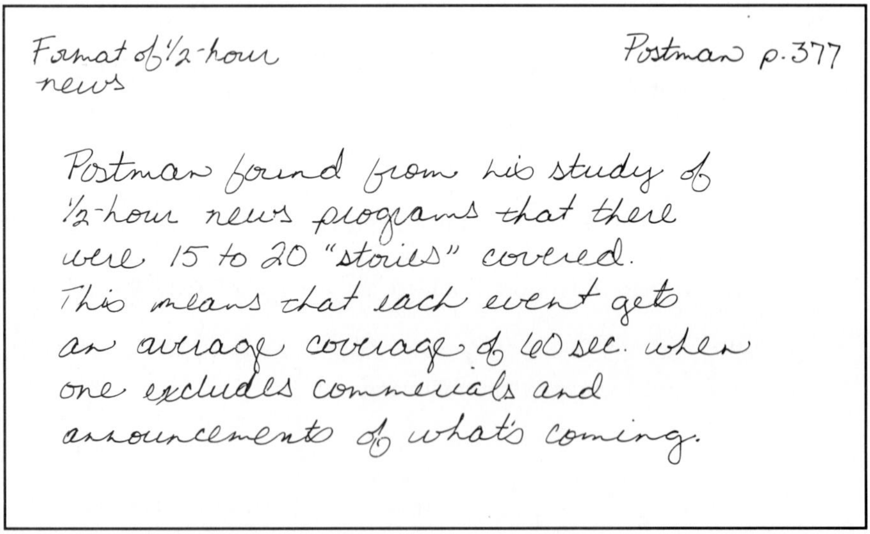

Format of ½-hour news   Postman p. 377

Postman found from his study of ½-hour news programs that there were 15 to 20 "stories" covered. This means that each event gets an average coverage of 60 sec. when one excludes commercials and announcements of what's coming.

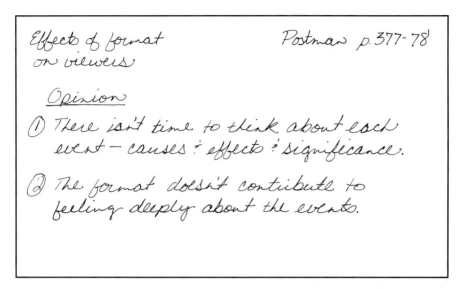

*Effects of format
on viewers*

Opinion

① *There isn't time to think about each
event — causes ÷ effects ÷ significance.*

② *The format doesn't contribute to
feeling deeply about the events.*

Postman p. 377-78

Figure 45 Paraphrase Note Card (Rough Paraphrase).

DIRECT-QUOTATION NOTES

Since most of your paper should be in your own words, most of your notes should be paraphrases rather than direct quotations. A paper that is a string of quotations "glued" together with a few transitional sentences is mere patchwork, not your own paper. The best way to resist using too many quotations is not to take notes that are directly quoted. Recording a direct quotation rather than a paraphrase only postpones the task of putting that information in your own words.

There are four legitimate uses of direct quotation in a research paper:

1. **To convey statistical information.** Paraphrasing a series of statistics without distorting the evidence can be difficult. Also, you may not be sure, at the note-taking stage, how much of the statistical information you will need to include in your paper.

2. **To give examples of a writer's ideas or style of writing.** When your purpose is to examine a writer's ideas or stylistic techniques, you must give specific examples of those ideas or techniques in direct quotation and then analyze them. For example, the student writing on Thomas Paine's skill as a persuasive writer should take notes from *Common Sense* in direct quotation, as examples of Paine's style.

3. **To cite an authoritative opinion.** When the opinion of an authority is especially helpful in support of a controversial thesis, it may be important to present that opinion in the authority's exact words. Certainly, if you intend to challenge an authority's views, you will want to give the reader the exact passage that you then dispute.

4. **To capture special phrasing.** At times a writer's views will coalesce in a phrase or sentence that cannot be paraphrased without changing the meaning or losing the power of the statement. Be careful, however, not to overuse this justification for quoting. Your paper should reflect not only your own thinking but also your own writing style. *If you cannot justify a direct quotation on the basis of these guidelines, paraphrase instead.*

When preparing a direct-quotation note, make sure that you compare your note word for word with the source to ensure accurate spelling and punctuation, as well as completeness. Then place all quoted material within quotation marks or, better yet, within double angle brackets—⟨⟨and⟩⟩—so that there is no doubt that you have someone else's words on the card.

When you have reason to quote, keep in mind as well that you are lifting a short passage out of a larger context. Be certain that what you quote is faithful to the entire source and does not misrepresent the writer's views on the topic. Figure 46 shows a direct-quotation note.

PHOTOCOPYING

Photocopying facilities in libraries make possible taking home entire articles and large sections of reference books that in the past students would have studied in the library. Keep in mind that photocopying provides the convenience of studying in your room, but it does not eliminate the need to take from each source only those key points that belong in your paper. Highlighting or in some other way indicating passages that you would, without photocopying, have noted in direct quotation can save time and be a guard against copying errors. But since most of the material you take from sources should be put in your own words, at some point you will have to paraphrase the information in those photocopies (just as you need to take notes on information in the books you have checked out). Probably some combination of strategies is in order: Photocopy key sources so that you can easily return to them, highlight segments to be quoted, and make paraphrase note cards for most of the information so that you can synthesize that material with ideas from other sources.

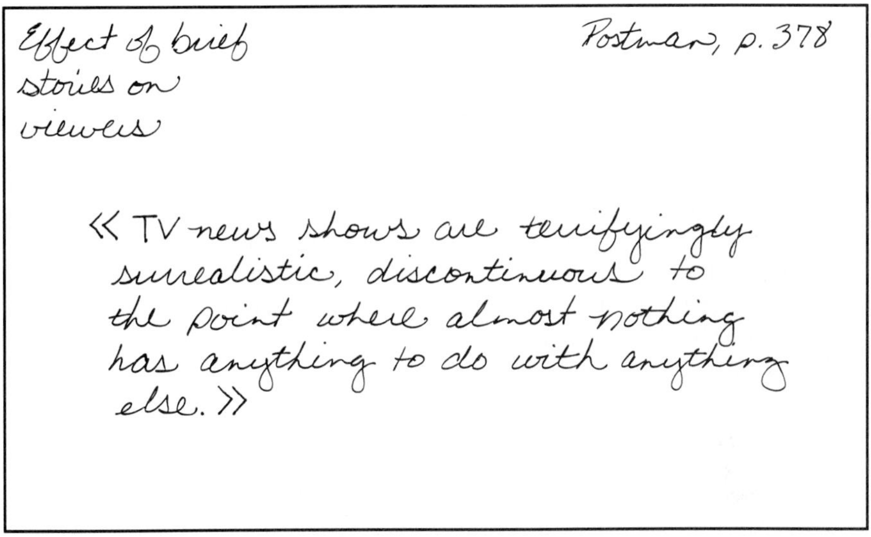

Effect of brief
stories on
viewers

Postman, p. 378

《 TV news shows are terrifyingly
surrealistic, discontinuous to
the point where almost nothing
has anything to do with anything
else. 》

Figure 46 Direct-Quotation Note.

COMPUTER NOTES

More and more writers have become comfortable composing papers at a computer and are not happy writing out notes on cards. Like these writers, you can compile your notes directly into a computer file, so long as you are indeed comfortable with the computer and have access to one throughout your research project. You can continue to add notes to one file as you work, or place each note in a separate file. In either case, make hard copies of your notes and cut them into separate "cards" so that you can organize them into the order of your outline. Then, with the note "cards" by you, you can compose at the computer, inserting noted information at appropriate places—not by retyping but by moving the information from one file to another. But if you have been using the computers in your school's writing center just for preparing final papers and are familiar with only the simplest word processing commands, you are probably wiser to write notes on cards.

The Note-Taking Process

The sample note cards drawing on Neil Postman's article serve as a good example of the note-taking process. Suppose you have decided to do

some primary research on the television, but you have not yet decided on
a focused topic. You begin by reading some articles on television, including Neil Postman's "Television News Narcosis." As a part of your preliminary reading, you prepare a summary note on Postman's article, as
illustrated in Figure 43.

After reading additional sources on the topic, you decide that you
want to update and extend Postman's analysis of television news
programs. You set up a plan for analyzing the format and content of
evening network news programs, but since you need to give credit to
Postman for the idea of the study and to test some of his conclusions,
you take several detailed notes, such as those shown in Figures 44–46.
Although you might initially record the sentence in Figure 46 as a direct
quotation, you should incorporate most of it into your paper in a
paraphrased form, perhaps quoting only the phrase "terrifyingly surrealistic."

Some sources will be more difficult to work with than Postman's
essay because the style of writing is technical or the ideas are complex or unfamiliar. The test of your grasp of complicated sources is
your ability to restate key ideas in your own words. Do not rely on
quoting as a way around the problem; if you quote passages that
you do not understand, you are not likely to produce a paper that
makes good sense. Suppose that you are writing a paper on the
characteristics of conservative thought in the United States after the
Civil War. In Richard Hofstadter's study of social Darwinism *(Social
Darwinism and American Thought)*, you read the following paragraph:

> [1] As a phase in the history of conservative thought, social
> Darwinism deserves remark. [2] Insofar as it defended the status
> quo and gave strength to attacks on reformers and on almost all
> efforts at the conscious and directed change of society, social
> Darwinism was certainly one of the leading strains in American
> conservative thought for more than a generation. [3] But it lacked
> many of the signal characteristics of conservatism as it is usually
> found. [4] A conservatism that appealed more to the secularist
> than the pious mentality, it was a conservatism almost without
> religion. [5] A body of belief whose chief conclusion was that the
> positive functions of the state should be kept to the barest mini-
> mum, it was almost anarchical, and it was devoid of that center of
> reverence and authority which the state provides in many conserva-
> tive systems. [6] Finally, and perhaps most important, it was a
> conservatism that tried to dispense with sentimental or emotional
> ties.

The sentences are complicated and some terms may be unfamiliar, but the paragraph does have a clear structure. It can be divided into the following sections and subsections that clarify Hofstadter's main points:

Sentences 1 and 2	Sentences 3, 4, 5, and 6
Social Darwinism was an important form of American conservatism. Its conservative characteristics were 1. Favoring the status quo. 2. Opposing social change. (This could lead to one note with the heading "Characteristics of conservative thought.")	It was unlike most other forms of conservatism because 1. It was secularly, not religiously, oriented. 2. It did not value governmental authority and wanted governmental functions to be limited. 3. It sought to eliminate sentimentality. (This could be another note with the heading "Characteristics of social Darwinism.")

Two valuable notes can be obtained by the patient student who takes time to understand the paragraph and distill from it the key points. This distilling process has several advantages: unnecessary direct quoting is avoided; excessive dependence on Hofstadter's language (hence plagiarism) is avoided; and the researcher actually learns about conservative thought.

WRITING ABOUT SOURCES

Understanding the importance of introducing students to some of the key scholars and significant issues in a particular area of study, instructors frequently assign projects that require students to write about the books and articles they have read on a specific topic. These assignments also prepare students for more advanced projects that must be based on a review of previous works on a topic. In other words, these assignments formalize into finished projects what is a part of any research assignment: reviewing what others have already written on your topic. Two formats used for writing about sources are the annotated bibliography and the review of literature. With either project, your purpose is to explain the sources themselves rather than to use them to develop a topic.

Preparing an Annotated Bibliography

An *annotation* is a brief note that explains the contents of a specific source. Preparing annotations of sources for a research project can help you evaluate the sources and provide an understanding of the state of scholarly debate on a particular subject. Jean-Michele's reading on the dinosaurs' extinction produced the following annotated bibliography. Examine it both for the writing style of the annotations and for the format of the bibliography.

                    Selected Annotated Bibliography
                         Jean-Michele Witiak

Alexander, R. McNeill. Dynamics of Dinosaurs and Other Ex-
     tinct Giants. New York: Columbia UP, 1989. 141-49.
     In his chapter "Death of the Giant Reptiles" Alexander
     examines two prevalent theories concerning dinosaur ex-
     tinction. One theory suggests that the earth was hit by
     an enormous meteorite, and the other theory is that
     there was a period of violent volcanic eruption.

Asimov, Isaac. Did Comets Kill the Dinosaurs? Milwaukee:
     Stevens, 1988. This book uses pictures to illustrate
     the possible ways that dinosaurs became extinct. Asi-
     mov believes that the rotating path of our galaxy
     caused the extinction by allowing collision to occur
     between the earth and another body.

Bakker, Robert T. The Dinosaur Heresies: New Theories Un-
     locking the Mystery of the Dinosaurs and Their Extinc-
     tion. New York: Morrow, 1986. Bakker, a paleontolo-
     gist, uses his personal observations and findings to
     present new ideas about the dinosaur world. Bakker
     examines the dinosaur, its habitat, its evolution,

and its extinction. He analyzes different theories on extinction, including his own: The increased exchange of species across the continents during the Cretaceous Period led to a biological disaster which killed off the dinosaurs.

Bradley, Franklyn M. <u>Dinosaurs, Asteroids, and Superstars: Why the Dinosaurs Disappeared</u>. New York: Crowell, 1982. This book discusses in simple terms information on the dinosaurs and possibilities for their extinction. The book orients us with the earth during the time of the dinosaur, as well as with the dinosaur itself. Bradley speculates on the various theories ranging from starvation to an asteroid collision and concludes that the dinosaur's decline is due to an event in space that influenced life on earth.

Kerr, Richard A. "Dinosaurs' Death Blow in the Caribbean Sea?" <u>Science</u> 18 May 1990: 815. In this article the author states that most scientists now believe the impact theory is the reason dinosaurs died out. The minority opinion, which claims volcanic activity may be the cause, points to the lack of a sufficient-sized crater. Kerr examines two possible crater sites in the Caribbean.

Lampton, Christopher. <u>New Theories on the Dinosaurs</u>. New York: Watts, 1989. Lampton examines the controversial new image of dinosaurs. He discusses the scientists and their understanding of dinosaurs. Lampton explains how fossils are preserved and how dinosaurs fit into the history of the earth.

Paul, Gregory S. <u>Predatory Dinosaurs of the World</u>. New York: Simon, 1988. In the chapter "A History of Predatory Dinosaur Success and Failure, and of Their Avian Descendants," Paul refutes the theories of stress causing thinner-shelled eggs and flowering plants poisoning the dinosaurs as reasons for their extinction. He does assert that continental drift and the consequence of mountain building and sea shrinkage may have coincided with volcanic or impact activities to lead to dinosaur extinction.

Sattler, Helen Roney. <u>Dinosaurs of North America</u>. New York: Lothrop, 1981. Sattler's chapter on extinction investigates different scientists' theories of the dinosaurs' extinction. Sattler rules out theories known to be incorrect, such as the theories claiming the dinosaurs to be huge, stupid, slow-moving animals, and explains possible theories. No one theory is given as an absolute; instead, Sattler offers a combination of theories as an answer.

Wilford, John Noble. <u>The Riddle of the Dinosaur</u>. New York: Knopf, 1987. Wilford examines the myths and truths that create our perception of the dinosaur. He writes about the early paleontologists as well as the recent discoveries that have revolutionized dinosaur theory. Lastly, Wilford discusses the contradictory theories on the extinction of the dinosaur, supporting the theory of a massive catastrophe rather than a maladaption.

Preparing a Review of the Literature on a Topic

As noted previously, a review of the literature presents the reading of key sources on a specific topic in an organized essay. In this examination of sources you need to go beyond the work of preparing an annotated bibliography. You need to shape your knowledge of individual sources into a discussion of the major issues in the debate on the topic. Individual sources should be grouped in some meaningful way to aid a reader's understanding of the topic's controversial issues. Aaron Knoll's reading on the dinosaurs' extinction led to the following polished and thoughtful review-of-the-literature essay. You can study it not only as a review of literature but also as a model for introducing material from sources, blending quoting and paraphrasing, and documenting in MLA style.

Aaron Knoll

English 111

December 13, 1990

The End of the Terrible Reptiles:
A Selected Review of the Literature

The dinosaurs reigned supreme over every land mass for entire geologic periods; yet sixty-five million years ago, at the end of the Cretaceous Period, the dinosaurs enigmatically disappeared, leaving their fossilized remains as the only indication that they ever existed. Scientists and nonexperts alike know that the dinosaurs became extinct, but no one knows exactly how or why. As a result, this mystery of dinosaur extinction has been the subject of considerable conjecture by scientists. Although a conclusive answer has yet to be given, many theories have been devised to decipher the enigma of dinosaur extinction. Most of those theories fall into one of two categories: extraterrestrial theories and terrestrial theories.

EXTRATERRESTRIAL THEORIES

Some of the most fantastic theories of dinosaur extinction involve extraterrestrial cataclysms: cosmic events such as an asteroid colliding with the earth, a comet colliding with the earth, or a supernova irradiating the earth. All the extraterrestrial theories have at least one element in common: they are all based on the discovery of abnormal amounts of the element iridium in the clay bed dividing the sediments left by the Cretaceous Period and later periods (Krishtalka 20). Although iridium is fairly scarce in rocks of the earth's crust, it is abundant in meteorites (Russell 499). These abnormal amounts of iridium were first discovered by Walter Alvarez who, ironically, was searching for a terrestrial solution to dinosaur extinction (Wilford 221). He and his father, Nobel Prize-winning physicist Luis Alvarez, announced in 1980 that there was an extraterrestrial connection between the abnormal amounts of iridium and the extinctions at the end of the Cretaceous (Wilford 227). Thus the asteroid theory of extinction was born (Krishtalka 21).

Of course, the iridium could have come from other extraterrestrial sources besides an asteroid. One theory, put forward by Dale Russell, is that the iridium was produced outside the solar system by an exploding star (500). The theory of a nearby star exploding in a supernova is by far the most fanciful extraterrestrial

theory; however, it warrants examination because of
its ability to explain the widespread extinctions of
the late Cretaceous Period (Colbert 205). Such an explosion, Russell states, could have blown the iridium
either off the surface of the moon or directly from the
star itself (500-01), while also producing a deadly
blast of heat and gamma rays (Krishtalka 19). Even
though this theory seems to explain the traces of iridium in the mass extinction, it does not explain why
smaller mammals, crocodiles, and birds survived (Wilford 220). As Edwin Colbert explains, the extinctions
of the late Cretaceous, although massive, were selective (205). So the supernova theory took a backseat to
the other extraterrestrial theories: those of asteroids and comets colliding with the earth. The authors
of the book The Great Extinction, Michael Allaby and
James Lovelock, subtitled their work The Solution
to . . . the Disappearance of the Dinosaurs. Their
theory: an asteroid or comet collided with earth
around sixty-five million years ago, killing billions
of organisms, and thus altering the course of evolution (157). This theory was hardly a new one when they
wrote it; the Alvarezes came up with it nearly three
years before. However, the fact that the theory of
collision with a cosmic body warrants a book describ-

ing itself as the solution to the extinction of dinosaurs calls for some thought: is the asteroid or comet
theory merely sensationalism, or is it rooted in fact?
Paleontologist Leonard Krishtalka declares that few
paleontologists have accepted the asteroid theory,
himself calling "some catastrophic theories . . .
small ideas injected with growth hormone" (22). However, other scientists, such as Allaby and Lovelock,
see the cosmic catastrophic theory as a solid one based
on more than guesswork (10-11).

The asteroid or comet theory has more to it than
just an asteroid smacking into the earth. As stated
before, the abnormal amounts of iridium have to be
taken into account, as well as the extinction of the
dinosaurs. The iridium would come from the asteroid or
comet itself, since asteroids are rich in that element
(Russell 499), but what about the extinction of the dinosaurs? It seems that the asteroid theorists have a
detailed explanation beginning with dust particles
filling the atmosphere and blocking the sun's rays for
three or four years, "thereby killing much of the
earth's plant life . . . [which] would have brought
about the disappearance of the plant-eating dinosaurs,
and in turn the carnivorous dinosaurs that depended
upon the giant herbivores" (Colbert 205). This total

destruction of the ecosystem has been likened to a "runaway nuclear winter" (Krishtalka 22). If an ecological catastrophe cannot explain dinosaur extinction, what other theories can account for the connection between iridium and the end of the dinosaurs?

TERRESTRIAL THEORIES

Lacking the ability to capture the public's imagination with such sensational theories as asteroids and comets falling from the sky, the terrestrial theories have mainly been the domain of paleontologists and geologists. Eminent paleontologist Robert T. Bakker believes this is so because "the solution [to dinosaur extinction] is . . . so obvious, so nonfantastic, that its very mundaneness comes as a jolt" (427). This mundane solution, according to Bakker, is found in the interchange of species over the continents (442). Another terrestrial theory is given by L. B. and Jenny Halstead and William Jaber who state that it was a combination of Continental Drift and an increase in global temperature (Halstead 162-64; Jaber 120-21). Still another theory, offered by Krishtalka, states that volcanic activity led to the dinosaurs' demise (26). Other theories which have been put forward include poisoning, a reversal in the earth's magnetic field, and the dinosaur's excessive size (Colbert 201-04).

Those theories dealing with poisoning, magnetic fields, and size can be dismissed at once. First, poisoning can be dismissed because it would not affect sea creatures that also died off (Bakker 430). Magnetic fields can also be given the cold shoulder because magnetic reversal has never been proven to cause harm and the extinction was so selective; why did the crocodiles survive and not the dinosaurs (Colbert 205)? Finally, the size theory can be ruled out easily: the dinosaurs existed successfully for a hundred and fifty million years while they were large (Colbert 203). A terrestrial cause needs to be one that would kill off all the dinosaurs without discrimination and without many traces.

The theory given by Krishtalka is similar to the extraterrestrial theories; the almost "nuclear winter" created by dust particles thrown up by volcanos causes the same reaction that an asteroid would have (26). However, the volcanic theory does the asteroid theory one better; it explains without a doubt where the iridium came from (Krishtalka 26). The iridium did not come from outer space; rather, it came from the center of the earth (26). But Krishtalka reminds readers that

even though his theory makes sense, the trail is sixty-
five million years cold, and no one may ever know the
final answers (26-27).

The next plausible theory is that Continental
Drift and global warming were the culprits that killed
off the dinosaurs. The Halsteads include a part of
Krishtalka's theory in theirs, the part about volcanic
activity (162-63), but nothing on the scale of
Krishtalka's global explosions (27). The Halsteads use
the dust from the volcanic activity as the instigator
for "the greenhouse effect," which would then either
melt the ice caps or begin another ice age (164).
Jaber ties all this into Continental Drift by explaining that the upheaval of the earth's crust during
Continental Drift caused the volcanos to erupt (120-
21). Although Jaber and the Halsteads have a detailed
chain of events which they believe occurred, Jaber
states that the "exact manner in which one set of factors influenced another . . . are unknown and may
never be known" (121).

The final, "heretical," theory is put forward by
Robert Bakker. His theory differs from every other because it does not use catastrophic or near-cata-
strophic events to explain dinosaur extinction;
rather, Bakker gives a biological reason for the de-

mise of the dinosaur (440-41). Bakker's theory is that dinosaurs became extinct because of the interchange of the species over the continents (442). Every species of animal, Bakker states, carries with it a unique load of disease and parasites (442). During the Late Cretaceous the time was ripe for species which never had encountered each other to meet: the shallow seas drained off and land bridges opened up (443). As these species intermingled, nothing less than biological disaster ensued (443). Bakker points the finger at disease and parasites for extinction of the dinosaurs, thus showing that an obvious and "mundane" theory can work (444). As for the iridium, Bakker shrugs that off to volcanic activity or even a meteor: "Maybe there is a place for an occasional bolt out of the blue to kill off the remnants of a weakened ecosystem" (444).

CONCLUSION

If the answer to the enigma of dinosaur extinction is ever to be discovered, much more research has to be done. However, it seems scientists have chosen one of two routes to dinosaur extinction: extraterrestrial or terrestrial. Whatever route a scientist chooses, his or her job is the same: play detective to find the murderer in a sixty-five-million-year-old crime.

Works Cited

Allaby, Michael, and James Lovelock. <u>The Great Ex-</u>
     <u>tinction: The Solution to One of the Great</u>
     <u>Mysteries of Science--the Disappearance of the</u>
     <u>Dinosaurs</u>. New York: Doubleday, 1983.

Bakker, Robert T. <u>The Dinosaur Heresies: New Theo-</u>
     <u>ries Unlocking the Mystery of the Dinosaurs</u>
     <u>and Their Extinction</u>. New York: Morrow, 1986.

Colbert, Edwin H. <u>Dinosaurs: An Illustrated History</u>.
     A Dembner Book. Maplewood: Hammond, 1983.

Halstead, L. B., and Jenny Halstead. <u>Dinosaurs</u>.
     Poole, Eng.: Blandford, 1981.

Jaber, William. <u>Whatever Happened to the Dinosaurs?</u>
     New York: Messner, 1978.

Krishtalka, Leonard. <u>Dinosaur Plots and Other In-</u>
     <u>trigues in Natural History</u>. New York: Morrow,
     1989.

Russell, Dale A. "The Mass Extinctions of the Late
     Mesozoic." <u>Scientific American</u> Jan. 1982. Rpt.
     in <u>The Writer's Stance</u>. Ed. Dorothy U. Sey-
     ler. New York: Random, 1988. 497-509.

Wilford, John Noble. <u>The Riddle of the Dinosaur</u>.
     New York: Knopf, 1987.

Chapter 5

Presenting and Documenting Research

This chapter presents many specific guidelines for the proper formatting of research essays. The chapter also explains and illustrates correct in-text documentation of sources according to MLA guidelines. Although you cannot expect to learn every detail given here prior to drafting your paper and meeting specific situations in your own writing, still you should study the chapter carefully enough to become familiar with its contents and to know what you must pay attention to when drafting and documenting your essay. Later, when revising and editing, you will want to check your draft against the required forms for quotations, for handling numbers, for documentation, and so on, presented here. You can eliminate much revision and avoid undetected errors if you will study the details of this chapter before you begin to write. For example, to avoid errors in documentation that can lead to plagiarism, it is essential to place parenthetical documentation in your draft as you write. So study the guidelines here and look closely at the examples to become familiar with the rules and to develop your visual sense of what "looks right."

REFERRING TO PEOPLE AND WORKS

Research papers call for frequent references to authors and to published works—whether literary figures and their writings analyzed in a literary study or the experts in a field of study and their books and articles you are drawing on to develop your study. Learn the conventions, reinforce these conventions of style by making it a habit to use correct form when taking notes, and check your draft against the guidelines for accuracy to demonstrate to instructors your desire to meet the expectations of readers in the scholarly community.

References to People

- In a first reference, give the person's full name (both the given name and the surname): Arthur Miller, Neil Postman, Thomas Paine. In second and subsequent references, use only the last name (surname): Miller, Postman, Paine.
- Do not use Mr., Mrs., or Ms. Special titles (President, Chief Justice, Dr.) may be used in the first reference with the person's full name.
- Never refer to an author by her or his first name. Write Dickinson, not Emily; Whitman, not Walt.

References to Titles of Works

Titles of works must *always* be written as titles. Titles are indicated by capitalization and by either quotation marks or underlining. (Underlining in handwritten or typed papers represents italic type in printed works.)

CAPITALIZING TITLES

- The first and last words are capitalized.
- The first word of a subtitle is capitalized.
- All other words in titles are capitalized except
  - Articles (a, an, the).
  - Coordinating conjunctions (and, or, but, for, nor, yet, so).
  - Prepositions of five or fewer letters (e.g., in, for, with); prepositions of more than five letters are capitalized (e.g., Between, Through, Before).

TITLES REQUIRING QUOTATION MARKS

Titles of works published *within* other works—e.g., within a book, magazine, or newspaper—are indicated by quotation marks.

essays	"Once More to the Lake"
short stories	"Young Goodman Brown"
poems	"The Road Not Taken"
articles	"Playing Dumb"
chapters	"Locating Sources"
lectures	"Henry VIII"
TV episode	"Resolved: Drug Prohibition Has Failed" (one debate on the TV show *Firing Line*)

TITLES REQUIRING UNDERLINING (ITALICS IN PRINT)

Titles of works that are separate publications and, by extension, titles of items such as works of art and films are underlined.

plays	A Raisin in the Sun
novels	War and Peace
nonfiction books	A Brief History of Time
textbooks	Doing Research
book-length poems	The Odyssey
magazines	Psychology Today
journals	Modern Fiction Studies
newspapers	New York Times
pamphlets	So You'd Like to Do Something about Water Pollution
ballets	Swan Lake
films	The Wizard of Oz
operas	Tosca
paintings	The Birth of Venus
sculptures	The Dying Slave
ships	Andrea Doria
recordings	Eine Kleine Nachtmusik
TV programs	Nightline

DOCUMENTING SOURCES

Depending on your course of study and specific research assignment, you may need the guidance of some but not all sections of this chapter. You may, for example, be quoting sources but not using charts in the essay on which you are currently working. Everyone, though, will need to study the first part of this section on documentation, because all researchers need to understand how to avoid misrepresenting material taken from sources.

All research essays using secondary sources *must* contain correct documentation, but not all researchers will use the MLA documentation patterns presented in the second part of this section. Those using APA style, footnote/endnote style, or a scientific style will find guidelines for documentation in Chapter 7. Whatever documentation pattern you use, if you have prepared an accurate set of bibliography cards (see Chapter 3) and your note cards contain all necessary information (see Chapter 4), then the formal documentation needed in your essay should not be difficult to prepare. Your goal must be to make all references to sources accurate, consistent with the required style, and concise. Follow the guidelines for documentation *exactly* as they are presented in this chapter for MLA style or in Chapter 7 for other styles. Handling the patterns of documentation correctly takes, more than other skills, discipline and patience. But there are challenges of intellect and writing skills in working borrowed material into your paper without misrepresenting either the sources or your indebtedness to the source.

Avoiding Misleading Acknowledgment of Sources Within the Paper

Until you give cause for question, your instructor will assume that you are a sincere and conscientious student, that you have done your own reading, note-taking, and writing. If you are such a student, you do not want to be penalized for unintentional plagiarism that is the result of careless note-taking or careless writing. Remember that plagiarism is a form of stealing: It is the presentation of someone else's information, ideas, or opinions as your own.

Plagiarism usually occurs in one of two ways: (1) a researcher takes notes carelessly, neglecting to put down precise page references, and then uses the information anyway, without properly documenting the sources; (2) a researcher presents borrowed material in such a way that even though the paper contains documentation, he or she misrepresents the nature of indebtedness to the source. The note-taking procedures explained in Chapter 4 will keep you from the first pitfall. The smooth integration of borrowed material from several sources is a challenging writing task that will be discussed in Chapter 6, but the part of this task that relates to appropriate documentation will be examined here. This examination will help you avoid the second cause of plagiarism.

Usually you will want to identify quoted or paraphrased material by author. You may even include the author's credentials ("According to Dr. Hays, a geologist with the Department of the Interior, . . .") or the location of the material ("The president, as quoted by *Time*, feels . . ."). These *introductory tags* give your reader a context for the borrowed information and serve as part of the documentation within the body of the paper, distinguishing between your words and the borrowed material within the paragraph. (See pages 216–217 for a discussion of varying word choice in introductory tags.) Be sure that a tag clarifies rather than distorts an author's relationship to his or her ideas and your relationship to the source. Here are three guidelines to follow to avoid misrepresenting borrowed material:

1. Be careful when you vary such standard introductions as "Smith says" or "Jones states" that you do not select alternatives that are misleading. Substituting "Smith implies" for "Smith says" misrepresents Smith's attitude toward his material.

2. If you vary the pattern of acknowledgment by mentioning Jones after you have incorporated her ideas into your paragraph, be sure that your reader can tell precisely which ideas in the passage belong to Jones. If your entire paragraph is a paraphrase of Jones's views, it isn't fair to conclude with "This idea is presented by Jones." Which of the several ideas in the paragraph is Jones's?

3. Be sure that your paraphrase notes are in your own words so that you do not incorporate Smith's ideas into your paper in his style of writing. To use Smith's words and/or sentence structure, even in a condensed version, is to steal Smith's work.

In general, providing a parenthetical reference at the end of a paragraph to indicate your source is not sufficient if you have misrepresented your dependence on that source in the body of your paragraph. Indeed, this "end of every paragraph" approach to documentation reflects a failure to synthesize and/or to guide readers through the research essay. Some paragraphs should combine information from several sources.

Other paragraphs will present ideas from one source combined with your analysis and discussion of those ideas. The placing of introductory tags and parenthetical references and the appropriate use of connecting words should make the patterns of synthesis and analysis clear to readers.

The paragraph below from Robert E. Spiller's *The Cycle of American Literature* will serve as the basis for the examples that follow of adequate and inadequate acknowledgment of sources. After reading Spiller's paragraph, study the three examples of student writing with these questions in mind: (1) Which example represents adequate acknowledgment? Why? (2) Which examples do not represent adequate acknowledgment? (3) In exactly what ways is each misleading paragraph flawed?

> Fiction and drama turned to classicism more slowly and reluctantly than did poetry and criticism, in some degree even avoiding its extremes completely. The generation of novelists who became prominent in the thirties, in addition to Wolfe and Hemingway, included James T. Farrell, John Steinbeck, Erskine Caldwell, and William Faulkner. Naturalists all in their primary inspiration, these men also developed in varying degrees the possibilities of symbolism and moved generally in the direction that Sherwood Anderson rather than Dreiser had indicated, toward fantasy and away from literal realism. At first unnoticed, the silvery laughter of the comic spirit began to be heard above the voices of tragedy, corruption, and death, with which their work was most concerned. As the theme of illusion which had so obsessed O'Neill came more and more to supplant that of reality, their art grew increasingly self-conscious and objective. From the most realistic of them all (Farrell) to the most symbolic and purely aesthetic (Faulkner) there is progress in technical virtuosity and philosophical depth. American fiction, like American poetry and drama, reached its highest point of achievement in the equilibrium of conflicting forces that characterized the mid-thirties, rather than in either extreme.

Student ¶1

Who were the important novelists in the 1930s? The

most prominent were Wolfe, Hemingway, Farrell,

Steinbeck, Caldwell, and Faulkner. Although they were

all influenced by the naturalists, they all, though

some more than others, developed into symbolic writers. They followed Anderson rather than Dreiser in focusing more on fantasy than on realism with the result that they became more consciously interested in technical innovations and at the same time more philosophical. The best works were those that found a balance between reality and fantasy. This attitude is emphasized by Robert Spiller, a critic of American literature (217).

Student ¶2

We can agree that the writers who became prominent in the thirties, besides Wolfe and Hemingway, were Farrell, Steinbeck, Caldwell, and Faulkner. Naturalists in their primary inspiration, these writers also examined the possibilities of symbolism and moved in the direction of Anderson rather than Dreiser, that is, toward fantasy and away from realism. The silvery laughter of the comic muse was heard in their novels, and their art grew more self-conscious and objective and more philosophically deep. We may agree with Robert Spiller that their fiction reached its highest achievement in the balance of conflicting forces that characterized the mid-thirties, rather than in either extreme (217).

Student ¶3

According to Robert Spiller, "American fiction . . . reached its highest point of achievement in the

equilibrium of conflicting forces that characterized
the mid-thirties." He observes that the most important
writers (Wolfe, Hemingway, Farrell, Steinbeck,
Caldwell, and Faulkner) were "naturalists all in their
primary inspiration," but they moved "toward fantasy
and away from literal realism" and "developed . . .
the possibilities of symbolism." The result, Spiller
asserts, was "progress in technical virtuosity and
philosophical depth" (217). Spiller presents a sound
analysis of stylistic characteristics, but his
assertion that these writers represent progress in
philosophical depth is open to debate.

Although only the third example demonstrates adequate acknowledgment of the writer's indebtedness to Spiller, if most of the student's
paper "leaned" this heavily on sources, there would be little of the student's own analysis in the paper. The extensive quoting and paraphrasing
is appropriate in this case, however, because the student is going to challenge part of Spiller's views. The student wisely presents Spiller's key
points in his own words before moving on to make clear what point she
will challenge.

MLA In-Text (Parenthetical) Citations

Most documentation, according to MLA style, will be in the form of parenthetical references to author and page number, or just to page number
if the author has been mentioned in an introductory tag, as in the student paragraphs above. Since a reference only to author and page number is an incomplete form of citation, whatever is cited in parentheses
must refer to a specific source presented fully in a Works Cited list that
follows the text of the paper. Make certain that you do not omit from
your Works Cited any sources you refer to in your paper. Before examining the various patterns of parenthetical documentation illustrated below,
review the following general guidelines.

Guidelines for Using Parenthetical Documentation

- The purpose of documentation is to make clear exactly what material in a passage has been borrowed and from what source the borrowed material has come.
- Parenthetical documentation requires specific page references for borrowed material.
- Parenthetical documentation is required for both quoted and paraphrased material.
- Parenthetical documentation provides as brief a citation as possible consistent with accuracy and clarity.
- Parenthetical documentation can be as brief as author and page number because it depends for its completeness on a citation in the Works Cited list. Each parenthetical reference must clearly connect to a full citation in the Works Cited list.

The Simplest Patterns of Parenthetical Documentation

The simplest parenthetical reference can be prepared in one of three ways:

1. Give the author's last name (full name in a first reference to an author) in the text of your paper, and place the relevant page number(s) in parentheses following the borrowed material.

   > Allen observes that, during the 1920s, urban tastes spread to the country (146).

2. Place the author's last name and the relevant page number(s) in parentheses immediately following the borrowed material.

   > During the 1920s, "not only the drinks were mixed, but the company as well" (Allen 82).

3. On the rare occasion that you cite an entire work rather than borrowing from a specific passage, give the author's name in the text and omit any page numbers.

   > Tuchman argues that there are significant parallels between the fourteenth century and our time.

Each one of these brief references is complete *only* if the appropriate full citation is found in the Works Cited; thus:

```
Allen, Frederick Lewis. Only Yesterday: An Informal His-

     tory of the Nineteen-Twenties. New York: Harper,

     1931.

Tuchman, Barbara W. A Distant Mirror: The Calamitous 14th

     Century. New York: Knopf, 1978.
```

The three patterns illustrated above are appropriate in each of the following situations:

1. The work is not anonymous—the author is known.
2. The work is by one author.
3. The work cited is the only work used by that author.
4. No other author in the bibliography has the same last name.
5. The borrowed material is either quoted or paraphrased.

PLACEMENT OF PARENTHETICAL DOCUMENTATION

The simplest placing of a parenthetical reference is at the end of the appropriate sentence *before* the period, but, when you are quoting, *after* the quotation mark.

```
During the 1920s, "not only the drinks were mixed, but

the company as well" (Allen 82).
```

Observe that no punctuation is used between the author's name and the page number.

If the borrowed material occurs someplace other than at the end of your sentence, place the parenthetical reference *after* the borrowed material but *before* any subsequent punctuation. This placement will more accurately show what is borrowed and what is your own work.

```
Sport, Allen observes about the 1920s, had developed

into an obsession (66), another similarity between the

1920s and the 1980s.
```

If a quoted passage is long enough to require setting off in display form, then place the parenthetical reference at the end of the passage, *after* the last period. (Remember that long quotations in display form do *not* have quotation marks.)

```
It is hard to believe that when he writes about the
influence of science, Allen is describing the 1920s,
not the 1980s:
            The prestige of science was colossal. The
            man in the street and the woman in the
            kitchen, confronted on every hand with new
            machines and devices which they owed to the
            laboratory, were ready to believe that
            science could accomplish almost anything.
            (164)
```

And to complete the documentation for all three examples:

```
                        Works Cited
Allen, Frederick Lewis. Only Yesterday: An Informal His-
    tory of the Nineteen-Twenties. New York: Harper,
    1931.
```

PARENTHETICAL DOCUMENTATION FOR COMPLEX SOURCES

Not all sources can be cited in one of the three simplest forms described above, for not all fit the five cases listed on page 160. Works by two or more authors, for example, will have to be cited with somewhat fuller references. Each sample form of parenthetical documentation below is completed with the full reference in the Works Cited.

Two Authors, Mentioned in the Text

```
Kehl and Heidt examine the "rhetoric of cow" in both
advertising and political speeches (208-10).
```

Two Authors, Not Mentioned in the Text

Both advertisers and politicians use the "rhetoric of cow" (Kehl and Heidt 208-10).

Works Cited

Kehl, D. G., and Donald Heidt. "The Rhetoric of Cow and the Rhetoric of Bull." <u>Rhetoric Society Quarterly</u> Sum/Fall 1985. Rpt. in <u>Read, Reason, Write</u>. 3rd ed. Dorothy U. Seyler. New York: Random, 1986. 391-96.

A Book in Two or More Volumes

Sewall analyzes the role of Judge Lord in Dickinson's life (2: 642-47).

OR

Judge Lord was also one of Dickinson's preceptors (Sewall 2: 642-47).

Note: The number before the colon always signifies the volume number; the number(s) after the colon represent page number(s).

Works Cited

Sewall, Richard B. <u>The Life of Emily Dickinson</u>. 2 vols. New York: Farrar, 1974.

A Book or Article Listed by Title

The current CBS presentation of "The Autobiography of Miss Jane Pittman" provides viewers with . . . ("Viewpoints" 65).

According to the Concise Dictionary of American Biography, William Jennings Bryan's 1896 campaign stressed social and sectional conflicts (117).

Works Cited

"Viewpoints." Rev. of "The Autobiography of Miss Jane Pittman" (film shown on CBS, 31 Jan. 1974). Time 4 Feb.
1974: 65.

Concise Dictionary of American Biography. New York: Scribner's, 1964.

A Work by a Corporate Author

According to the report of the Institute of Ecology's
Global Ecological Problems Workshop, the civilization of
the city can lull us into forgetting our relationship to
the total ecological system on which we depend (13).

Although corporate authors may be cited parenthetically by name and
page number as with any other author, your presentation will be more
graceful if corporate authors are introduced in the text. Then only page
numbers will be in parentheses.

Works Cited

Institute of Ecology. Man in the Living Environment. Madison: U of Wisconsin P, 1972.

Two or More Works by the Same Author

During the 1920s, "not only the drinks were mixed, but
the company as well" (Allen, Only Yesterday 82).

According to Frederick Lewis Allen, the early
1900s were a period of complacency in America (The Big
Change 4-5).

In The Big Change, Allen asserts that the early
1900s were a period of complacency (4-5).

If your Works Cited list contains two or more works by the same author, the
fullest parenthetical citation will include the author's last name, followed by

a comma; the work's title, shortened if possible; and the page number(s). If
the author's name appears in the text—or the author and title both, as in
the third example above—omit these items from the parenthetical citation.

Works Cited

Allen, Frederick Lewis. <u>The Big Change</u>. New York: Harper,

    1952.

---. <u>Only Yesterday: An Informal History of the Nineteen-</u>

    <u>Twenties</u>. New York: Harper, 1931.

Two or More Works in One Parenthetical Reference

Several writers about the future agree that big

changes will take place in work patterns (Toffler

384-87; Naisbitt 35-36).

Separate each author cited parenthetically with a semicolon. But if the
parenthetical citation would be disruptively long, cite the works in a "See
also" note rather than in the text.

Works Cited

Naisbitt, John. <u>Megatrends: Ten New Directions Transform-</u>

    <u>ing Our Lives</u>. New York: Warner, 1982.

Toffler, Alvin. <u>The Third Wave</u>. New York: Bantam, 1981.

COMPLETE PUBLICATION INFORMATION IN PARENTHETICAL REFERENCE

Occasionally you may want to give complete information about a source
within parentheses in the text of the paper. Then a Works Cited list is not
used. Square brackets are used for parenthetical information within parentheses. This approach may be appropriate when a paper refers to only
one or two sources, even if many references are made to the few sources,
as in a literary study. For example:

Edith Wharton establishes the bleakness of her

setting, Starkfield, Massachusetts, not through

description of place but through her main character,

Ethan, who is described as "bleak and unapproachable"
(Ethan Frome [New York: Scribner's, 1911] 3. All
subsequent references are to this edition.). Later
Wharton describes winter as "shut[ting] down on
Starkfield" and negating life there (7).

ADDITIONAL-INFORMATION FOOTNOTES OR ENDNOTES

At times you may need to provide additional useful information, explanation, or commentary that is not central to the development of your paper. These additions belong in content footnotes or endnotes, but use them sparingly and never as a way of advancing your thesis. Many instructors object to content footnotes or endnotes and prefer only parenthetical references in student papers.

"SEE ALSO" FOOTNOTES OR ENDNOTES

More acceptable to most readers is the footnote (or endnote) that refers to other sources of evidence for or against the point being established in the paper. Such footnotes or endnotes can be combined with parenthetical documentation. The footnotes (or endnotes) are usually introduced with "See also" or "Compare," followed by the citation. For example:

Chekhov's debt to Ibsen is indeed obvious and should
be recognized, as should his debt to Maeterlinck and
other playwrights of the 1890s who were concerned with
the inner life of their characters.[2]

    [2]See also Eric Bentley, In Search of Theatre (New
York: Vintage, 1959) 330; Walter Bruford, Anton
Chekhov (New Haven: Yale UP, 1957) 45; and Raymond
Williams, Drama from Ibsen to Eliot (New York: Oxford
UP, 1953) 126-29.

PRESENTING DIRECT QUOTATIONS

As discussed in Chapter 4, most notes should be paraphrases so that most of your paper is in your own words and style. Still, there are times that quoting directly from sources is appropriate, even essential (e.g., in literary studies). When you need to quote from sources, make certain that you adhere to the following guidelines and conventions.

General Guidelines

1. **Quote accurately.** Take time to compare what you have written with the original. Pay attention to spelling and punctuation.
2. **Enclose all quoted material in quotation marks** and do not change words or punctuation within the quoted material.
3. **Keep quoted passages brief,** avoiding quoted passages of more than a few key lines. Long quoted passages throughout a paper are a quick visual signal to instructors that students have not learned much about their topics and are just trying to fill pages.
4. **Introduce quoted passages with the author's name and other appropriate information to provide a context for readers.** Consider the following examples.

Ineffective Long Quotation "Dumped" on Reader

"What a piece of work is man! He flushes fields, levels forests, covers waterways, creates swamps, drains swamps, changes the course of rivers. But at times his surgery on the land seems the work of a brilliant surgeon operating with a hatchet and buck knife, his mistakes and excuses sutured with leftover string" (Grove 159).

It is true that we have destroyed a majority of this country's wetlands, but just maybe with our intelligence, we can find a way to restore some of the loss and repair some of the damage with more than leftover string.

(Never let a long quotation rest by itself as a complete paragraph. Providing documentation at the end of the quotation is insufficient context for readers. These last two paragraphs of a paper on preserving wetlands should have been revised into one with a clear context for the quotation that includes identifying the author *before* quoting.)

Effective Context for Quotation

> In developing this country, we have demonstrated
> great intelligence and skills. As Noel Grove puts it,
> man "flushes fields, levels forests, . . . changes the
> course of rivers" (159). Unfortunately, we have also
> destroyed most of the country's wetlands; our "surgery
> on the land," to use Grove's metaphor, "seems the work
> of a brilliant surgeon operating with a hatchet and buck
> knife" (159). We need to employ our surgical skills and
> knowledge of the patient to repair the damage to wet-
> lands and restore some of the duck's lost habitats.

5. **Combine quoting and paraphrasing when possible,** working key passages into sentences of your own. Consider the following examples.

Ineffective Long Quotation

> Eliot shows Prufrock's anxiety in these lines:
>
> > And I have known the eyes already, known
> > > them all--
> > The eyes that fix you in a formulated
> > > phrase,
> > And when I am formulated, sprawling on a
> > > pin,
> > When I am pinned and wriggling on the wall,
> > Then how should I begin
> > To spit out all the butt-ends of my days and
> > > ways?

(Simply quoting lines of the poem without discussion does not do the job of analysis. The reader is left to figure out how the lines reveal anxiety. Instead, the writer should provide that explanation, as in the revision below.)

Effective Blend of Quoting and Analysis

```
Eliot has Prufrock reveal his anxiety and self-
consciousness when he worries about "the eyes that fix
you in a formulated phrase," eyes that will dissect
him as if he were an insect "sprawling on a pin," a
specimen "pinned and wriggling on the wall."
```

Form for Quotations

WORDS ADDED TO QUOTED PASSAGES

Quoted passages must be reproduced exactly. Any words added to a quoted passage to make the meaning clear must be placed in *square brackets,* not parentheses. Add *[sic]* immediately after the necessary word or phrase to alert readers to an error in the original. Add words when necessary to clarify a quoted passage.

Original: "The most important common feature of American fiction today is that it has all been produced in the interval between two world wars."From Joseph Warren Beach, *American Fiction 1920-1940* (New York: Macmillan, 1941), 11.

Incorrect: Joseph Warren Beach says that "the most important common feature of American fiction between 1920 and 1940 is that it has all been produced in the interval between two world wars" (11).

Correct: Joseph Warren Beach says that "the most important common feature of American fiction today [between 1920 and 1940] is that it has all been produced in the interval between two world wars" (11).

LOWERCASE FOR CAPITALS

When quoted material forms only part of a sentence, the first quoted word is not capitalized, even if it was capitalized in the original source. *Exception:* The quoted passage follows an introduction that ends in a colon.

Incorrect: In his book Taking a Stand Against Environ-
              mental Pollution, David Newton asserts that
              "Every living organism, from the simplest
              to the most complex, affects the environ-
              ment and is in turn affected by it" (13).

Correct: In his book Taking a Stand Against Environ-
              mental Pollution, David Newton asserts that
              "every living organism, from the simplest
              to the most complex, affects the environ-
              ment and is in turn affected by it" (13).

Also correct: David Newton explains our relationship to
                the environment thus: "Every living or-
                ganism, from the simplest to the most
                complex, affects the environment and is
                in turn affected by it" (13).

PUNCTUATION WITH QUOTED MATERIAL

1. **Do not quote unnecessary punctuation.** When quoted material comes at the end of a sentence, use only the punctuation appropriate to complete the sentence.

Original: "Trust thyself: every heart vibrates to
              that iron string." From Ralph Waldo Emerson,
              "Self-Reliance."

Incorrect: Emerson's faith in self-reliance is summed
              up in two words: "Trust thyself:."

Correct: Emerson's faith in self-reliance is summed
              up in two words: "Trust thyself."

2. **Place commas and periods *inside* the closing quotation mark.**

   Adhering to his own words "trust thyself," Emerson was

   an optimist, believing that the "filths of nature the

   sun shall dry up."

3. **Place colons and semicolons *outside* the closing quotation mark.**

```
Rousseau believed that "the words 'slavery' and
'right' are contradictory"; his thinking was in
advance of his time.
```

4. **Depending on the structure of your sentence, use a colon, a comma, or no punctuation before a quoted passage.** A colon provides a formal introduction; use it sparingly for emphasis and to introduce a long quotation. Use a comma only when sentence structure requires it. A quotation presented in a "that" clause is not preceded by a comma.

Original: "Hence a wise leader cannot and should not keep his word when keeping it is not to his advantage or when the reasons that made him give it are no longer valid." (From Machiavelli's *The Prince*)

(a): Machiavelli argues for pragmatism thus: "a wise leader cannot and should not keep his word when keeping it is not to his advantage" (51).

(b): "Hence a wise leader cannot and should not keep his word," Machiavelli asserts, "when keeping it is not to his advantage" (51).

(c): Machiavelli insists that "a wise leader cannot and should not keep his word when keeping it is not to his advantage" (51).

ELLIPSIS POINTS

To reduce the length of direct quotations, omit irrelevant portions. Indicate omitted words by using ellipsis points (three spaced dots: . . .). If the omitted material comes at the end of a sentence, a fourth dot is needed to serve as the period that completes the sentence. If a parenthetical reference is given, the period follows the parenthetical reference, as the third example illustrates.

1. Robert T. Bakker believes this is so because "the solution [to dinosaur extinction] is . . . . so obvious, so nonfantastic, that its very mundaneness comes as a jolt" (427).

(Observe the use of an interpolation in square brackets to clarify the quoted material.)

2. As Colbert explains, "the dinosaurs were not failures; they dominated the earth for more than one hundred million years. . . . ." They could not have become extinct, Colbert concludes, merely because they were too big (201).

3. Colbert argues that "the dinosaurs were not failures; they dominated the earth for more than one hundred million years . . . ." (201).

The use of ellipsis points between sentences that are continuously quoted indicates that one or more complete sentences have been omitted.

4. "It is unlikely," Colbert asserts, "that dinosaurs became extinct because a comet collided with the earth. . . . . While this theory explains the demise of the dinosaurs and the marine plankton, it fails to explain how . . . . so many animals managed to survive" (205).

Indicate that one or more lines of poetry have been omitted by using a line of spaced dots about the length of the omitted line(s).

5. Prufrock reveals the inaction of the anti-hero in his contrast to Hamlet:

> No! I am not Prince Hamlet, nor was meant to be;
>
> Am an attendant lord, one that will do
>
> To swell a progress, start a scene or two,
>
> . . . .
>
> Almost, at times, the Fool.

(11. 111-119)

Single Quotation Marks

Use single quotation marks (the apostrophe key on your keyboard) to identify quoted material within quoted material.

1. In <u>The Social Contract</u>, Rousseau argues that "the words 'slavery' and 'right' are contradictory; they cancel each other out."

Periods are placed inside both the single and the double closing quotation mark, unless the sentence concludes with a parenthetical reference, as the following examples illustrate.

2. Lester Thurow complains that "when it comes to empirical analysis of consumer choice, economists retreat to the doctrine of 'revealed preferences.'"

3. Lester Thurow complains that "when it comes to empirical analysis of consumer choice, economists retreat to the doctrine of 'revealed preferences'" (449).

Display Form for Long Quotations

If quoted material runs to more than four typed lines, present it in *display form*. Indent the quoted material ten spaces from the left margin and, when typing, continue to double-space. Quotation marks are not used (the indenting signals a direct quotation). If the quotation includes more than one paragraph, indicate the beginning of a new paragraph by indenting an additional three spaces. Place a parenthetical reference two spaces *after* the final period. Long quotations need an introduction that identifies the author and (usually) concludes with a colon.

Daniel Boorstin conveys his dismay over the effects of television through the following effective metaphor:

> A new miasma—which no machine before could emit—enshrouds the world of TV. We begin to be so accustomed to this foggy world, so at home and solaced and comforted within and by its blurry edges, that reality itself becomes slightly irritating. (374)

Form for Quoting Poetry

1. When quoting two lines of poetry, or a portion of two lines, separate the lines with a slash (/) and retain the capital letter that (usually) begins the second line. Note that there is a space on either side of the slash. In the following example the first quoted word is not capitalized because it is not the first word in the poetic line.

```
Browning's Duke reveals his arrogance when he says:

"and I choose / Never to stoop."
```

2. More than two lines of poetry should be presented in display form and reproduced in the *exact* form of the original lines. As with most long quotations, introduce the quoted material and conclude the introduction with a colon. Line numbers are usually given for passages from long poems.

```
The "tight" lines near the poem's end reinforce the

image of Lowell's tightly-controlled speaker who seems

to be willing herself to repress her feelings, to meet

the expected patterns of her life:

                I shall go

                Up and down

                In my gown.

                Gorgeously arrayed,

                Boned and stayed.

                      (97-101)
```

Form for Quoting Drama

If you are quoting from a prose play, follow the guidelines for quoting prose passages. If you are quoting from a poetic drama, follow the guidelines for quoting poetry. Whether in prose or poetry, short passages from one character can be worked into the text, but long passages, or passages involving two speakers, should be reproduced in display form using the conventional pattern for indicating the speakers. For prose dramas, provide act and scene number (or indicate the appropriate section of the play and conclude with a parenthetical reference, as in the first example). For poetic dramas give act, scene, and line numbers. Use arabic numerals separated by periods, as shown in the examples.

1. Emotional language can be found in part of Charley's
   speech to Biff and Happy during the Requiem:

   > Willy was a salesman. And for a salesman
   > there is no rock bottom to the life. He don't
   > put a bolt to a nut, he don't tell you the law
   > or give you medicine. He's a man way out
   > there in the blue, riding on a smile and a
   > shoeshine. And when they start not smiling
   > back--that's an earthquake. . . . Nobody dast
   > blame this man. A salesman is got to dream,
   > boy. It comes with the territory

2. Creon shows his paranoia early in the play when he ac-
   cuses the Sentry of taking bribes from those Creon believes to be plotting against him: "from the very beginning ▌ There have been those who have whispered together, ▌ Stiff-necked anarchists" (1.110-112).

3. In the following exchange Iago subtly plants suspicion
   of Cassio in the mind of Othello:

   > Oth. Was not that Cassio parted from my
   >   wife?
   > Iago.Cassio, my lord! No, sure, I cannot
   >   think it
   >   That he would steal away so guilty-
   >   like,
   >   Seeing you coming.

```
    Oth.                            I do believe 'twas he.
                                    (3.3.37-40)
```

(Note that Othello's last remark is a continuation of line 40. His words are placed on a new line but moved to the right of "coming.")

Style for Quotations

Handling quotations effectively is an important part of many research tasks. You have just reviewed guidelines for presenting direct quotations in proper form. In addition to getting the form right, you need to pay attention to the style of sentences containing quoted material. Review the following four general guidelines and study the examples to avoid confusion or grammatical errors when quoting.

1. **Do not distort the meaning or tone of the original material by quoting too little.**

    Original: Strauss tells his friends his wounds may be "incurable."

    Misleading: Strauss is said to have "incurable" "wounds."

    Better: Strauss said that his wounds "may be 'incurable.' "

    The use of the passive "is said" in the misleading version leaves the speaker's identity unknown. In addition, the misleading version does not make clear that "incurable" is Strauss's term and that it is qualified with "may be."

2. **Do not distort or confuse meaning by quoting out of context or giving so little information that readers cannot evaluate the significance of quoted material.**

    Misleading: Some words and phrases Evans and Novak use to attack the liberals are "left-wing," "seized on the incident," "first opening to attack," and "assault."

The writer is trying to present evidence that the language used by columnists Evans and Novak to describe liberals is slanted or pejorative. But only the first word, "left-wing," which is a label, can be understood out of context. The other three phrases all reveal some aggressive action, but since the reader is not given enough of the description of the action, it is impossible to tell that the writers are indeed describing the action in a pejorative way.

3. **Do not distort the meaning of a quoted passage by writing a misleading introduction to the quotation.**

Original: Naturalists all in their primary
              inspiration, these men also developed
              in varying degrees the possibilities of
              symbolism and moved generally in the
              direction that Sherwood Anderson rather
              than Dreiser had indicated, toward
              fantasy and away from literal realism.
              (Robert E. Spiller, *The Cycle of American Literature*,
              p. 217)

Misleading: Spiller asserts that the writers of the
              1930s "moved . . . toward fantasy"
              because they were naturalists (217).

This is misleading because Spiller states that the writers were "naturalists" *and* that they "moved . . . toward fantasy," but he does not say that one caused the other.

4. **Weave quoted passages smoothly into sentences and without grammatical error.** Quotations must not distort the grammar, syntax, or logic of the complete sentence. Words, phrases, or clauses quoted in a series must maintain parallel structure, and quoting must be accomplished without leading to incomplete or illogical statements. Here are several examples.

Sentence   Just below the picture a title to the
fragment: article, "Watergate Notoriety Pays Off
                for Some."

Revised: Just below the picture is the title of
                the article: "Watergate Notoriety Pays
                Off for Some."

Not parallel:	<u>Time</u> states that legalized abortion may help to solve such problems as "overpopulation," "the number of unwanted babies," and "probably lower the suicide rate of pregnant women."
Revised:	<u>Time</u> states that legalized abortion may help to solve such problems as "overpopulation," "the number of unwanted babies," and the high "suicide rate of pregnant women."
Tense shift:	As Mrs. Mallard looks out of the window she feels that "there was something coming to her."
Revised:	As Mrs. Mallard looks out of the window she feels that there is "something coming to her."
Person shift:	The duke says that "I choose / Never to stoop."
Revised:	The duke says that he chooses "never to stoop."
Illogical structure:	<u>Time</u>'s description is ". . . prose style is a cross between 'Dear Abby' and early Chinese fortune cookie."
Revised:	<u>Time</u> describes the style as "a cross between 'Dear Abby' and early Chinese fortune cookie."
Illogical word choice:	Other unrealistic (?) words used by <u>U.S. News & World Report</u> are "topple," "jockeying for power," and "unofficial kingmaker." (Revision is not possible. Only the writer knows what this sentence was supposed to mean.)

Many of the problems illustrated here can be solved by quoting less of a passage and using more of your own words. The revisions illustrate this principle.

USING PUNCTUATION CORRECTLY

This brief guide to punctuation emphasizes the required uses. Remember that while some uses are a matter of personal style, other uses are necessary, and consistency is essential.

Commas

1. **Use commas between items in a series.**

   Professors Alleyne, Cromwell, and Johnson appeared on the panel.

2. **Use commas with coordinating conjunctions** *(and, or, but, for, nor, yet, so)* **that join independent clauses.**

   Biff's initiation is sudden and devastating, but Chick develops more slowly.

3. **Use commas between adjectives that, individually, modify the same noun.**

   Tabloids contain unreliable, titillating stories.

4. **Use commas around parenthetical elements, or interrupters.**

   Huck, an outsider in his society, does not grow up.

   Scholarly journals, on the other hand, require the volume number and year in parentheses.

5. **Use commas after long introductory phrases or clauses.**

   Although this survey does not cover a large number of participants, some conclusions can be drawn.

6. **Use commas around nonrestrictive phrases or clauses.**

   The painting, which was admired by the judges, received first prize.

   Walker's painting, hanging on the far wall, received first prize.

But: Do not use commas around restrictive elements.

```
The painting that won first prize has been sold.

Shaw's Pygmalion is the source for the musical My

Fair Lady.
```

Other uses of commas—in dates, for example—and the placing of commas with quoted material and in bibliographic citations are explained in Chapter 3 or earlier in this chapter.

Colons and Semicolons

Colons and semicolons have very different uses; do not confuse them.

1. **Use colons to introduce examples or explanations of what has been said.**

```
The rules are simple: take drugs or break curfew and

you are off the team.
```

2. **Use colons to introduce quoted passages in display form or to introduce a list of items when preceded by such formal expressions as** *the following* **or** *as follows.*

```
The steps in the experiment are as follows:

1. . . . (etc.)
```

3. **Use semicolons to separate two independent clauses, two complete thoughts that could be separated by a period.**

```
There is much compromise in growing up; Chick learns

to compromise on some issues, but not all.
```

4. **Use semicolons in compound sentences if the clauses are long and contain commas within them.**

```
Managing to "have its cake and eat it too," Time, on

one level, is delivering news to the masses; but, on

another level, it is serving up its own opinion for

readers to digest.
```

Periods

1. **Use periods to end complete sentences, endnotes, footnotes, bibliographic citations, and captions of figures (charts, maps, photographs, etc.).**

2. **Use periods between related numbers—for example, to separate act, scene, and line numbers for plays (3.2.6-8).** Place periods outside the closing parenthesis, unless the statement within the parentheses is a complete sentence. Place periods within the closing quotation mark.

Exclamation Points

Rarely if ever use exclamation points in research essays. A clear, forceful statement is sufficient.

Hyphens

1. **Use hyphens to form compound adjectives (*twentieth-century* music) and compound nouns (*anti-intellectual, know-how*).** *Note:* Check a recent dictionary for the correct form of a compound noun: open (*fruit tree*), hyphenated (*ill-favored*), or closed (*notebook*).

2. **Do not hyphenate words at the end of a line. Neither APA nor MLA approves of dividing words. Either leave the line short or use right justification so that words on the line are automatically spaced to create an even right margin.** If you must divide a word between two lines, divide it between syllables and never leave only two letters on either one of the lines.

Dashes

A dash is formed by typing two hyphens without spacing. Use dashes--as illustrated here--to separate a shift in thought or parenthetical material. (Alternatives for parenthetical material include commas and parentheses.)

Brackets

1. **Use brackets around interpolations within quoted material.**

   "Ever since the 1830s, these diaries [fossil bones]

   have been telling the scientific community about

   dinosaurs' growth."

2. **Use brackets around a phonetic transcript of a word.**

   Weltanschauung [velt'än shou'oŏng]

3. **Use brackets as a sign of aggregation in mathematical equations:**
   $[(a + b - c)/(x - y)]$.
   Do not confuse square brackets with parentheses.

Parentheses

1. **Use parentheses to enclose added elements in a sentence.**

   Turning to the remaining types of social interaction

   (with friends, strangers, children). . . .

2. **Use parentheses to enclose series headings.**

   After controls, the following variables remain

   significant: (1) age, (2) education. . . .

3. **Use parentheses when first giving an abbreviation.**

   Studies of rapid eye movement (REM). . . .

4. **Use parentheses with in-text citations.**

   Price-Williams et al. (1969) found. . . .

PRESENTING NUMBERS

There are a few basic rules for presenting numbers in written works—and many exceptions and variations. To grasp the basic rules keep in mind that the goals are clarity and consistency. Thus, when you are presenting many kinds of numbers, you may have to ignore one rule in order to maintain consistency throughout your paper. Variations of general rules are often associated with the writing context; works written in the humanities will treat some numbers differently than texts in scientific and technological fields. You may find that you can solve a specific writing problem best by studying the examples given here for a model that corresponds to your particular use of numbers.

Words and Numerals

In determining when to write numbers as words or as numerals, the choice is between *words* and *arabic numerals*. MLA style now requires the use of arabic numerals for chapter, section, and volume numbers of works; for act, scene, and line numbers in plays; and for canto, stanza, and line numbers of poems. (The acceptable uses of Roman numerals are explained below.)

1. **Use words for whole numbers under 10.**

   She began writing five years ago.

2. **Write as figures (arabic numerals) numbers from 10 up.** This rule applies to cardinal, ordinal, and percentage numbers.

   There were 18 in the first and 26 in the second group.

   He graduated 126th [or 123d] in his class of 450.

   Tuition costs have increased 11%.

   Variation: In discussions using numbers infrequently, the numbers may be expressed in words if they can be written in no more than two or three words; thus: *fifteen hundred, eleven percent.*

3. **Use arabic numerals for partial numbers below 10.**

   8¼   8.66   3.14

4. **Regardless of its size, write out any number that begins a sentence.**

   Thirty-six percent of those interviewed responded with a "yes" to question 1.

(*Note:* Never use a symbol such as "%" with a number written out.)

Eighteen fifty-nine was the year that Darwin revolutionized the field of biology.

(If the sentence is awkward, recast it:

Darwin revolutionized the field of biology in 1859.)

5. **Express very large numbers by combining numerals and words.**

   4.5 billion years ago

6. **Spell out round numbers (e.g., approximations) and numbers that are even hundred thousands.**

   The dinosaurs became extinct some sixty-five million years ago.

   The rally was attended by two hundred thousand fans.

7. **Write as numerals numbers below 10 that appear in the same context as numbers from 10 up.**

   In 3 out of 15 case studies. . . .

   Compare lines 8, 25, and 56.

8. **Use numerals with abbreviations and symbols.**

   65 mph   125 km   200 lb   5%

   3" × 5"   70°–80°   6 p.m. $2.50

9. *Scientific and technical usage.* **Express physical quantities in numerals, regardless of size.**

   4 cubic feet   8 cubic centimeters

   120 volts   60 miles

10. **Use the numeral "1" on your keyboard, not the lowercase "l" or the uppercase "L."**

11. **Place commas between the third and fourth digits from the right, the sixth and seventh, and so on.**

    2,000   20,000   2,200,200

Exceptions: Commas are not used with page numbers, addresses, and years of four digits.

```
On page 3210. . . .

8333 Little River Turnpike

The Norman Conquest of 1066. . . . (BUT: 14,000 B.C.)
```

Percentages, Mixed Numbers, and Money

1. **Write percentages, mixed numbers, and decimal numbers as numerals.**

   ```
   20%   2¹/₂   3.14
   ```

2. **Use an initial zero for decimal numbers less than 1.00.**

   ```
   0.6   0.617
   ```

   Variations: (*a*) If the decimal fraction can never be 1.00 or greater, no zero is used: n = .32 or p < .08.
   (*b*) In some common decimal usages, such as batting averages, no zero is used:

   ```
   He batted only .223 last year.

   The murder weapon was a .38-caliber gun.
   ```

3. **To write amounts of money, follow the rules for words and numerals.**

   ```
   Tickets cost five dollars each.

   The fund-raiser netted $675.

   The painting sold for $3.6 million.
   ```

   (Combine figures and words for large numbers.)

4. **Be consistent when writing amounts of money.** If you use words for the amount, write out the unit of currency (five dollars); if you use a numeral, then use the appropriate symbol for the unit of currency ($675; 6¢). Do *not* use both symbol and word ($675 dollars). If some amounts are in dollars and cents, then use the decimal point and zeros for whole dollar amounts in the

same context: She sold the necklace for $49.50, the earrings for $15.00.

Dates

1. **Be consistent when writing dates.** Use either the day-month-year pattern or the month-day-year pattern throughout. (*Note:* MLA style requires the day-month-year pattern with months abbreviated in the Works Cited.) Punctuate dates correctly, according to the following examples:

   She was born on 5 May 1938. (No punctuation.)

   She was born on May 5, 1938, and graduated in 1959.

   (Commas before and after the year.)

   Iraq invaded Kuwait in August 1990. (No punctuation.)

2. **Write the year alone in figures:** 1945.

3. **Place** B.C. after the date, A.D. before the date.

   Octavian became the Emperor Augustus in 27 B.C. and

   ruled until his death in A.D. 14.

4. **Use words, without capitalization, for decades and centuries:** during the sixties, the twentieth century.
   Variation: It is now acceptable to identify a decade in figures: the 1960s, the '60s.

5. **Hyphenate centuries when they are used as adjectives.**

   sixteenth-century thought

   twentieth-century music

Inclusive Numbers

1. **Follow these rules for figures used to indicate a continuous sequence of numbers. Separate numbers by a hyphen.**
   From 1 through 99, write all digits: 4-16, 67-95
   From 100 up, write only the last two digits of the second number, unless more are needed:
   226-42, 695-720, 2003-07, 1863-912

2. **Express inclusive numbers according to the following models:**

the winter of 1990-91   BUT: from 1990 to 1992

the years 1914-1918   BUT: between 1914 and 1918

A.D. 312-37   BUT: A.D. 200-235

119-14 B.C.

43 B.C. — A.D. 17

Roman Numerals

1. Use lowercase (i, iv) Roman numerals to number the pages of a preface or introductory material or to cite pages that are so numbered.
2. Use capital Roman numerals for major divisions of an outline and for titles of persons (Henry VIII, Elizabeth I).

Equations

Write equations as simply as possible, preferably on one line rather than two whenever possible; thus:

$$(x + y)/(3x-y) \quad \text{NOT:} \quad \frac{x + y}{3x - y}$$

Word processing software allows you to reproduce many mathematical symbols (such as Σ and ∞). If you cannot reproduce needed symbols on your keyboard, type as much of the quotation as possible and fill in the rest in ink.

PRESENTING TABLES AND ILLUSTRATIONS

Although tables and illustrations or figures (e.g., charts, graphs, maps, diagrams, photographs) are never a substitute for clear and thorough discussions, they are effective and efficient means for presenting statistical material or showing relationships and processes. When you plan to use one or more figures in a paper, follow both the general guidelines and the specific instructions for the type of figure you will use.

General Guidelines

1. Select the type of graphic best suited to illustrating the material you want to present.

2. Make a table or illustration simple and clear; use several, if necessary, rather than one that seeks to show too much information.

3. Prepare tables with the characters on any keyboard. Prepare illustrations either by using computer graphics software or by working neatly by hand, in ink, using a ruler, a compass, and/or templates.

4. Place tables and/or figures in your text as near as possible to your discussion of the material. *Exception:* If your project contains complex or numerous tables and/or illustrations, you may want to group them in an appendix. (When following MLA style, place an appendix between the end of the text and the Works Cited. See Chapter 7 for variations in other documentation styles.)

5. Number tables and illustrations consecutively throughout the paper, and label them appropriately: Table 1, Table 2, etc., or Figure 1, Figure 2, etc. Do not abbreviate Table; Figure may be abbreviated Fig.

6. Every table or figure needs *(a)* a number, *(b)* a caption that simply and clearly explains what it shows, and *(c)* a reference to it in the text. *Always refer to the table or figure before it appears in the paper, and always refer to it by its label—either "Table" or "Figure" and its number; thus: "See Figure 3."* Do not write "the following Table" or "the Table below."

7. A table or figure with its caption should be clear without textual discussion; additionally, the textual discussion of the material should be clear without the table or figure. Do not repeat all the information in a table or figure, but explain the general points that the table or figure illustrates. The following textual discussion and Figure 47, both from "Demographics Are Us, Revisited," by Jerry B. Reid (*Radiologic Technology* Mar./Apr. 1991), illustrate the guideline.

Of those employed full or part time, most are in hospital settings. (See Table 1.) The percentage employed by hospitals has decreased somewhat since 1972 for all three disciplines [radiography, nuclear medicine, and radiation therapy]. In 1972 it was 72 percent for radiography vs. 65 percent in 1990, 92 percent for nuclear medicine technology as opposed to 85 percent in 1990 and 89 percent for radiation therapy technology, which was 75 percent in 1990.

Table 1
Employment Setting
(Active Part or Full-Time)

		RAD			NMT			RTT		
		Male	Female	Total	Male	Female	Total	Male	Female	Total
Hospital	1972	—	—	72%	—	—	92%	—	—	89%
	1990	80%	60%	65%	85%	86%	85%	76%	75%	75%
Clinic	1972	—	—	9%	—	—	4%	—	—	4%
	1990	7%	15%	13%	3%	4%	4%	9%	10%	10%
Private Office	1972	—	—	15%	—	—	1%	—	—	3%
	1990	6%	21%	17%	5%	7%	6%	8%	11%	11%
Educator	1972	—	—	—	—	—	—	—	—	—
	1990	2%	1%	1%	1%	1%	1%	2%	2%	2%
Other	1972	—	—	4%	—	—	3%	—	—	4%
	1990	5%	3%	3%	5%	2%	3%	4%	2%	2%

Note: Dash indicates data not available.

Figure 47 Illustration of Table That Is Discussed in Text.

8. Place any explanatory notes below tables or illustrations. Introduce an explanatory note that refers to the entire table or figure with the word "Note" followed by a colon. Introduce an explanation of some specific element within the table or figure by using a superscript *letter* (not number) both after the specific element and before the note.

9. Tables and figures taken from sources must be documented. Introduce documentation with the label "Source" and a colon. Give author and page number, as for any in-text citation, and provide complete documentation in the Works Cited. When a table or figure is followed by both source information and explanatory notes, give the source information first.

Tables

Tables gather a series of related numbers together. They are the easiest figures to prepare because they can be typed as part of the text. Still, take time to align columns and space the material attractively. Prepare tables according to the following guidelines. Use Figures 47 and 48 as models.

1. Place the label and caption *above* the table. The label comes first, typed flush with the left margin. Double-space and then type the caption, again flush with the left margin. Capitalize the words of the caption according to the rules for titles (see page 152).
2. Use a line to separate the table caption and column headings. Use either a caption or a number for each column heading. Keep column headings brief; use two lines if necessary, as shown in Figure 48.
3. For tables with several parts, experiment with a combination of broken lines, solid lines, and double solid lines to aid your visual presentation.

Figure 48 Illustration of a Table with an Explanatory Note.

Table 1
Incidences of Bias by Category

Bias Category	Positive Connotation	Negative Connotation
Contextual	9	3
Adjective	1	4
Attribution	4	3
Photographic	8	3
Opinion	21	9
Total	43	22

Note: Adverbial bias omitted for lack of occurrences.

Bar Charts

Bar charts, also relatively easy to prepare and to read by those not expert in statistics, show quantitative relationships and highlight comparisons between two or more factors. Figure 49 gives an example. Follow these guidelines to prepare a bar chart.

1. Decide on the width of each bar on the basis of the number needed and whether the bars will be spaced or connected. (Note that in Figure 49 a combination of spacing and connection has been used. Spacing aids readability when a number of points of difference are shown.) Take time to create a balanced, neat visual.
2. Label each axis with numbers or captions. Keep captions (bar headings) brief; use two lines if necessary.
3. Place the label (e.g., Figure 1) and the caption *below* the bar chart. Place the label flush with the left margin. Put the caption either on

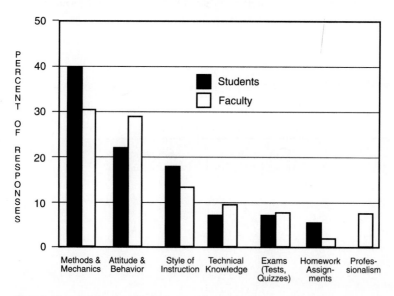

Figure 1. Characteristics of good instruction, as defined by faculty and students, arranged by category.
Source: Higgins, Jenkins, and Lewis (13).

Figure 49 Example of a Bar Chart.

the same line (as in Figure 49) or on a separate line a double space below the label. Captions for figures usually end in a period.

4. Bars can be shaded or patterned differently to highlight differences.

5. If shading or patterns are used, a legend will be needed. The legend can be placed within the lines framing the chart, as in Figure 49, or below the caption.

Pie Charts

A pie chart is a circle divided into segments. Each segment represents a portion of a whole; thus the segments must add up to a total of something—a group of people, an amount of money, and so on. A pie chart is a good visual for emphasizing differences in relationship to a whole. Prepare a pie chart according to these guidelines and use Figure 50 as your model.

1. Limit segments to no more than six. To accomplish this, combine small amounts into an "other" segment.

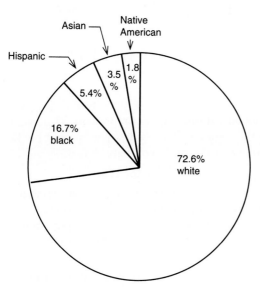

Figure 50 The Federal Work Force by Race or Ethnicity for 1990. Source: Office of Personnel Management, 1990.

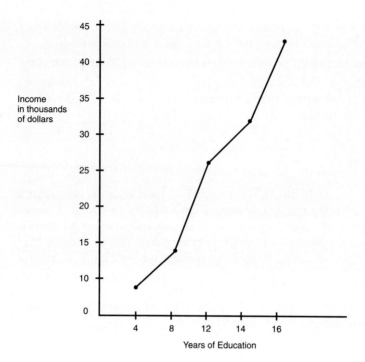

Figure 51 Median Income of Households in Relation to Educational Level.
Source: Statistical Abstracts, Table 718 (445).
Note: Depicts householders 25 years or older as of March 1988.

2. Draw segments proportionally. If one segment represents 32 percent of the total "pie," then the segment at its widest part should be 32 percent of the circumference of the circle you have drawn.

3. Place the pie chart's label and caption *below* the chart.

4. Give each segment a label, written horizontally, not on an angle. Labels may be placed within segments if there is room; they may also be placed outside. Alternatively, the percentage numerals may be placed within the segments and the captions outside.

5. Segments may be shaded to emphasize differences, but avoid using colored pencils.

Line Charts (Graphs)

Line charts, or graphs, are ideal for showing trends or changes over time or for showing a frequency distribution—a distribution relationship of two variables, such as the number of participants per age group. Follow these guidelines when preparing a line chart. (See Figure 51.)

1. Place the figure number and caption *below* the graph.
2. Label each axis.
3. If you are showing changes over time, put time periods on the horizontal axis. Then put the subject of the graph—such as numbers of people or dollar amounts—on the vertical axis.
4. If you are showing a frequency distribution, place the method of classification on the horizontal axis and the frequency on the vertical axis. Thus if you wanted to show the distribution by age of the residents of a particular area, you would place age labels (0, 10, 20, etc.) on the horizontal axis and numbers of residents (0, 5,000, 10,000, etc.) on the vertical axis.

Flowcharts

Flowcharts show qualitative rather than quantitative relationships. They are good for marking a series of steps in a process or procedure, for indicating a sequence of events or ideas, for revealing causal relationships, and for instructing. Prepare flowcharts according to the following guidelines, using Figure 52 as a model.

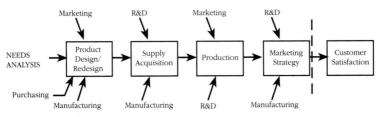

Figure 52 Customer Satisfaction Chain.
Source: Craven and Shipp. "Market Driven Strategies for Competitive Advantage." *Business Horizons* Jan./Feb. 1991: 58.

1. Place the figure label and caption *below* the chart.

2. Select the shape—or shapes—to be used from a template. Prepare the chart with even space between shapes as much as possible, depending on the chart's complexity. Connect all shapes with lines and arrows to show the pattern of movement through the steps or stages. Experiment with different shapes and flow patterns to find the most effective version.

3. Give each shape a label. The label is usually placed *within* the shape.

4. For simple flowcharts, arrange the shapes in a single horizontal or vertical line.

5. For complex patterns that involve "either/or" decision points or looping, use a combination of horizontal and vertical patterns of movement. Add "yes" and "no" terms above horizontal flow lines and beside vertical flow lines at the decision points.

Chapter 6

Writing the Paper

As you near the end of your reading and note-taking and study Chapter 5 to become familiar with forms for presenting and documenting research, you may begin to worry about putting all your work together into a unified paper. You can ease your mind by remembering that the research process is not significantly different from the process of writing other essays. When selecting and focusing other writing topics, you search through the ideas, examples, and opinions you already have. Depending on the topic, you may also look over text material or class notes or a reference source. Then, as a due date approaches, you structure your ideas and material into a plan and write a first draft. This is the process you have been following with your research project, only you have searched through sources for facts and ideas, or perhaps you have conducted interviews or experiments to obtain facts upon which to reflect. And if throughout your study you have continued to think about what your topic needs and how you might approach it, you have been developing and refining a plan all along. Now you need to settle on a thesis and develop a detailed organization to guide your writing, and then draft the paper.

ORGANIZING THE PAPER

To make decisions about your paper's organization, a good place to begin is with the identifying phrases at the top of your note cards. They represent subsections of your topic that emerged as you studied sources and took notes. They will now help you organize your paper. Here are some guidelines for getting organized to write:

1. **Arrange note cards by identifying phrases and read them through.** Read personal notes as well. Work all notes into one possible order as suggested by the identifying phrases. In reading through all cards at one time, you may discover that some notes now seem irrelevant. Set them aside, but do not throw them away yet. Some additional note-taking may be necessary to fill in gaps that have become apparent. You know your sources well enough by now to be able to find the additional material that you need.

2. **Reexamine your tentative thesis or statement of purpose and the preliminary outline that guided your research.** Consider: As a result of reading and reflection, do you need to alter or modify your thesis in any way? Or, if you began with a research question, what now is your answer to the question? What, for example, was the impact of Prohibition on the 1920s? Or, is Catherine Barkley a Hemingway hero? You need to decide.

3. **Write a thesis.** To produce a unified and coherent essay with a clear central idea and a "reason for being," you need a thesis. And your thesis statement will help you decide on a structure for the paper. Write a thesis that conforms to these guidelines:

   • *It is a complete sentence, not a topic or statement of purpose.*

      Topic: General Lee's strategy for the Battle of Chancellorsville.

      Thesis: General Lee's success at the Battle of Chancellorsville was the result of his skill as a military leader.

   • *It is limited and focused.*

      Unfocused: Prohibition affected the 1920s in many ways.

      Focused: Prohibition was more acceptable to rural than urban areas because of differences in religious values, in patterns of socializing, in cultural backgrounds, and in the economic impact of prohibiting liquor sales.

- *It can be supported by your research.*

  Unsupportable: *Time* magazine does not like George Bush.

  Supportable: A study of *Time*'s coverage of President Bush during the 1990–91 winter months reveals a favorable bias during the Persian Gulf war but a negative bias after the war.

- *It establishes a new or interesting approach to the topic that makes your research worthwhile.*

  Not Inventive: A regional shopping mall should not be built adjacent to the Manassas Battlefield.

  Inventive: Putting aside an appeal to our national heritage, one can say, simply, that the building of a regional shopping mall adjacent to the Manassas Battlefield has no economic justification.

4. **Write down the organization revealed by the way you have grouped note cards and compare this organization with your preliminary plan.** The note-card organization will be fuller—more detailed—than your preliminary outline. If you have deleted sections or reordered them, justify those changes in your own mind. Consider: Does the new, fuller plan now provide a complete and logical development of your thesis? If, for example, your thesis asserts that there were *four* areas of Prohibition's effects on urban and rural America, then your organization must show that all *four* areas of impact will be examined for *both* urban and rural America. In short, you need eight sections for your plan in addition to an introduction and a conclusion.

5. **Think once more about your purpose in writing.** First, will your thesis and organization guide you to a paper that meets your research assignment requirements? Second, will they help you produce a paper that accomplishes your purpose and gives emphasis to your approach to the topic? If your approach to the "effect of a law" topic is to show differing effects in different parts of the country, then you need a contrast structure superimposed on a structure that examines effects one by one. Another student, having selected the Glass-Steagall Act of 1933, will not use a contrast structure but will perhaps order the several effects of the act on banking and investment procedures either from short-term to long-term effects or from least to most important.

WRITING FORMAL OUTLINES

For many researchers, a clear thesis and a revised and expanded version of their preliminary outline are all they need as a guide to drafting their paper. Others benefit from preparing a detailed formal outline because they write better if they see the paper's complete and logical structure before beginning to write. If you decide to use a formal outline—or if your research assignment requires one—remember that you can change the outline as you write. It is still only a guide, one that should help, not hinder, your writing. If you are submitting the outline with your paper, make certain to revise it to correspond to any changes made while drafting.

Conventional Outline Patterns

If you are preparing a formal outline, then select one of the standard patterns and follow the conventions of logic and form. The most common pattern combines roman numerals, letters, and arabic numerals to show major sections and subdivisions of the paper. The outline takes this form:

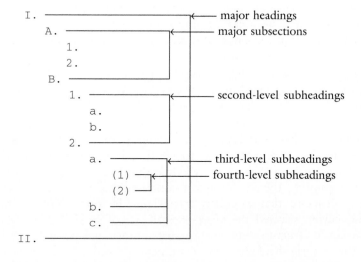

When typing the outline, align all headings and subheadings of equal weight by indenting those of the same weight the same number of spaces. (Begin major headings—the roman numerals—five spaces from the left margin.) Place a period after each letter or number, except for the fourth-level subheadings within parentheses. Allow two spaces after the period or parenthesis before typing words. Capitalize the first letter of the first word of each heading and subheading. Remember that each subdivision requires at least two parts; for example, if there is a 1. under A., there must also be a 2. But any subsection may have more than two parts, and some subsections may not be divided at all.

An alternative pattern is the *decimal outline,* found with papers in business and the sciences. This pattern uses only numbers, with subsections indicated by adding onto the original section number; thus:

```
1. _____
     1.1. _____
          1.1.1. _____
          1.1.2. _____
     1.2. _____
     1.3. _____
2. _____
```

Outline Styles

An outline's headings and subheadings can be written as *paragraphs, sentences,* or *topics.* You need to select one and then maintain that style throughout the outline. The paragraph outline is rarely used for relatively short papers. There is also a danger with the paragraph outline that you will write so much that the outline will begin to resemble the paper, yet, lacking specifics and documentation, it cannot be transformed without change into the paper.

Some instructors encourage use of the sentence outline as a strategy for eliminating headings that are too brief or vague to be helpful. If you are more used to writing topic outlines but are expected to produce a sentence outline, you can begin with topic headings and then expand them into complete sentences. This process, one that forces you to develop assertions about each section, can help clarify your thinking about the topic, not just about the ordering of its parts. One portion of a topic outline has been turned into sentences to illustrate the sentence outline:

Sentence Outline

II. Practical and economic issues demonstrate that building the shopping mall is a bad idea.

   A. An examination of existing shopping facilities shows that additional shopping facilities are not needed.

   B. The argument that the mall will bring new jobs to the area is unconvincing because the unemployment rate in the county is very low and the income needed to live in the county is greater than could be obtained from clerking jobs.

   C. The increased county revenues from sales would be more than offset by the cost of providing and maintaining the new road system that would be needed to provide access to the proposed new mall.

   D. The increased traffic generated by another mall would create a level of congestion adversely affecting all retailers in the area.

The Topic Outline

The built-in advantages of the paragraph and sentence outlines—specific headings in parallel structure—must also be established in a topic outline for that outline to be helpful to you and to meet expected conventions of form. Here are guidelines for preparing a useful and correct topic outline.

USE PARALLEL STRUCTURE

When writing a topic outline, put headings of equal rank in parallel structure. That is, select a noun or noun phrase *(access to the media)*, a gerund phrase *(obtaining media access)*, or an infinitive phrase *(to obtain media access)*. Observe the lack of parallel structure in the following:

   I. Steps in picking up a new sport

      A. Good equipment   *(noun)*

      B. To take lessons   *(infinitive)*

      C. Practicing   *(gerund)*

USE SPECIFIC HEADINGS

Vague headings put off the task of deciding what you want to say in each section of the paper, so make each heading concrete and content-filled so that it will guide you through the paper. Avoid using "Introduction" and "Conclusion." They are useless labels, since every paper has to begin and end. In the sample topic outline below, one student, Tom Finley, uses "Background of the controversy" instead of "Introduction" and "Solutions to the controversy" instead of "Conclusion." Observe as well that Tom does not settle for "Background" only but develops the first section with several specific subheadings. Similarly, Tom lists specific solutions in the outline's final section.

FOLLOW CONVENTIONS OF FORM

Since a topic outline does not contain complete sentences, do *not* place a period after each heading. Additionally, capitalize only the first word of each heading. Title the page "Outline"; place your thesis statement, labeled "Thesis," after the title; and double-space throughout.

SAMPLE TOPIC OUTLINE

```
                          Outline


Thesis: The building of the William Center, a re-

        gional shopping mall adjacent to the Man-

        assas Battlefield cannot be justified on

        practical and economic grounds.

     I. Background of the controversy

        A. History of the shopping mall plan

        B. Explanation of the controversy

           1. Those favoring the mall

           2. Those opposing the mall

    II. Practical and economic arguments against

        the mall

        A. Analysis of existing shopping facili-

           ties
```

   B. Analysis of "new jobs for the area" ar-
      gument

   C. Cost of services in relation to new rev-
      enues

   D. Problems of traffic congestion

   E. County tax problems

III. Solutions to the controversy

   A. National park site

   B. Roads completed before mall

   C. Original office park plan

DRAFTING THE PAPER

Embrace your opportunity, finally, to draft your paper. You have been reading and writing (on note cards) and thinking (in your thesis and outline) about your topic for some time. Look forward, now, to putting all your new knowledge and ideas together in a format that can be shared with others.

Guidelines for the Drafting Process

Here are some strategies for getting started—and for getting through the drafting process successfully.

Allocate Enough Time

Good writing takes time and a commitment to revision. Consider how much time you will need to complete an entire first draft. Working with note cards and being careful about documentation make research paper writing more time-consuming than writing undocumented essays. A 10- or 12-page paper may take two or three afternoons or evenings to draft; a 20-page paper will obviously take longer. You should start writing, then, *at least* five days before your paper is due to allow time away from the draft before revising. You also need to calculate the time needed to type and proofread the final version. If you have drafted on a word processor, preparing the final version will not be a lengthy process, because you will not have to retype the entire paper after revising and editing. If you are typing from a handwritten draft and you are not a strong typist, allow 20 or 30 minutes a page. If you are paying someone to type your paper, you must schedule this service *in advance,* and you will need to allow the typist from two days to a week to complete your project. Do not sell short many weeks of research by trying to draft, revise, and complete a finished paper all in one day.

Prepare to Document as You Draft

Although you may believe that stopping to include parenthetical documentation as you write will cramp your writing, you really cannot wait until completing the draft to add the documentation. The risk of failing to document accurately is too great. Remember that parenthetical documentation is brief; take time to place in parentheses the author's name and relevant page number (or just the page number as appropriate) as you compose. Then, when your paper is finished and you are preparing your list of works cited, go through the paper carefully to make certain that there is a work listed for *every* parenthetical reference. Including documentation as you compose applies equally to writers using either the number style or the footnote or endnote style of documentation. A parenthetical number is just as quickly placed in a draft as a parenthetical author and page reference. If you are using footnotes or endnotes, write out citations on a separate sheet of paper for each number you place in your draft. (If composing at a word processor, read the directions for preparing footnotes; once the procedure is mastered, footnote preparation at the keyboard is simple.)

Have All Materials Within Reach

Whether working in your room or in a computer lab or writing center, you need to have all relevant materials at hand. Make sure that you have all note and bibliography cards and your outline with you, as well as books and photocopied articles for checking the accuracy of direct quotations. If writing in longhand, you will also need paper, pencils, and a dictionary. If using one of the school's word processors, you will probably need to take your own formatted disk with you, and you may need to supply your own paper for a printer that processes single sheets. A few minutes spent collecting materials can save much time and considerable frustration.

Take Care of the Writer

Try, as much as possible, to provide the writer—you—with an environment conducive to the task of writing. Some writers can concentrate with background music; few can make much progress with a blaring stereo or television. An even greater challenge to concentration is conversation that you can hear but are not a part of. So, turn down the music and work when roommates are not around. If necessary, take your materials to a quiet study room or the library. Or plan to use the computer lab at times when it is not crowded (usually morning hours are best).

Remember that no paper needs to be written from top to bottom. If you have trouble getting started with the opening paragraph, skip it and move on to the body of the essay. After you write several pages, a clever opening may occur to you. If you get stuck, take a short break: stretch, look out the window, get something to eat. Ten minutes of relaxation may be just what you need to get back in gear. After composing a few pages, and certainly after breaks, read over what you have written thus far. This strategy will help you maintain a coherent style and inspire you to keep pressing forward.

Writing Style

Specific suggestions for composing the parts of your paper will follow, but first here are some general guidelines for research paper style.

Use the Proper Person

Research papers are written primarily in the third person *(she, he, it, they)* to create objectivity and to direct attention to the content of the paper. You are not likely to use the second person *(you)* at all, for the second person occurs in instructions, in works such as texts that focus on what readers should understand or do. The usual question is over the appropriateness of the first person *(I, we)* in research essays. Although you want to avoid writing "as *you* can see," do not try to skirt around the use of *I* if you need to distinguish your position from others you have presented. It is better to write "I" than "it is the opinion of this writer" or "the researcher learned" or "this project analyzed."

Use the Proper Tense

When you are writing about people, ideas, or events of the past, the appropriate tense to use is the past tense. When writing about current times, the appropriate tense is the present. Both may occur in the same paragraph, as the following paragraph illustrates:

Fifteen years ago "personal" computers were all but unheard of. Computers were regarded as unknowable, building-sized mechanized monsters that required a precise 68 degree air-conditioned environment and eggheaded technicians with thick glasses and white lab coats scurrying about to keep the temperamental and fragile egos of the electronic brains mollified. Today's generation of computers is accessible, affordable, commonplace, and much less mysterious. A computer that used to require two rooms to house is now smaller than a briefcase. A computer that cost hundreds of thousands of dollars fifteen years ago now has a price tag in the hundreds. The astonishing progress made in computer technology in the last few years has made computers practical, attainable, and indispensable. Personal computers are here to stay.

In the above example when the student moves from computers in the past to computers in the present, he shifts tenses accurately. When we write about sources, however, the convention is to use the present tense *even* for works or authors from the past. The idea is that the source, or the author, *continues* to make the point or use the technique into the present—that is, every time there is a reader. Use of the *historical present tense* requires that you write "Lincoln selects the biblical expression 'Fourscore and seven years ago'" and "King echoes Lincoln when he writes 'five score years ago.'" Observe, in the following paragraph, the use of the present tense, except in the first sentence, which refers to a past event.

Two weeks after the opening of <u>Death of a Salesman</u>, Arthur Miller's essay "Tragedy and the

Common Man" was published in the New York Times. In
that widely reprinted piece, Miller stands in direct
contradiction to at least one premise of Aristotle's.
Miller writes that "the common man is as apt a subject
for tragedy in its highest sense as kings were" (143).
Miller reinterprets and updates the traditional
definition of tragedy when he describes "the tragic
right" as a "condition in which the human personality
is able to flower and realize itself" (145). Miller
concludes by challenging his contemporaries to
recognize that modern tragedy indeed exists in "the
heart and spirit of the average man" (147).

USE VOCABULARY APPROPRIATELY

Although a research paper is more formal than a personal essay, it is still
your writing, so it should sound like your writing. Avoid current slang
expressions *(hang-up, okay, gross)* unless they are a part of your study, but
do not seek unfamiliar, unnecessary five-dollar words or stilted sentence
patterns on the mistaken notion that research papers are supposed to
sound pompous.

On the other hand, as you explore a topic in a particular field, you
need to learn the special terms of that field relevant to your topic. As you
read and took notes, you should have studied definitions of terms to
make certain that you would be able to use them correctly. In a literary
analysis, for example, you may need to discriminate accurately among
such terms as *image, metaphor,* and *symbol.* In his review of the literature
on the dinosaurs' extinction, Aaron Knoll must understand the process
of photosynthesis and discuss *comets, asteroids,* and *supernovas* as well as
iridium deposits at the *K-T boundary.* Indeed, in many research projects,
part of the task is to clarify, refine, or illustrate the meaning of a specialized concept such as *identity formation* in psychology or *surrealism* in
art. The surest way to convince an instructor that you are only copying
from sources but have not really learned about your topic is to string together key terms incorrectly.

Writing Good Beginnings

General guidelines for effective introductions apply to research papers as well as essays. The best introduction is one that presents your subject in an interesting way to gain the reader's attention, states your thesis, and gives the reader an indication of the scope and limits of your paper. In a short research essay, you may be able to combine an attention-getter, a statement of subject, and a thesis in one paragraph. More typically, especially in longer papers, the introduction will expand to two or three paragraphs. In the physical and social sciences, the thesis may be withheld until the conclusion, but the opening introduces the subject and presents the researcher's hypothesis, often posed as a question. Since students sometimes have trouble with research paper introductions in spite of knowing these general guidelines, several specific approaches are explained and illustrated in the following pages.

PRESENT AN EXAMPLE OR ANECDOTE

Begin with a brief example or anecdote to dramatize your topic. One student introduced her study of the nightly news with this attention-getter:

> When I watched television in the first weeks
> after moving to the United States, I was delighted by
> the relaxing display of the news programs. It was
> different from what I was used to on German
> television, where one finds a stern-looking man
> reading the news without any emotion. Here the
> commentators laugh or show distress; their tone with
> each other is amiable. Watching the news in this
> country was a new and entertaining experience for me
> initially, but as my reading skills improved, I found
> that I preferred reading newspapers to watching
> television news. Then, reading Neil Postman's attack
> on television news shows in "Television News Narcosis"

```
reminded me of my early experience with American TV
and led me to investigate the major networks'
presentation of the news.
```

In her second paragraph, the student completed her introduction by explaining the procedures used for analyzing network news programs.

Relate to the Known

In the opening to her study of car advertisements, a student reminds readers of the culture's concern with image:

```
    Many Americans are highly image conscious.
Because the "right" look is essential to a prosperous
life, no detail is too small to overlook. Clichés
about first impressions remind us that "you never get
a second chance to make a first impression," so we
obsessively watch our weight, firm our muscles, sculpt
our hair, select our friends, find the perfect houses,
and buy our automobiles. Realizing the importance of
image, companies compete to make the "right" products,
that is, those that will complete the "right" image.
Then advertisers direct specific products to targeted
groups of consumers. Although targeting may be labeled
as stereotyping, it has been an effective strategy in
advertising.
```

Challenge a Popular Attitude

Challenging a popular attitude or assumption is an effective attention-getting opening. For a paper on the advantages of solar energy, a student began:

```
    America's energy problems are serious, despite
the popular belief that difficulties vanished with the
```

end of the Arab oil embargo in 1974. Our problems

remain because the world's supply of fossil fuels is

not limitless.

DEFINE KEY TERMS

Terms and concepts central to your project need defining early in your paper, especially if they are challenged or qualified in some way by your study. The following opening paragraph demonstrates an effective use of definition:

William Faulkner braids a universal theme, the

theme of initiation, into the fiber of his novel

Intruder in the Dust. From ancient times to the

present, a prominent focus of literature, of life, has

been rites of passage, particularly those of childhood

to adulthood. Joseph Campbell defines rites of passage

as "distinguished by formal, and usually very severe,

exercises of severance." A "candidate" for initiation

into adult society, Campbell explains, experiences a

shearing away of the "attitudes, attachments and life

patterns" of childhood (9). This severe, painful

stripping away of the child and installation of the

adult is presented somewhat differently in several

works by American writers.

PROVIDE BACKGROUND

You can effectively begin by giving readers background information needed to create a context for understanding the discussion. A student arguing against the building of a shopping mall next to the Manassas Battlefield began with the following brief history of the controversy:

The developer, Hazel-Peterson, said he wanted to

build a low-rise, campus-styled office park in rapidly

growing Prince William County. So the County Board of
Supervisors approved the rezoning of a 542-acre site
located adjacent to Manassas Battlefield Park, near
Interstate-66 and the proposed VA-234 bypass
interchange (see map, page 2), to a Planned Mixed-Use
Development designation (PMD). Under PMD zoning, the
developer is not limited to his original plan but can
build just about anything he wants, and, more than a
year after the zoning change, Hazel-Peterson had a
change of heart--or financial advice--and decided that
it really wanted to build a 1.2 million square foot
regional mall at the site known as the William Center.
Not surprisingly, a controversy has developed over the
use of these 542 acres next to the Manassas
Battlefield.

REVIEW THE LITERATURE

A review of the relevant literature on a topic is an essential part of the
report of research in the sciences and social sciences. This review, a part
of the paper's introduction, is not usually given in the opening paragraph. In shorter papers, and in research essays in other fields, a brief review of the literature can be an opening-paragraph strategy, as illustrated
in the following:

Since opening on Broadway on February 10, 1949,
Arthur Miller's <u>Death of a Salesman</u> has been one of
the world's most discussed plays. Essays, reviews,
interviews, retrospectives, indeed entire volumes have
been dedicated to the examination of Miller's play.
Every facet of each production, every nuance of
dialogue, every opinion of the author has been put
under the critic's microscope. In this immense body of

words, the dominating question emerges: Is <u>Death of a</u>
<u>Salesman</u> a tragedy? Commentators have drawn parallels
between this play and some of the classical tragedies
of ancient Greece and Elizabethan England (Fuller 243;
Bierman et al. 265). Arthur Miller himself has written
in defense of his play as a tragedy (143-47). Others
have disputed his claim, citing the work of Aristotle
(Clark 222; Hynes 284). To resolve the conflict, we
need first to examine both Aristotle's and Miller's
definitions of tragedy and then see how they allow us
to understand and define the play itself.

Present Facts

Beginning with important, perhaps startling, facts, evidence, or statistics is an effective way to introduce a topic, provided the details are relevant to the topic. Observe the following example:

Teenagers are working again, but not on their
homework. Over 40 percent of teenagers have jobs by
the time they are juniors (Samuelson A22). And their
jobs do not support academic learning since almost
two-thirds of teenagers are employed in sales and
service jobs that entail mostly carrying, cleaning,
and wrapping (Greenberger and Steinberg 62-67), not
reading, writing, and computing. Unfortunately, the
negative effect on learning is not offset by improved
opportunities for future careers.

State and Expand the Thesis

Some topics do not lend themselves to arresting beginnings, and some writers get blocked trying to devise clever openings. Remember that presenting a clear statement of the paper's thesis, developed in several sentences, is always one appropriate way to get started. In a study of *The Great Gatsby*, one student began this way:

> F. Scott Fitzgerald's novel <u>The Great Gatsby</u> examines one man's attempt to realize his dream. Fitzgerald skillfully uses a number of symbols, including colors, cars, and names, to develop and support his observations on the American dream. Gatsby, a self-made man, is himself a symbol of the American dream. While reading this novel, however, one comes to realize that for Fitzgerald the American dream is flawed. Although Gatsby attains great material wealth, he is never able to change his past and gain acceptance into the world of Daisy Buchanan. The American dream's flaws are underscored by Fitzgerald's use of symbolic colors, cars, and names throughout the novel.

Avoiding Ineffective Openings

Follow these guidelines for avoiding openings that most readers find ineffective or annoying.

1. **Do not restate the title** or write as if the title were the first sentence in paragraph 1. First, the title of the paper appears at the top of the first page of text. Second, it is a convention of writing to have the first paragraph stand independent of the title.
2. **Do not begin with "clever" visuals** such as artwork or fancy lettering.
3. **Do not begin with humor** unless it is part of your topic.
4. **Do not begin with a question that is just a gimmick, or one that a reader may answer in a way you do not intend.** Asking "What are the advantages of solar energy?" may lead a reader to answer

"None that I can think of." A straightforward research question ("Is *Death of a Salesman* a tragedy?") is appropriate.

5. **Do not open with an unnecessary definition quoted from a dictionary.** "According to Webster, solar energy means . . ." is a tired, overworked beginning that does not engage readers.

6. **Do not start with a purpose statement:** "This paper will examine. . . ." Although a statement of purpose is a necessary part of a report of empirical research, such a report should open not with an immediate purpose statement but rather with some interesting introduction to the research subject.

Composing Main Paragraphs

As you compose the body of your paper, keep in mind that you want to (1) maintain unity and coherence, (2) guide readers clearly through source material, and (3) synthesize source material and your own ideas. These are three demanding writing goals that take planning and practice on your part. Do not settle for paragraphs in which facts from note cards are just loosely run together. Review the following discussion and study the examples to see how to present what you have learned and want others to understand about your topic.

PROVIDE UNITY AND COHERENCE

Paragraph unity is achieved when every sentence in a paragraph relates to and develops the paragraph's main idea or topic sentence. If you have a logical organization, composing unified paragraphs is not a problem. Unity, however, does not automatically produce coherence; that takes attention to wording. Coherence is achieved when readers can follow the connection between one sentence and another and between each sentence and the topic sentence. Strategies for achieving coherence include repetition of key words, the use of pronouns that clearly refer to those key words, and the use of transition and connecting words. Observe these strategies at work in the following paragraph.

```
Perhaps the most important differences between
the epiphanic initiations of Robin and Biff and that
experienced by Chick are the facts that Chick's
epiphany does not come all at once and it does not
```

devastate him. Chick learns about adulthood--and
enters adulthood--piecemeal and with support. His
first eye-opening experience occurs as he tries to pay
Lucas for dinner and is rebuffed (15-16). Chick
learns, after trying again to buy a clear conscience,
the impropriety and affront of his actions (24). Lucas
teaches Chick how he should resolve his dilemma by
setting him "free" (26-27). Later, Chick feels outrage
at the adults crowding into the town, presumably to
see a lynching, then disgrace and shame as they
eventually flee (196-97, 210). As in most lives,
Chick's passage into adulthood is a gradual process;
he learns a little bit at a time and has support in
his growing. Gavin is there for him, to act as a
sounding board, to lay a strong intellectual
foundation, to confirm his beliefs. Chick's initiation
is consistent with Joseph Campbell's explanation: "all
rites of passage are intended to touch not only the
candidate, but also every member of his circle" (9).
Perhaps Gavin is affected the most, but Chick's mother
and father, and Lucas as well, are influenced by the
change in Chick.

Coherence is needed not only within paragraphs but between paragraphs
as well. Submitting an outline does not eliminate the writer's responsibility to guide readers through the entire paper, connecting paragraphs and
showing relationships by the use of transitions. Sometimes writers purposely avoid transition words or phrases because they seem awkward or
heavy-handed, as they can be if writers unwisely choose "My first point is
. . . ," "My second point is . . . ," and so on. But transitions can be
smooth and still clearly signal shifts in the paper's subtopics from one

paragraph to another. The following opening sentences of four paragraphs from a paper on the advantages of solar energy illustrate smooth transitions:

¶7   Owners of private solar-heated homes,
construction companies, and researchers all seem to
agree that, despite the initial high cost, the system
offers tremendous savings over a period of years.

¶8   Private homeowners and builders are not the
only ones who are experimenting with solar energy
systems. Several government buildings, including
schools, are testing this new form of heating and
cooling.

¶9   The prospects of solar energy seem so promising
that many cities and states are also beginning to plan
for its increased use.

¶10   Important as well is the support and
recognition members of Congress are giving to the
further development of solar energy.

Without repeating the same phrase—"Also using solar energy are"—three times, the student guides her readers from private-home use of solar energy to public-building use, to government use, to congressional support.

GUIDE READERS THROUGH SOURCE MATERIAL

To understand the importance of guiding readers through source material, consider first the following paragraph from a paper on the British coal strike in the 1970s:

The social status of the coal miners was far from
good. The country blamed them for the dimmed lights
and the three-day work week. They had been placed in

```
the position of social outcasts and were beginning to

"consider themselves another country." Some businesses

and shops had even gone so far as to refuse service to

coal miners (Jones 32).
```

Who has learned that the coal miners felt ostracized or that the country blamed them? As readers we cannot begin to judge the validity of these assertions without some context provided by the writer. Most readers are put off by an unattached direct quotation or some startling observation that is documented correctly but given no context within the paper. Using introductory tags that identify the author of the source and, when useful, the author's credentials helps guide readers through the source material. The following revision of the paragraph above provides not only context but also sentence variety:

```
    The social acceptance of coal miners, according

to Peter Jones, British correspondent for Newsweek,

was far from good. From interviews both in London

shops and in pubs near Birmingham, Jones concluded

that Britishers blamed the miners for the dimmed

lights and three-day work week. Several striking

miners, in a pub on the outskirts of Birmingham,

asserted that some of their friends had been denied

service by shopkeepers and that they "consider[ed]

themselves another country" (32).
```

When you use introductory tags, try to vary both the words you use and their place in the sentence. Look, for example, at the first sentence in the sample paragraph above. The tag is placed in the middle of the sentence and is set off by commas. The sentence could have been written two other ways:

```
    The social acceptance of coal miners was far from

good, according to Peter Jones, British correspondent

for Newsweek.
```

OR

According to Peter Jones, British correspondent

for <u>Newsweek</u>, the social acceptance of coal miners was

far from good.

Whenever you provide a name and perhaps credentials for your source, you have these three sentence patterns to choose from. Make a point to use all three options in your paper. Word choice can be varied as well. Instead of writing "Peter Jones says" throughout your paper, consider some of the many options you have:

Jones *asserts*	Jones *contends*	Jones *attests to*
Jones *states*	Jones *thinks*	Jones *points out*
Jones *concludes*	Jones *stresses*	Jones *believes*
Jones *presents*	Jones *emphasizes*	Jones *agrees with*
Jones *argues*	Jones *confirms*	Jones *speculates*

Observe that not all the words in this list are synonyms; you cannot substitute *confirms* for *believes*. Select, first, the term that most accurately conveys the writer's relationship to his or her material. Then, when appropriate, vary word choice as well as sentence structure.

The use of introductory tags to provide a context for understanding material from sources is a convention in research paper writing for good reason. Readers need to be told how they are to respond to the sources used. They need to know which sources you accept as reliable and which you disagree with, and they need to see you distinguish clearly between fact and opinion. Statistical information and undisputed facts can be presented with parenthetical documentation citing author and page number, but ideas and opinions from sources need introductory tags and then some discussion from you. Your goal is to create clear and smooth transitions between information from different sources and between borrowed material and your own ideas.

Synthesize Source Material and Your Own Ideas

A smooth synthesis of source material is aided by an introductory tag and parenthetical documentation because they mark the beginning and ending of material taken from a source. But a complete synthesis requires something more: your ideas about the source and the topic. To understand the point, consider, first, the problems in another paragraph from the British-coal-strike paper:

> Some critics believed that there was enough coal
> in Britain to maintain enough power to keep industry
> at a near-normal level for thirty-five weeks (Jones
> 30). Prime Minister Heath, on the other hand, had
> placed the country's usable coal supply at 15.5
> million tons (Jones 30). He stated that this would
> have fallen to a critical 7 million tons within a
> month had he not declared a three-day work week (Jones
> 31).

This paragraph is a good illustration of random details strung together for no apparent purpose. How much coal did exist? Whose figures were right? And what purpose do these figures serve in the paper's development? Note that the entire paragraph is developed with material from one source. Do sources other than Jones offer a different perspective? This paragraph is weak for several reasons: (1) it lacks a controlling idea (topic sentence) to give it purpose and direction; (2) it relies for development entirely on one source; (3) it lacks any discussion or analysis by the writer.

By contrast, the following paragraph, taken from the review-of-the-literature paper in Chapter 4, demonstrates a successful synthesis:

> Of course, the iridium could have come from other
> extraterrestrial sources besides an asteroid. One
> theory, put forward by Dale Russell, is that the
> iridium was produced outside the solar system by an
> exploding star (500). The theory of a nearby star
> exploding in a supernova is by far the most fanciful
> extraterrestrial theory; however, it warrants
> examination because of its ability to explain the
> widespread extinctions of the late Cretaceous Period

(Colbert 205). Such an explosion, Russell states, could have blown the iridium either off the surface of the moon or directly from the star itself (500-01), while also producing a deadly blast of heat and gamma rays (Krishtalka 19). Even though this theory seems to explain the traces of iridium in the mass extinction, it does not explain why smaller mammals, crocodiles, and birds survived (Wilford 220). As Edwin Colbert explains, the extinctions of the late Cretaceous, although massive, were selective (205). So the supernova theory took a backseat to the other extraterrestrial theories: those of asteroids and comets colliding with the earth. The authors of the book The Great Extinction, Michael Allaby and James Lovelock, subtitled their work The solution to . . . the disappearance of the dinosaurs. Their theory: an asteroid or comet collided with earth around sixty-five million years ago, killing billions of organisms, and thus altering the course of evolution (157). This theory was hardly a new one when they wrote it; the Alvarezes came up with it nearly three years before. However, the fact that the theory of collision with a cosmic body warrants a book describing itself as the solution to the extinction of dinosaurs calls for some thought: is the asteroid or comet theory merely sensationalism, or is it rooted in fact? Paleontologist Leonard Krishtalka declares that few paleontologists have accepted the asteroid theory,

```
himself calling "some catastrophic theories . . .

small ideas injected with growth hormone" (22).

However, other scientists, such as Allaby and

Lovelock, see the cosmic catastrophic theory as a

solid one based on more than guesswork (10-11).
```

This paragraph's synthesis is accomplished by several strategies: (1) the paragraph has a controlling idea; (2) the paragraph combines information from several sources; (3) the information is presented in a blend of paraphrase and short quotations; (4) information from the different sources is clearly indicated to readers; and (5) the student explains and discusses the information.

You might also observe the very different lengths of the two sample paragraphs just presented. Although the second paragraph is very long, longer than a typical paragraph, still it is not unwieldy because it achieves unity and coherence. By contrast, body paragraphs of only three sentences are probably in trouble. They are not likely to develop an idea from several sources or provide the needed analysis of sources to produce the synthesis that readers expect. If you find yourself composing a number of short paragraphs, stop and reexamine your organizational plan. If the problem is not in the logic of your plan, then ask yourself if you are providing the necessary explanation and discussion of material from sources.

Writing Good Conclusions

Sometimes ending a paper seems even more difficult than beginning one. You know you are not supposed to just stop, but every ending that comes to mind sounds more corny than clever. Perhaps you are trying too hard for a "catchy" ending that really may not be appropriate for a complex and serious research essay. If you have trouble, try one of the following types of endings.

RESTATE AND EXTEND THE THESIS

Do not just repeat your thesis as it was stated in paragraph 1, but expand on the original wording and emphasize the thesis's significance. Here is the conclusion of the solar energy paper:

The idea of using solar energy is not as far-fetched as it seemed years ago. With the continued support of government plus the enthusiasm of research groups, environmentalists, and private industry, solar energy may become a household word quite soon. With the increasing cost of fossil fuel, the time could not be better for exploring this use of the sun.

And from the *Death of a Salesman* paper:

Willy Loman, in the twentieth-century definition of a tragic hero, fits. No matter how convoluted his circumstances, his dreams, his existence, Willy Loman struggles for success, not just in business, but in his perception of life. And Willy's pursuit of success is not selfish. He wants to be a good provider for his family and a role model for his sons. He knows, too, that he has failed his sons, especially Biff, and is tortured by this failure in spite of denials. He knows that the car is a piece of junk, that people don't like him, but he sees no alternative except to hold on tighter to America's success myth--until he has squeezed the life out of it and it has choked him. The final ironic metaphor of the play, that Willy Loman's life is used up just as his debts are about to be paid off, also fits. Willy Loman's story, Arthur Miller's Death of a Salesman, is indeed a tragic one.

CLOSE WITH A QUOTATION

End with a quotation that effectively summarizes and drives home the point of your paper. Researchers are not always lucky enough to find the ideal quotation for ending a paper. If you find a good one, use it. Better yet, present the quotation and then add your comment in a sentence or two. The conclusion to a paper on the dilemma of defective newborns is a good example:

> Dr. Joseph Fletcher is correct when he says that "every advance in medical capabilities is an increase in our moral responsibility" (48). In a world of many gray areas, one point is clear. From an ethical point of view, medicine is a victim of its own success.

PRESENT DISCUSSION OR SUGGESTIONS FOR FURTHER STUDY

Conclusions of empirical reports will contain a discussion of the new data or the results of the experiment. This discussion can go beyond an explanation of the result's significance to suggest further research. In a review of the literature on a given issue, the paper can also conclude with suggestions for further study. In a paper that examined the empirical work conducted on infants' preference for infant-directed speech, the student ended with directions for further research. (Note that documentation is not in MLA style but in APA style—appropriate for a paper in the social sciences.)

> Possibly the most important area of study to focus on is how we can use infants' auditory preferences to understand later language learning. For example, do the specific features of motherese help infants gain knowledge of segmentation of speech? Studies should determine whether infants benefit from features such as exaggerated use of pitch contouring and differential stress. Although some research has sought to examine this issue, more work needs to be done. Also, future research may look at how auditory preferences change ontogenetically, and how they may relate to other aspects of development (Cooper & Aslin, 1989).

PRESENT SOLUTIONS

If you have researched a current problem, you can present your solutions to the problem in a final paragraph. The student opposing a mall adjacent to the Manassas Battlefield concluded with several solutions:

> Whether the proposed mall will be built is clearly in doubt at the moment. What are the solutions to this controversy? One approach is, of course, not to build the mall at all. To accomplish this solution, now, with the rezoning having been approved, probably requires an act of Congress to buy the land and make it part of the National Park. Another solution, one that would please the County and the developer and satisfy citizens objecting to traffic problems, is to build the needed roads before the mall is completed. A third approach is to allow the office park of the original plan to be built, but not the mall. The local preservationists had agreed to this original development proposal, but now that the issue has received national attention, they may no longer be willing to compromise. Whatever the future of the William Center, the present plan for a new regional mall is not acceptable.

Avoiding Ineffective Conclusions

Follow these guidelines to avoid conclusions that most readers consider ineffective and annoying.

1. **Do not introduce a new idea.** If the point belongs in your paper, you should have introduced it earlier.

2. **Do not just stop or trail off,** even if you feel as though you have run out of steam. A simple, clear restatement of the thesis is better than no conclusion.

3. **Do not tell your reader what you have accomplished:** "In this paper I have explained the advantages of solar energy by examining the costs. . . ." If you have written well, your reader knows what you have accomplished.

4. **Do not offer apologies or expressions of hope.** "Although I wasn't able to find as much on this topic as I wanted, I have tried to explain the advantages of solar energy, and I hope that you will now understand why we need to use it more" is a disastrous ending.

5. **Do not end with a vague or confusing one- or two-sentence summary of complex ideas.** The following sentences make little sense: "These authors have similar and different attitudes and ideals concerning American desires. Faulkner writes with the concerns of man towards man whereas most of the other writers are more concerned with man towards money."

Choosing a Title

You should give some thought to your paper's title since that is what your reader sees first and what your work will be known by. A good title provides information and creates interest. Make your title informative by making it specific. If you can create interest through clever wording, so much the better. But do not confuse "cutesiness" with clever wording. Better to be just straightforward than to demean a serious effort with a "cutesy" title. Study the guidelines in Chapter 5 for presenting titles of works to make certain that capitalization is correct. Review the following examples of acceptable and unacceptable titles.

Vague:	A Perennial Issue Unsolved
	(There are many; which one is this paper about?)
Better:	The Perennial Issue of Press Freedom Versus Press Responsibility
Too Broad:	Earthquakes
	(What about earthquakes? This title is not informative.)
Better:	The Need for Earthquake Prediction

Too Broad:	The Scarlet Letter
	(Never use just the title of the work under discussion; you can use the work's title as a part of a longer title of your own.)
Better:	Color Symbolism in The Scarlet Letter
Cutesy:	Babes in Trouble
	(The slang "Babes" makes this title seem insensitive rather than clever.)
Better:	The Dilemma of Defective Newborns

REVISING THE PAPER

After completing a first draft, catch your breath, pat yourself on the back, and then "gear up" for the next—and equally important—step in the writing process: revision. Revision actually involves three activities that can best be approached as three separate steps to revising your paper. *Revising,* step 1, means *rewriting:* actually adding text, deleting text, or moving parts of the draft around. Next comes *editing,* a rereading to correct errors from misspellings to awkward sentences. Finally, you need to *proofread* the typed copy. Trying to combine the first two steps often leads to incomplete revision; trying to ignore the third step can lead to a lower grade than the research and writing deserve because easily corrected mistakes are overlooked.

Rewriting

If you have composed your first draft at a word processor, print a hard copy that is double- or—better—triple-spaced so that you have room for revision. When composing a handwritten draft, you can prepare a similar working draft by skipping lines or leaving wide margins. Read your draft through and make changes—adding, deleting, moving parts around—as a result of answering the following questions:

PURPOSE AND AUDIENCE

1. Is my draft long enough to fulfill assignment requirements and my purpose?

2. Are terms defined and concepts explained appropriately for my audience?

CONTENT

1. Do I have a clearly stated thesis?
2. Have I presented sufficient evidence to support my thesis?
3. Are there any irrelevant sections that should be deleted?

STRUCTURE

1. Are paragraphs ordered to develop the topic logically?
2. Does the content of each paragraph help develop the thesis?
3. Is everything in each paragraph on the same subtopic to create paragraph unity?
4. Do body paragraphs have a balance of information and analysis, of source material and my own ideas?
5. Are there any paragraphs that should be combined? Are there any very long paragraphs that should be divided? (Length alone is not a reason to divide; check long paragraphs for unity.)

These questions guide your revision of the large elements of the paper. Clearly, if your draft is too short to meet requirements, you have a problem to solve *before* turning to issues of style or grammar. If you are facing too short a paper, examine your outline and note cards again to see if you have overlooked material you had intended to include. Then, with the questions on structure as your guide, examine each body paragraph for incomplete development. Consider: Are you assuming that the reader has information or understanding that it is really your task to provide?

Make any large-scale revisions involving length, content, organization, and paragraphing first. If you composed at a computer, you know how to add text, delete text, and move parts around with the BLOCK and MOVE commands. If your draft is handwritten, add above the line and in the margin, marking each place to add material with a caret (∧). You can circle an entire paragraph and draw an arrow to mark its new placement, or cut the paragraph out and tape it to a new sheet that you place in front of the page to which the paragraph will be added. With handwritten drafts, be especially careful to make changes that can be read.

After rewriting, read the entire draft through *again* to assess length, content, order, and paragraph unity. Complete this first step of revision by judging your draft according to the following questions:

COHERENCE

1. Have connecting words been used and key terms repeated to produce paragraph coherence?
2. Have transitions been used to show connections between paragraphs?

SOURCES

1. Have I paraphrased instead of quoted whenever possible?
2. Have I avoided long quotations?
3. Have I used introductory tags to create a context for source material?
4. Have I used verbs in introductory tags that accurately represent the author's relationship to the material?
5. Have I documented *all* borrowed material, whether quoted or paraphrased?
6. Are parenthetical references properly placed after borrowed material?

After making the additional revisions generated by the above questions, you will be ready for the editing step. If you have been working with a handwritten draft, this is the time to type your paper into a word processor so that you can take advantage of its editing features. If you are going to turn over a handwritten paper to a typist, you may want to make a fresh copy at this point, especially if you have already made extensive changes. Remember that further changes are likely when you edit.

Editing

Although you may have corrected various errors and stylistic weaknesses as you made major revisions to the first draft, you are wise to examine the now completed second draft for specific "smaller"—but still important—kinds of problems. Students often assert that they would be happy to edit their papers if they only knew what to look for. Their point is well taken. What often passes for *editing* is an examination of content primarily, what you have just done to *revise* your first draft. Here are five specific elements of writing that you should examine, one by one, to perform a thorough editing of your paper.

TONE

Read your second draft through to assess the paper's tone. Have you avoided humor or sarcasm, except as a part of your topic? Have you avoided condescending to or ridiculing readers? ("As everybody understands, surrealism refers to" is the kind of expression that needs deleting.) Do you maintain the appropriate level of seriousness throughout? (Do not be flip; do not complain about difficulties finding sources.)

SENTENCE STYLE

Examine your draft *sentence by sentence,* testing your sentences against the following questions:

1. Are the sentences grammatically complete, except for those fragments purposely used for emphasis? Look specifically for any beginnings with words such as *because* and *although*. These words introduce dependent clauses, which must be attached to an independent clause to make a complete sentence.

2. Are there instances of wordiness, clichés, trite expressions, or inflated phrases that can be eliminated? Examine your writing for phrases such as the following, and observe the simpler alternatives that can be substituted.

Wordy, Trite, Inflated	Revision
very unique	unique
the study tends to suggest	the study suggests
in this day and age	today, now, currently
conduct an examination of	examine
at the present time	now
fewer in number	fewer
of great importance	important
in today's modern society	today

3. Do you need to increase sentence variety? Consider varying both length and structure. Begin some sentences with dependent clauses or phrases to avoid having most start with subject and verb.

4. Most important, do sentences present ideas clearly, and with precision? Look specifically at uses of *this* and *which*. (If you are editing at a word processor, use the SEARCH function to find all uses of any given word.) Do not use *this* to refer vaguely to a complex idea in the preceding sentence, and avoid attaching a *which* clause, as a vague comment, to a complex statement. For example:

```
Huck never becomes an adult citizen of society despite

the broad experience he has in that society, which is

why he differs from Chick.
```

What noun does the clause modify? You probably need two sentences:

```
Huck never becomes an adult citizen of society despite

the broad experience he has in that society. His lack

of growth sets him in contrast to Chick.
```

DISCRIMINATORY LANGUAGE

Edit to eliminate all discriminatory language—language that stereotypes people by race, sex, nationality, religion, age, or handicap. Most people recognize ethnic or racial slurs and would not write such statements, but sometimes attitudes about young, old, or handicapped people can slip unnoticed into writing, and of course sexist writing is a particular problem because English lacks a neuter pronoun to refer to people. Remember that it is unacceptable to use *he* to refer to a noun that could be male or female. Here are some ways around the problem of sexist writing.

- Use "people," "humans," or "human beings" instead of "man."
- Use "spouse" or "family" instead of "wife," or use "families," as appropriate.
  Sexist: "The pioneer and his wife opened up the West."
  Nonsexist: "Pioneer families opened up the West."
- Use nonsexist terms for types of workers. Instead of "manpower" use "workers," "staff," or "personnel." Instead of "policeman" use "police officer"; instead of "housewife" use "homemaker"; and so on.
- Eliminate "he" or "his" to refer to a noun that could be male or female by pluralizing the noun and then using the plural pronoun "they" or "their." Alternatively, recast the sentence to avoid the use of a pronoun. "He or she" can be used sparingly, but not more than once in a sentence.
  Sexist: "A good manager has learned how to motivate *his* employees."
  Nonsexist: "Good managers have learned how to motivate *their* employees."
  Nonsexist: "A good manager has learned how to motivate employees."

WORD CHOICE

Examine your word choice and edit as necessary according to your answers to these questions:

1. Are specialized terms used correctly?

2. Have I avoided an excessive use of specialized terms and selected instead, where possible, simpler words?

3. Have I used, as much as possible, specific, concrete words instead of general, abstract words? Look specifically for too much reliance on such words as *thing, factor, aspect.*

4. Have I used correctly those troublesome words called homonyms: *there, their, they're; you're, your; where, were; its, it's; affect, effect;* and so on? Use the word processor's SEARCH function to check each use of both abstract words (question 3) and the particular words that give you trouble.

5. Have I avoided contractions as too informal for research essays? (SEARCH the apostrophe ['] to find and change any contractions.)

PUNCTUATION

Finally, review the guidelines in Chapter 5 for punctuation usage and for all other technical issues such as presenting titles and quotations.

Proofreading

When your editing is completed, prepare a final draft of your paper according to the format described below. Try to print your final copy on either a daisy wheel or laser printer, or on a dot matrix printer with second-strike capability so that the final copy looks good and is easily read. If you are preparing your paper on a typewriter, work with a new ribbon. With either process, select quality paper. Then proofread the final copy carefully, making necessary corrections neatly in ink. If a page has several errors, print a corrected page or retype the page. It is especially important that you carefully proof a paper typed by someone else from your handwritten copy. Remember: You are responsible for the work you hand in, and you will be receiving the grade, not the typist.

PREPARING THE COMPLETE PAPER

Your paper, when submitted, may contain some or all of the following parts, in the order given, depending on your requirements. All papers will contain parts 4 and 7. Adhere to the guidelines for each part included in your project. (Double-space all parts of your paper.)

1. **A title page,** with your title, your name, the course name or number, your instructor's name, and the date—all centered. Place each

item on a separate line and double-space between lines. Do *not* underline your title or put it in quotation marks, but handle any title(s) within your title appropriately. If your paper does not contain either an outline or an abstract, you may omit a separate title page. With this pattern, place your name, the name of the course, and the date on the first page of text, in the upper left corner, before the paper's title. Center the title on the page and double-space all these elements. (See page 242 for an example.)

2. **An outline** or statement of purpose, if required. If the outline is more than one page, number the pages with small roman numerals (i.e., i, ii, iii).

3. **An abstract,** if required. The abstract, a summary of your paper in about 100 words, can be placed below the title on page 1 of your text, but more often it is placed on a separate page after the title page (and outline, if there is one) and before the first page of text. Title the page "Abstract." (See page 269 for a sample.)

4. **The body, or text, of your paper.** Begin the first page of text with the title of the paper centered 1 inch from the top. If you have not used a separate title page, center the title after the identifying information in the upper left corner of the page. Number all pages consecutively, placing the numeral "1" on the first page in the upper right corner of the page ½ inch from the top of the sheet. A running head is usually used with the page number. MLA style requires the author's last name (see page 234); APA style requires a short title (see page 269).

5. **Content endnotes if used.** Content notes can be presented as footnotes on appropriate pages of text, or they can be grouped as endnotes on one or more pages following the end of the text of the paper. Title the page "Notes," continue to number pages consecutively, and double-space throughout. Indent the first line of each note five spaces, and begin each note with a raised (superscript) numeral that corresponds to the numeral placed within the text. (See page 165 for a discussion of content notes.)

6. **An appendix if needed.** Use an appendix for a number of visuals, lengthy tables of statistics or mathematical proofs, or detailed results of questionnaires that support a discussion within the text. Do not have a separate appendix for a few tables or charts that can easily be placed within the text of the paper. If you use an appendix, title a new page "Appendix" and continue to number pages consecutively and double-space throughout. If you have more than one appendix, title them "Appendix A," "Appendix B," and so on.

7. **Your Works Cited list.** Begin a new page titled "Works Cited," and continue to number pages consecutively and to double-space throughout. See Chapter 3 (or Chapter 7) for citation formats and pages 240 and 256 for sample Works Cited pages.

SAMPLE RESEARCH PAPER 1: A SHORT LITERARY ANALYSIS

The following paper, in MLA style, illustrates the use of a few sources but many page references to one literary work. Alan's essay was written for a 200-level American literature course and was based in part on class discussion of *Intruder in the Dust* as an example of an initiation novel. Alan demonstrates considerable skill in literary analysis and shows, by his references to Nathaniel Hawthorne and Arthur Miller, that he remembers previously studied works and recognizes them as also employing an initiation theme. The ability to go beyond class discussion and to make connections with other works or concepts will be rewarded in any field of study.

Peterson 1

Alan Peterson

American Literature 242

May 5, 1990

Faulkner's Realistic Initiation Theme

    William Faulkner braids a universal theme, the theme of initiation, into the fiber of his novel <u>Intruder in the Dust</u>. From ancient times to the present, a prominent focus of literature, of life, has been rites of passage, particularly those of childhood to adulthood. Joseph Campbell defines rites of passage as "distinguished by formal, and usually very severe, exercises of severance." A "candidate" for initiation into adult society, Campbell explains, experiences a shearing away of the "attitudes, attachments and life patterns" of childhood (9). This severe, painful stripping away of the child and installation of the adult is presented somewhat differently in several works by American writers.

    One technique of handling this theme of initiation is used by Nathaniel Hawthorne in his story "My Kinsman, Major Molineaux." The story's main character Robin is suddenly awakened to the real world, the adult world, when he sees Major Molineaux "in tar-and-feathery dignity" (Hawthorne 528). A terrified and

---

Margin annotations:

Appropriate heading when separate title page is not used. (See page 231.)

Center title. Double-space throughout.

Opening ¶ introduces subject, presents thesis, and defines key term—initiation.

Student combines paraphrase and brief quotations in definition. (See pages 166–68.)

Summary and analysis combined to explain initiation in Hawthorne's story.

amazed Robin gapes at his kinsman as the large and colorful crowd laughs at and ridicules the Major; then an acquiescent Robin joins with the crowd in the mirthful shouting (Hawthorne 529). This moment is Robin's epiphany, his sudden realization of reality. Robin goes from unsophisticated rube to resigned cynical adult in one quick scene. Hawthorne does hold out hope that Robin will not let this event ruin his life, indeed that he will perhaps prosper from it.

Transition to second example establishes contrast with Hawthorne.

A similar, but decidedly less optimistic, example of an epiphanic initiation occurs in Arthur Miller's play Death of a Salesman. Miller develops an initiation theme within a flashback. A teenaged Biff, shockingly confronted with Willy's infidelity and weakness, has his boyhood dreams, ambitions--his vision--shattered, leaving his life in ruins, a truth borne out in scenes in which Biff is an adult during the play (1083-84, 1101). Biff's discovery of the vices and shortcomings of his father overwhelm him. His realization of adult life is a revelation made more piercing when put into the context of his naive and overly hopeful upbringing. A ravaged and defeated Biff has adulthood

¶ concludes with emphasis on contrast.

wantonly thrust upon him. Unlike Hawthorne's Robin, Biff never recovers.

William Faulkner does not follow these examples

when dealing with the initiation of his character

Chick in <u>Intruder in the Dust</u>. In Robin's and Biff's

cases, each character's passage into adulthood was

brought about by realization of and disillusionment

with the failings and weaknesses of a male adult play-

ing an important role in his life. By contrast, Chick's

male role models are vital, moral men with integrity.

Chick's awakening develops as he begins to comprehend

the mechanisms of the adult society in which he would

be a member.

> Transition to Faulkner's story by contrast with Hawthorne and Miller.

Faulkner uses several techniques for illustrating

Chick's growth into a man. Early in the novel, at the

end of the scene in which Chick tries to pay for his

dinner, Lucas warns Chick to "stay out of that creek"

(Faulkner 16).[1] The creek is an effective symbol: it is

both a physical creek and a metaphor for the boy's ten-

dency to slide into gaffes that perhaps a man could

avoid. The creek's symbolic meaning is more evident

when, after receiving the molasses, Chick encounters

Lucas in town. Lucas again reminds Chick not to "fall

in no more creeks this winter" (24). At the end of the

novel, Lucas meets Chick in Gavin's office and states:

> Footnote first parenthetical reference to inform readers that subsequent citations will exclude the author's name and give only the page number. (See pages 164–65.)

---

[1] Subsequent references to Faulkner's novel cite page
numbers only.

[0]"you ain't fell in no more creeks lately, have you?"
(241). Although Lucas phrases this as a question, the
answer is obvious to Lucas, as well as to the reader,
that indeed Chick has not blundered into his naive boyhood quagmire lately. When Lucas asks his question,
Chick's actual falling into a creek does not occur to
the reader.

Note
transition.
(See pages
214–15 on
transitions.)

Another image Faulkner employs to show Chick
growing into a man is the single file line. After
Chick gets out of the creek, he follows Lucas into the
house, the group walking in single file. In the face of
Lucas's much stronger adult will, Chick is powerless
to get out of the line, to go to Edmonds's house (7).
Later in the novel, when Miss Habersham, Aleck Sander
and Chick are walking back from digging up the grave,
Chick again finds himself in a single file line with
a strong-willed adult in front. Again he protests,
then relents, but clearly he feels slighted and won-
ders to himself "what good that [walking single file]
would do" (130). The contrast between these two scenes
illustrates Chick's growth, although he is not yet
a man.

Note
interpolation
in square
brackets.
(See page
168.)

Faulkner gives the reader other hints of Chick's
passage into manhood. As the novel progresses, Chick is
referred to (and refers to himself) as a "boy" (24), a

Peterson 5

"child" (25), a "young man" (46), "almost a man" (190),

a "man" (194), and one of two "gentlemen" (241). Other

clues crop up from time to time. Chick wrestles with

himself about getting on his horse and riding away, far

away, until Lucas's lynching is "all over finished

done" (41). But his growing sense of responsibility

and outrage quell his boyish desire to escape, to bury

his head in the sand. Chick looks in the mirror at

himself with amazement at his deeds (125). Chick's

mother serves him coffee for the first time, des-

pite the agreement she has with his father to with-

hold coffee until his eighteenth birthday (127).

Chick's father looks at him with pride and envy

(128-29).

> Good use of brief quotations combined with analysis. (See pages 166–68.)

    Perhaps the most important differences between

the epiphanic initiations of Robin and Biff and that

experienced by Chick are the facts that Chick's epiph-

any does not come all at once and it does not devastate

him. Chick learns about adulthood--and enters adult-

hood--piecemeal and with support. His first eye-

opening experience occurs as he tries to pay Lucas for

dinner and is rebuffed (15-16). Chick learns, after try-

ing again to buy a clear conscience, the impropriety

and affront of his actions (24). Lucas teaches Chick

how he should resolve *his* dilemma by setting him "free"

> Character- istics of Chick's gradual and positive initiation explained. Observe coherence techniques. (See pages 213–15.)

(26-27). Later, Chick feels outrage at the adults crowding into the town, presumably to see a lynching, then disgrace and shame as they eventually flee (196-97, 210). As in most lives, Chick's passage into adulthood is a gradual process; he learns a little bit at a time and has support in his growing. Gavin is there for him, to act as a sounding board, to lay a strong intellectual foundation, to confirm his beliefs. Chick's initiation is consistent with Joseph Campbell's explanation: "all rites of passage are intended to touch not only the candidate, but also every member of his circle" (9). Perhaps Gavin is affected the most, but Chick's mother and father, and Lucas as well, are influenced by the change in Chick.

> Student concludes by explaining the values Chick develops in growing up.

In Intruder in the Dust, William Faulkner has much to say about the role of and the actions of adults in society. He depicts racism, ignorance, resignation, violence, fratricide, citizenship, hope, righteousness, lemming-like aggregation, fear, and a host of other emotions and actions. Chick learns not only right and wrong, but that in order to be a part of society, of his community, he cannot completely forsake those with whom he disagrees or whose ideas he challenges. There is much compromise in growing up; Chick

Peterson 7

learns to compromise on some issues, but not all. Gavin's appeal to Chick to "just don't stop" (210) directs him to conform enough to be a part of the adult world, but not to lose sight of, indeed instead to embrace, his own values and ideals.

Works Cited

Paging is continuous.	

Campbell, Joseph. <u>The Hero with a Thousand Faces</u>.

     Princeton: Princeton UP, 1949.

Place Works Cited on separate page.	

Faulkner, William. <u>Intruder in the Dust</u>. New York:

     Random, 1948.

Hawthorne, Nathaniel. "My Kinsman, Major Molineaux."

Double-space throughout.	

     1832. Rpt. in <u>The Complete Short Stories of</u>

     <u>Nathaniel Hawthorne</u>. New York: Hanover/Doubleday,

     1959. 517–30.

Use hanging indention.	

Miller, Arthur. <u>Death of a Salesman</u>. New York: Viking,

     1949. Rpt. in <u>An Introduction to Literature</u>. 9th

     ed. Ed. Sylvan Barnet, Morton Berman, and William

     Burto. Boston: Little, 1985. 1025–111.

SAMPLE RESEARCH PAPER 2:
A STUDY OF ADVERTISING
INVOLVING PRIMARY RESEARCH

The following paper, in MLA style, illustrates the formal research essay format that includes a separate title page, an outline, the use of tables within the text, and an appendix, as well as a Works Cited page recording secondary sources used.

Which Ride Do You Choose at Consumer World?

by

Joan Rice

English 112
Dr. Dorothy U. Seyler
March 25, 1991

Outline

Thesis: A comparison of auto advertising through magazine ads in selected publications and an evaluation by random survey reveal the advertising
industry's awareness of the changing sociological patterns in America.

I. Introduction

    A. Explanation of car advertising as a research
topic

    B. Explanation of research procedures

II. Analysis of car ads by magazine category

    A. Car ads in men's magazines

    B. Car ads in women's magazines

    C. Car ads in news magazines

    D. Car ads in general interest magazines

    E. Car ads in magazines of the arts, sciences,
and people

III. Analysis of questionnaire results

    A. Magazine preferences of those surveyed

    B. Influence of advertising on car purchases of
those surveyed

IV. Conclusions from analysis and questionnaire

    A. Differences between current ads and those
studied by Martin ten years ago

    B. Strategies generally used in today's car ads

> Number preliminary pages with small roman numerals.

> Begin with a thesis statement, and use one standard outline pattern consistently. (See pages 198–202.)

Which Ride Do You Choose at Consumer World?

The visitor to Disney World is promised a fun-filled, fanciful, and exciting experience. The prospective car buyer is promised the same experience at "Consumer World," the fantasy world created by American advertising. Ad campaigns to sell a new car model have long used a Disney World approach to capture the buyer's fancy and promote a promise of fun and excitement. Have advertising strategies to target and sell to specific audiences changed significantly in the last decade? In a study of car ads completed almost 10 years ago, Clark Martin concludes that there is stereotyping by auto manufacturers, particularly in women's magazines. He also notes that advertising of a specific model seldom changes from one magazine to another (164). My analysis of auto advertising in selected magazines, updating Martin's findings, reveals the various techniques advertisers now employ to target a specific audience, display the product, and convey the message.

To organize the research on automotive advertising, I designated the period of November and December 1990, the beginning of the model year. My selection of eight magazines is from a list of the top 30 in circulation in the United States, as indicated in The World

---

Page numbers and running heads in upper right corner.

Repeat title on first page of text.

Double-space throughout. (See page 230.)

The student introduces her topic—car ads—in the context of updating a previous study. (See pages 210–11.)

Student continues her introduction by explaining the methods used in her study.

Rice 2

<u>Almanac and Book of Facts 1991</u> (312). Two other maga-
zines, <u>Connoisseur</u> and <u>Vanity Fair</u>, were added because
of their growing circulation and appeal. I chose
<u>Sports Illustrated</u> and <u>Playboy</u> because their advertis-
ers aim appeals to male readers. <u>Woman's Day</u> and <u>Better
Homes and Gardens</u>, two widely circulated publications,
appeal primarily to the female consumer. The weekly
news magazines selected, <u>Time</u> and <u>Newsweek</u>, are from
the last week in November and in December 1990. A category of broad appeal includes <u>Reader's Digest</u> and
<u>Vanity Fair</u>. The final category encompasses arts, sci-
ences, and people. The <u>Smithsonian</u> and <u>Connoisseur</u>
represent this category. For each category of magazines I analyzed the type of vehicles shown and the
content of the ads, and compared the ads with those in
other categories.

A review of the car ads in <u>Sports Illustrated</u>
could lead to the inference that American highways
have been converted to race tracks. From the 27 ads in
the two issues selected, seven ads depict autos with a
racing theme or trucks with a "he-man" appeal. An emphasis is placed on awards received in various auto
races (Indy 500, Baja 1000, NASCAR, etc.) and on the
names and photos of prominent race car drivers. D. G.
Kehl and Donald Heidt, in their article "The Rhetoric

The
student
begins her
analysis of
ads in
men's
magazines.

An
introductory
tag is used
to present
ideas on
advertising.
Brief
quotations
are blended
with
paraphrase.
(See pages
166–68.)

of Cow and the Rhetoric of Bull," assert that "cow
rhetoric" is often employed when the writer "relies on
a barrage of scientific or pseudo-scientific, or technical jargon" while "bull rhetoric" represents "gener-
alization, overstatement, and repetition" (392). The
testimonial and use of exaggeration are forms of
"bull" in the racing car ads, and "cow" is expressed in
the use of racing jargon. Using a different kind of
cow, Honda draws attention to the public's concern for
the environment by "recycling" some of their prior ads
selling fuel-efficient models and informing buyers

A long
quotation is
shortened
by use of
ellipses.
(See pages
170–71.)

that they "can actually have fun while . . . saving the
planet." Ford's promotional theme of "Quality is Job
1" is handled in a provocative way. When this ad appears in <u>Sports Illustrated</u>, the employee is female.
The reverse is found in magazines appealing to women.
<u>Playboy</u> magazine proved to be a surprise. It contained
only one ad for the Volkswagen GTI in the December issue, and an ad in the November issue for a Danbury Mint
replica of the 1957 Bel Air Chevrolet. It would appear
that auto advertisers are not trying to sell their
products in this magazine. <u>Sports Illustrated</u>, on the
other hand, includes a diversity of car styles in its
various ads.

Women's magazines contain fewer auto ads than

Rice 4

<u>Sports Illustrated</u>. <u>Woman's Day</u> contains an ad for the
Pontiac Grand Am, depicting it as a sedan with all the
features of a sports car. There are two other ads in
this magazine for sedans highlighting family safety
and comfort. The Chevrolet Corsica ad features a
mother and child playing on the lawn with the statement that their car is "one thing you don't have to
worry about." <u>Better Homes and Gardens</u> had a total of
six ads featuring an all-purpose vehicle, a station
wagon, and several sedans. Ford quotes several auto
magazines prominently in their station wagon ad, appealing to the intelligence of the female buyer. By
contrast, a Chrysler ad is packed with blatant emotional appeal. This two-page ad features a full-page
profile shot of a pregnant woman with the facing page
showing the woman holding her new-born baby. The text
of the ad relates the history of an auto accident and
the fact that two lives were saved by the air bag in
the Dodge Spirit the pregnant woman was driving. In
his article "Over-the-Counter Lies," Richard Cohen
discusses Lee Iacocca's reluctance to commit to the
compulsory inclusion of air bags. Cohen reports that
the purpose of a secret meeting held in 1971, involving Iacocca, Henry Ford II, and President Nixon, was to
dissuade the President from supporting a mandatory

> The transition to women's magazines is developed by contrast.

> The student develops this paragraph by analyzing representa- tive ads, by introducing material from her reading, and then by drawing a conclusion about changes in car ads in women's magazines.

requirement for air bags in every auto (3). Ironically, Iacocca is now prominent in taking credit for this safety feature. The appearance of a variety of ads in these two popular women's magazines reveals that manufacturers and advertisers are slowly becoming aware of the buying power of women and their influence on auto purchases.

The Time and Newsweek issues contain a total of 22 auto ads, featuring a variety of types and price ranges, designed to appeal to a broad cross-section of the public. The ads range from the Dodge Colt station wagon featuring convenience and efficient gas mileage to the Volvo station wagon touting the vehicle as a "safety deposit box for your valuables [family]." The Chevrolet Geo ad displays two teenaged girls draped over the "peppy little runabout," while the Lincoln Continental ad compares the auto to a commute in the Concorde jet. Toyota features two self-effacing public service advertisements. An article on the Chesapeake Bay Foundation and the Christmas in April program draws attention to and informs you that Toyota took part in the sponsorship of the programs. Only the company name appears at the bottom of the two-page article. Not surprisingly, a broad spectrum of products, appealing to a diverse market, and employing a variety of selling strategies are found in the news magazine category. After all, "advertising," as S. I. Hayakawa reminds us, "is a symbol-manipulating occupation" (168). "The symbols of youthful gaiety" sell not only "soft drinks" (168) but Chevy Geos as well. The Lincoln Continental, Ford wants us to believe, provides a first-class ride.

> An introductory tag is placed in mid-sentence to vary sentence patterns. Hayakawa's ideas about advertising are connected directly to the student's study. (See page 216.)

Placing Reader's Digest and Vanity Fair in the same broad category might seem to be an eclectic choice. The former is an established publication with a conservative readership and high volume circulation. Vanity Fair is directed to a younger and more affluent audience seeking a tony magazine. The intention here is to encompass the male and female audience of all ages. Predictably, the ads displayed in Reader's Digest include all-purpose vehicles, station wagons, trucks, and lower priced sedans. Vanity Fair advertisers concentrate on luxury models and one all-purpose vehicle, the expensive Range Rover. The two different Range Rover ads follow the automakers' trend to photograph their products on the top of a mountain. The headline on both ads causes the reader to do a double take and read the whole text to the last sentence to understand the point of the headline: "At last. A

Range Rover that won't last forever." This statement with a photo of the "Alpine White" vehicle featuring a front bull bar (bumper) and an individually numbered badge tells buyers little about the features of the vehicle but urges them to call their nearest dealer quickly. In case buyers should have any doubt about the reliability of the vehicle, four seals of approval by appointment from the queen are shown in the middle of the ad. Kehl and Heidt would undoubtedly agree there is more "bull" here than the bull bar on the Range Rover (391-96). An analysis of the broad category indicates a stereotyping of the advertising to the readership of each magazine. Reader's Digest will appear in the family doctor's waiting room, while Vanity Fair will be displayed in the specialist's office.

In the arts, sciences, and people category Smithsonian and Connoisseur magazines display large numbers of luxury car ads. Smithsonian's 29 ads include some all-purpose vehicles and station wagons but no trucks. Connoisseur contains only luxury auto ads including the Jaguar and Bentley. The model names--Vanden Plas, Allante, and Torfeo--are examples of a recent Madison Avenue trend used respectively by Jaguar, Cadillac, and Oldsmobile, all displayed in Connoisseur. Marcus

Rice 8

Mabry discusses the use of foreign words in American advertising in his article in <u>Newsweek</u>. He reports the intent is to add an aura of snob appeal, enhance name recognition, and recapture some of the market lost to Japanese manufacturers (58). There is a tendency in the ads in these two magazines toward a glossier display, more verbiage, and more expensive products. The other ads in these magazines are similar, indicating the intention to reach a well-educated and affluent sector of society.

In addition to the above analysis, I also conducted a random survey during March 1991 which was specifically designed to ascertain the influence of car advertising in magazines and other media on consumer purchasing. The participants were questioned regarding gender, age, year of auto purchase, magazines read, and possible influence of other media on their purchase. (See Appendix.) Some conclusions can be drawn from this survey of 35 people. First, <u>Smithsonian</u> and <u>Time</u> are the magazines most widely read by the men and women surveyed. <u>Smithsonian</u> received five male votes and nine female votes, while <u>Time</u> received four male votes and ten female votes. <u>Sports Illustrated</u> received one male vote. Further, the female participants indicated a preference for

Having completed her analysis of ads by magazine type, the student introduces her survey of car owners and buyers.

The student explains survey results.

Rice 9

the magazines in the news category (15) over those in the women's magazine category (8). Male participants gave the news magazine and arts, sciences, and people categories six votes each. Of the 35 participants in the survey, 12 indicated that they do not routinely read any of the listed publications. (See Table 1.)

Survey results are also presented in two tables. (See pages 186–89.)

Table 1. Evaluation of Readership of Selected Magazines

Magazines	Male	Female
Better Homes and Gardens	0	3
Connoisseur	1	0
Newsweek	2	5
Playboy	0	0
Reader's Digest	1	4
Smithsonian	5	9
Sports Illustrated	1	0
Time	4	10
Vanity Fair	1	0
Woman's Day	0	5
None of the listed magazines	4	8

Answers to other questions revealed that the largest number of men and women involved (17) in the survey are in the 50-to-64-year-old category. A total of 21 of the 35 auto purchases were made more than two years ago. When responding to the question of influence by the various media, nine participants indicated magazines may have influenced their purchase. However, 24 participants indicated they were not influenced by any of the media. (See Table 2.)

Rice 10

Clearly, manufacturers and their advertising agencies do heed the results of their market research, for changes in car advertising have taken place over the last decade. Today, women's publications include some auto advertising and, except for the emotional appeal in the Chrysler air bag ad in <u>Better Homes and Gardens</u>, the themes are similar to the ads in other magazines. Although there is a notable emphasis in <u>Sports Illustrated</u> on racing and macho themes, there is also a variety of auto advertising in this publication. <u>Playboy</u>, with only one car ad, represents a change from Martin's study. In general, the majority of ads feature messages on safety, reliability, mileage, and style choice. In the total of 118 ads studied, only 18 featured people as part of the display, allowing the consumer's imagination to fill in the occupant. Some displays feature black and white rather than color, some use drawings, and a few feature the employer and employee relationship or a public service message without a vehicle. I found almost no duplication of ads from one magazine to another, contrary to Martin's findings. The ads featured in a magazine cater to the audience for that publication, a justifiable marketing practice.

The student begins her conclusion by bringing together her general points about car ads and relating these to Martin's study of 10 years ago.

Rice 21

Table 2. Supporting Data Indicating Influence on
        Car Purchase

Respondents by Age

AGE	21-29	30-39	40-49	50-64	65-older
MALE	0	2	4	5	1
FEMALE	2	2	6	12	1

Auto Purchasing History

	In Past Year	In Past Two Years	In Past Five Years
MALE	4	1	7
FEMALE	3	6	14

Influence of Advertising on Purchase

	Mag- azines	News- papers	Radio	Tele- vision	No Influence
MALE	4	2	1	2	8
FEMALE	5	3	1	5	16

Final points about car ads connect ad analysis and the survey.

Foreign competition and federal government regulations have compelled the automotive and advertising
industries to focus on quality and truthfulness in
selling their products. Although auto manufacturers
invest millions of dollars each year in clever, inno-
vative magazine advertising in an attempt to sell
their cars, at least some of today's consumers make a
commitment after talking with other car owners, reading comparative analyses in Consumer Reports, shopping
the dealerships, and evaluating the economic factors
of a purchase. The consumer of the nineties may be less
easily swayed by the fun-filled, fanciful, and exciting experience at "Consumer World."

Rice 12

Appendix
Questions Used in Random Survey

I am preparing a research paper on the marketing of cars through magazine advertising. The following information will be collated for use in the research paper. Please circle your responses.

1. Survey participant: Female   Male

2. Age group: 21-29   30-39   40-49   50-64
   65 or older

3. Have you purchased a new car:

   In past year   In past two years
   In past five years

4. Do you routinely read or browse through one or more

   of the following magazines?

   <u>Better Homes and Gardens</u>   <u>Connoisseur</u>
   <u>Newsweek</u>   <u>Playboy</u>   <u>Reader's Digest</u>
   <u>Smithsonian</u>   <u>Sports Illustrated</u>   <u>Time</u>
   <u>Vanity Fair</u>   <u>Woman's Day</u>
   None of the listed magazines

5. Do you think your auto purchase may have been in-

   fluenced by advertising in one or more of the fol-

   lowing media?

   Magazines   Newspapers   Radio   Television
   No Influence

Thank you for participating in this survey.

Joan Rice

The student includes a copy of the question-naire used as an appendix. (See page 231.)

Rice 13

Works Cited

Cohen, Richard. "Over-the-Counter Lies." Washington
        Post Magazine. 3 Mar. 1991: 3.

Hayakawa, S. I., and Alan R. Hayakawa. Language in
        Thought and Action. 5th ed. San Diego: Harcourt,
        1990.

Kehl, D. G., and Donald Heidt. "The Rhetoric of Cow and
        the Rhetoric of Bull." Rhetoric Society Quarterly
        14 (1985). Rpt. in Read, Reason, Write. 3rd ed.
        Ed. Dorothy U. Seyler. New York: McGraw, 1991.
        391-96.

Mabry, Marcus. "Sprechen Sie Advertising?" Newsweek 10
        Dec. 1990: 58.

Martin, Clark. "Have You Taken the Bait?" in Read, Rea-
        son, Write. 3rd ed. Ed. Dorothy U. Seyler. New
        York: McGraw, 1991. 162-70.

The World Almanac and Book of Facts 1991. New York:
        Scripps, 1991.

A new page is started for the Works Cited. Only those works actually cited in the text are listed. Works are alphabetized; hanging indention is used; and double-spacing is used throughout. (See page 232.)

Chapter

7

Observing Other
Styles of Documentation

*A*lthough the research process is much the same regardless of the
area of study, the presentation of the results of research varies from
one discipline to another. Thus it is possible to explain, only once,
the process of selecting a topic, finding sources, studying and taking notes, and then drafting a paper, but a separate examination of the
various documentation styles is necessary to avoid confusion. As previously explained, the guidelines for documenting sources presented in
Chapters 3 and 5 follow the Modern Language Association style. The
MLA's parenthetical documentation providing author and page number
and completed with a list of works cited will be acceptable in many, but
not all, undergraduate courses in addition to language and literature
classes.

Because not all disciplines accept MLA style, you need to be aware of
three other styles of documentation, and of the fields of study that use
them, so that you can properly document research papers for any of your
courses, regardless of discipline. The three predominant styles of documentation in addition to the MLA *author/page style* are the *author/year*

257

style, used in the social sciences and also in some science fields; the *foot-note/endnote style,* used in a number of humanities fields; and the *number style,* used in some scientific and technical disciplines.

The *author/year style* of citation is similar to MLA style in that it identifies a source in parentheses within the text and then provides complete bibliographic information about each source in an alphabetized list at the end of the paper. This style of documentation gives special emphasis to the year of a source's publication, hence the label "author/year" style. The year is included in the in–text citation and is usually highlighted in the complete bibliographic citation by its placement after the author's name.

The *footnote/endnote* pattern of documentation offers the greatest variation from other documentation styles in that no bibliographic information is provided parenthetically in the text. Instead, a raised (superscript) numeral is placed after each reference to a source, and then complete bibliographic information is given, followed by a precise page reference to the borrowed material, either at the "foot" of the page on which the reference to the source occurs or at the "end" of the text in a listing of all notes in the order in which the references appear in the text. The format for presenting information is the same in footnotes and endnotes; the only difference is location.

The *number style* requires that each source used be given a number as it is referred to and that only the number appear, in parentheses within the text, whenever reference is made to the source. The research paper concludes with a list of references, supplying complete bibliographic information, organized usually in the order in which the sources are referred to in the text. (A variation of this pattern is to organize the references alphabetically.)

If documentation patterns were as simple as the previous paragraphs suggest, the rest of this chapter would be easy to organize and complete. The facts, however, are a bit more complicated. Within each of the three types of styles described above, variations in the presentation of information about sources can be found. Some disciplines have their own style manuals (as does the Modern Language Association), designating variations of the author/year pattern. Some disciplines that seem to be partially in the humanities and partially in the social sciences (government and/or political science is a perfect example) will sometimes use footnotes/endnotes, sometimes the author/year style. And in disciplines not guided by a specific manual, many variations can be found in the scholarly journals serving those fields. As a reader of scholarship in a field of study, you need to be prepared to find—and not be bothered by—variations in documentation among the journals, for all references provide the same key information: author, title, and facts of publication for the source. As a student doing research and preparing papers in different disciplines, you need to adhere to the style your instructor expects. For example, some educational journals, using essentially an author/year pattern of in–text citations, blend that style with MLA style in the full citation of sources in a list of references. However, some education instructors expect students to use the author/year style as presented in the manual of the American Psychological Association (APA style); others want to see footnotes/endnotes as illustrated in the *Chicago Manual of Style;* and a few may accept MLA style, knowing that it is the pattern students were taught in composition classes. *If your instructor does not specify a pattern of documentation when assigning a research paper, it is your responsibility as a student to have a specific style approved and then to follow that style consistently in your paper.*

In the following pages, the author/year, footnote/endnote, and number patterns will be explained and illustrated. Within each section, the disciplines usually using that section's pattern of documentation will be listed. Then, for those disciplines with their own style manuals, the variations found in those manuals will be explained and illustrated. APA style will also be illustrated in a sample student paper. The following guide will help you locate various fields of study.

GUIDE TO DOCUMENTATION PATTERNS

AUTHOR/YEAR STYLE

APA style (260–81):	anthropology	economics	political science
	archeology	education	psychology
	astronomy	linguistics	sociology
	business	physical education	

CBE (Council of Biology Editors) style (282–85):	biology	physiology
	botany	zoology

USGS (U.S. Geological Survey) style (285–87): geology

FOOTNOTE/ENDNOTE STYLE (287–95)

art	history	philosophy
dance	music	religion

NUMBER STYLE (295–304)
computer science   health and medicine
ACS (American Chemical Society) style (297–99): chemistry
AIP (American Institute of Physics) style (300–02): physics
AMS (American Mathematical Society) style (302–04): mathematics

AUTHOR/YEAR STYLE

As the guide above indicates, most disciplines in the social sciences, biological sciences, and earth sciences use some version of the author/year
style. Three style manuals establish formats for documentation, but the
Publication Manual of the American Psychological Association (3rd ed.
1983) establishes the predominant pattern, known as *APA style*. For
most papers in the social sciences you will use APA style.

APA Style: In–Text Citations

The simplest parenthetical reference can be presented in one of three
ways:

1. Place the year of publication within parentheses immediately following the author's name in the text.

   ```
   In a typical study of preference for motherese,

   Fernald (1985) used an operant auditory preference

   procedure.
   ```

Within the same paragraph, additional references to the author do not
need to repeat the year, if the discussion makes it clear that the same
study is the source drawn on by the researcher.

   ```
   Because the speakers were unfamiliar subjects,

   Fernald's work eliminates the possibility that it is

   the mother's voice per se that accounts for the

   preference.
   ```

2. If the author is not mentioned in the text, place the author's last
   name followed by a comma and the year of publication within parentheses after the borrowed information.

Even a newborn baby, only a few minutes old, often moves his eyes toward a source of sound and rarely moves them in the wrong direction (Wertheimer, 1961).

3. Cite a specific passage by providing the page, chapter, or figure number following the borrowed material. *Always* give specific page references for quoted material.

   • A brief quotation:

   Deuzen-Smith believes that counselors must be involved with clients and "deeply interested in piecing the puzzle of life together" (1988, p. 29).

   • A quotation in display form:

   Bartlett (1932) explains the cyclic process of perception:

   > Suppose I am making a stroke in a quick game, such as tennis or cricket. How I make the stroke depends on the relating of certain new experiences, most of them visual, to other immediately preceding visual experiences, and to my posture, or balance of posture, at the moment. (p. 201)

   (Indent a block quotation five spaces from the left margin and double-space throughout. To show a new paragraph within the block quotation, indent the first line of the new paragraph an additional five spaces. Note the placing of the year after the author's name, the page number at the end of the direct quotation.)

More complicated in-text citations should be handled as follows:

TWO AUTHORS, MENTIONED IN THE TEXT

Kuhl and Meltzoff (1984) tested 4- to 5-month-olds in an experiment . . .

TWO AUTHORS, NOT MENTIONED IN THE TEXT

. . . but are unable to show preferences in the presence of two mismatched modalities (e.g., a face and a voice; see Kuhl & Meltzoff, 1984).

Give both authors' last names each time you refer to the source. Connect their names with "and" in the text; use an ampersand (&) in the parenthetical citation.

More Than Two Authors

For works coauthored by three, four, or five people, provide all last names in the first reference to the source. Thereafter, cite only the first author's name followed by et al.

```
As Price-Williams, Gordon, and Ramirez have shown

(1969), . . .
```

OR

```
Studies of these children have shown (Price-Williams,

Gordon, & Ramirez, 1969) . . .
```

THEN

```
Price-Williams et al. (1969) also found that . . .
```

If a source has six or more authors, use only the first author's last name followed by et al. every time the source is cited.

Corporate Authors

In general, spell out the name of a corporate author each time it is used. If a corporate author has well–known initials, the name can be abbreviated after the first citation.

First in–text citation: (National Institutes of Health [NIH], 1989)
Subsequent citations: (NIH, 1989)

Two or More Works Within the Same Parentheses

When citing more than one work by the same author in a parenthetical reference, use the author's last name only once and arrange the years mentioned in order; thus:

```
Several studies of ego identity formation (Marcia,

1966, 1983) . . .
```

When an author, or the same group of coauthors, has more than one work published in the same year, distinguish the works by adding the letters *a, b, c,* and so on, as needed, to the year. Give the last name only once, but repeat the year, each one with its identifying letter; thus:

```
Several studies (Smith, 1990a, 1990b, 1990c) . . .
```

When citing several works by different authors within the same parentheses, list the authors alphabetically; alphabetize by the first author when citing coauthored works. Separate authors or groups of coauthors with semicolons; thus:

```
Although many researchers (Archer & Waterman, 1983;

Grotevant, 1983; Grotevant & Cooper, 1986; Sabatelli &

Mazor, 1985) study identity formation . . .
```

APA Style: Preparing the List of References

Every source cited parenthetically in your paper needs a complete bibliographic citation. In APA style, these complete bibliographic citations are placed on a separate page (or separate pages) after the text of the paper and before any appendices included in the paper. Sources are arranged alphabetically, and the first page is titled "References." Begin each source flush with the left margin and indent second and subsequent lines three spaces. Double–space throughout the list of references. Follow these rules for alphabetizing:

1. Organize two or more works by the same author, or the same group of coauthors, chronologically.

```
Marcia, J. E. (1966).
Marcia, J. E. (1983).
```

2. Place single–author entries before multiple–author entries when the first of the multiple authors is the same as the single author.

```
Grotevant, H. D. (1983).
Grotevant, H. D., & Cooper, C. R. (1986).
```

3. Organize multiple–author entries that have the same first author but different second or third authors alphabetically by the name of the second author or third and so on.

```
Gerbner, G., & Gross, L.

Gerbner, G., Gross, L., Jackson-Beeck, M., Jeffries-
     Fox, S., & Signorielli, N.

Gerbner, G., Gross, L., Morgan, M., & Signorielli, N.
```

4. Organize two or more works by the same author(s) published in the same year alphabetically by title.

FORM FOR BOOKS

A book citation contains these elements in this form:

```
Yalom, I. D. (1989). Love's executioner and other tales of
     psychotherapy. New York: Basic Books.
```

Authors: Give all authors' names, last name first, and initials. Separate authors with commas, use the ampersand (&) before the last author's name, and end with a period. For edited books, place the abbreviation "Ed." or "Eds." in parentheses following the last editor's name.

Date of Publication: Place the year of publication in parentheses followed by a period.

Title: Capitalize only the first word of the title and of the subtitle, if there is one, and any proper nouns. Underline the title and end with a period. Place additional information such as number of volumes or an edition in parentheses after the title, before the period.

```
Moody, K., & Logan, B. (Eds.). (1979). Television awareness
     training (2nd ed.).
```

Publication Information: Cite the city of publication; add the state (using the Postal Service abbreviation) or country if necessary to avoid confusion; then give the publisher's name, after a colon, eliminating unnecessary terms such as *Publishers, Co.,* and *Inc.* End the citation with a period.

Anderson, J. R., & Bower, G. H. (1973). <u>Human associative</u>
<u>memory</u>. New York: V. H. Winston.

Mitchell, J. V. (Ed.). (1985). <u>The ninth mental measure-</u>
<u>ments yearbook</u> (vol. 2). Lincoln: University of Ne-
braska Press.

U.S. Commission on Civil Rights. (1977). <u>Window dressing on</u>
<u>the set: Women and minorities in television</u>. Washing-
ton, DC: Author.

(Give a corporate author's name in full. When the organization is both author and publisher, place the word "Author" after the place of publication.)

Form for Articles

An article citation contains these elements in this form:

Wertheimer, M. (1961). Psychomotor coordination of audi-
tory and visual space at birth. <u>Science</u>, <u>134</u>, 1962.

Author: Same rules as for author(s) of books.

Date of Publication: Place the year of publication for articles in scholarly journals in parentheses, followed by a period. For articles in newspapers and popular magazines, give the year followed by month and day (if appropriate).

(1990, March).(See also example below.)

Title of Article: Capitalize only the title's first word, the first word of any subtitle, and any proper nouns. Place any necessary descriptive information immediately after the title in square brackets.

Scott, S. S. (1984, December 12). Smokers get a raw deal
[Letter to the Editor].

Publication Information: Cite the title of the journal in full, capitalizing according to conventions for titles. Underline the title and follow it with a comma. Give the volume number, underlined, followed by a comma, and then inclusive page numbers followed by a period. *If* a journal begins each issue with a new page 1, then also cite the issue number in parentheses immediately following the volume number. Do not use "p." or "pp." before page numbers when citing articles from scholarly journals; do use "p." or "pp." in citations to newspaper and magazine articles.

Price-Williams, D. R., Gordon, W., & Ramirez, W. (1969). Skill and conservation: A study of pottery-making children. Developmental Psychology, 1, 769.

Werker, J. F., & McLeod, P. J. (1989). Infant preference for both male and female infant-directed talk: A developmental study of attentional and affective responsiveness. Canadian Journal of Psychology, 43 (2), 230-246.

Hughes, M., & Gove, W. R. (1981, October). Playing dumb. Psychology Today, pp. 24-27.

FORM FOR AN ARTICLE OR CHAPTER IN AN EDITED BOOK

Gerbner, G., & Gross, L. (1980). The violent face of television and its lessons. In E. L. Palmer & A. Dorr (Eds.), Children and the Faces of Television: Teaching, Violence, Selling (pp. 149-162). New York: Academic Press.

Cite the author(s), date, and title of the article or chapter. Then cite the name(s) of the editor(s) in signature order after "In," followed by "Ed." or "Eds." in parentheses; the title of the book; the inclusive page numbers of the article or chapter, in parentheses, followed by a period; and the place of publication and publisher.

FORMS FOR DISSERTATIONS

Bolt, J. A. (1986). A study of the effects of a bibliographic instruction course on achievement and retention of college students. Dissertation Abstracts International, 47, 4219A. (University Microfilms No. AAS87-08161.)

If the microfilm of the dissertation was used, give the microfilm number as well as the volume and page numbers of *DAI.*

Kuhlthau, C. C. (1983). The library research process: case studies and interventions with high school seniors in advanced placement English classes using Kelly's theory of constructs (Doctoral dissertation, Rutgers University, 1983). <u>Dissertation Abstracts International</u>, <u>44</u>, 1961A.

Sample Paper in APA Style

In the following paper in APA style, Adam examines the concept of identity formation and argues for a modification of the prevailing concept. As explained in Chapter 4, the "testing of a concept" research topic is frequently assigned in courses in many fields. The paper conforms to APA style and format for this type of topic and illustrates the following elements: title page, running head, abstract, author/year in–text citations, subheadings in the text, and list of references. Papers in the social sciences that are reports of empirical research may also contain tables and appendices, and the texts of such papers will adhere to the report structure described in Chapter 5.

Identity Formation 1

Sample title for a paper in APA style.

A Developmental Systems Perspective on Identity
Formation

Adam Wilhite

Virginia Polytechnic Institute and State University

Running head: IDENTITY FORMATION

Identity Formation 2

Abstract

A central integrating construct for understanding psychological development during adolescence is the concept of ego identity. Identity formation, an important activity of the adolescent in this society, occurs, in the prevailing conceptualization, when the individual moves from identity diffusion to identity achievement. The model of identity formation should be understood as a developmental process. This is a dynamic and complex process involving a considerable amount of intra-individual variability.

Observe placement of running head and page numbers.

A sample abstract, required in many kinds of research essays in social science and science fields. (See page 231.)

A Developmental Systems Perspective on Identity
Formation

Student
begins by
explaining
the concept
that he will
challenge
and expand
on. (See
page 125.)

A central integrating construct for understanding
psychological development during adolescence is the
Eriksonian concept of ego identity (Waterman, 1984).
Ego identity denotes an inner solidarity of self-imag-
es and ideals. It gives individuals a sense of who they
are and in what direction they are headed (Adams,
1977). There is a commitment to goals, values, and beliefs which develops over time and gives a direction,
purpose, and meaning to life. In this way, a sense of
identity creates a developmental continuity between
the past, present, and anticipated future. Finally,
the identity provides a framework for the organization
of behavior while it provides a motivation for behaviors which often support the identity itself (Waterman, 1984).

Observe
forms of
author/
year
citations.
(See pages
260–63.)

Although Grotevant (1983) asserts that identity
consolidation is rarely achieved before late adolescence or early adulthood, the process of searching for
an identity is the expected occupation of the adolescent in this society. In fact, Adams (1977) feels that
the American culture offers the adolescent a time during which economic obligations are withheld so that
the adolescent may experiment with various roles. Dur-

Identity Formation 4

ing this time the individual should move through a pro-

cess which will eventually produce an identity. Iden-

tity formation should be understood as a developmental

process.

THE CONCEPT OF IDENTITY FORMATION

Identity formation has long been conceptualized

as a transition from one polar alternative, identity

diffusion, through to another, identity achievement

(Marcia, 1966). In the original psychoanalytic concep-

tualization, this transition was propelled by an iden-

tity crisis, yet many adolescents do not seem to expe-

rience such a crisis (Grotevant & Cooper, 1986). Not-

withstanding, Marcia (1983) characterized this period

as the most significant period of disorganization nat-

urally occurring in a person's life.

Grotevant and Cooper (1986) point out that this

pursuit of identity formation requires multiple per-

spective taking and the active consideration of alter-

native possibilities. They also name occupational

choice, political beliefs, religious and philosophical

beliefs, sex roles, interpersonal relationships, val-

ues, and sexual identity as some of the content areas

within the larger construct of identity. Bernard

(1981) discusses how a serious consideration of alter-

Subheadings are frequently used in papers in the social sciences.

natives within each of these content areas leads to a relatively firm choice, a commitment. Archer and Waterman (1983) claim that individuals who have made such a commitment to an identity are more likely to engage in productive work and relationships.

Marcia (1966) described, measured, and validated four identity statuses. The presence of crisis and commitment in the two content areas of occupation and ideology were gauged through a variety of self-report measures and a semi-structured interview. The four statuses of identity formation are identity diffusion, foreclosure, moratorium, and identity achievement.

Identity diffusion is characterized by a lack of commitment (Marcia, 1966) and a lack of effort on the part of the individual even to explore the possibilities of achieving identity (Adams, 1977; Archer & Waterman, 1983). Bernard (1981) explains that the identity diffused person has either not experienced the identity crisis or has gone through the crisis without making a commitment.

Foreclosure, in Marcia's (1966) model, is a commitment made without having experienced the crisis and without exploring the possibilities. Most often, this identity has been supplied to the individual by the society or is the identity of the parents. Marcia de-

Identity Formation 6

scribes such a person as having a rigid personality which would be threatened by any situation in which parental values are nonfunctional.

Moratorium is the status in which the person is reacting to the identity crisis by actively seeking information to help with the selection of an identity (Archer & Waterman, 1983). Issues that are considered to be adolescent preoccupy this person (Marcia, 1966). Gathering information, experimenting with roles, and discussing possibilities are the main methods used in moratorium to consider identity elements (Waterman, 1984).

The goal of this entire process is identity achievement. Identity achievement individuals have experienced a crisis period, have considered all the choices, and have made a commitment to an occupational and ideological viewpoint on their own terms (Marcia, 1966).

IDENTITY FORMATION AS A DEVELOPMENTAL PROCESS

It is important to view this model of identity formation as a developmental process. These statuses are but labels to help characterize the major stages that seem to be required for individuals to develop and establish their own sense of identity. I am basing this on the assumption that all people who have

Having explained the concept, the student now develops his view of the concept.

achieved an identity have passed through a moratorium
in which many possibilities have been explored. If
they have not done so, then they are either identity
diffused or they have accepted an identity without serious exploration and are therefore foreclosed.

To glean the most useful scientific knowledge
from Marcia's (1966) model of the developmental stages
of the identity construct, a developmental systems approach should be implemented. Valisner (1987) provides
a number of issues which should be considered when one
is attempting to use a developmental systems approach
to study a construct which has long been studied in
more limited ways.

Psychologists have commonly separated the person
or the psychological phenomena being studied from the
surrounding environment. This seems necessary in order
to separate the phenomena being studied from other
phenomena. However, development occurs in an open system that is dependent upon exchange relationships with
the environment. Biological, psychological, and social
systems are open systems and are context dependent
(Valisner, 1987).

Although many researchers (Archer & Waterman,
1983; Grotevant, 1983; Grotevant & Cooper, 1986; Sabatelli & Mazor, 1985) study identity formation from in-

Observe
citing of
multiple
sources.
(See page
263.)

Identity Formation 8

dividual development and family system theory perspectives and cite the contribution of the family to identity achievement, they are taking an interactionist perspective in which the identity and the environment merely affect one another. From a developmental systems perspective, these factors cannot merely affect one another because the individual is existing in a system which has no clear boundaries between the environment and psychological phenomena. And, any effect which the environment has on the development of the identity will immediately feed back into that environment, consequentially changing the environmental context. There can be no separation.

An example can be obtained from examining Waterman's (1984) assertion that one of the sources of identity elements is the "latent" abilities generated from the physiological constitution of the individual. Gottlieb (1976) explains that there is a bidirectional structure-function relationship wherein the genetic material, the developing structure, and the function of that structure feed back and forth through the process, leaving no possibility of any one part of the system creating a main effect for development. Therefore, a genetic predisposition to be large and muscular could be a factor in a person's choice of a "pro-

The student develops a detailed example to illustrate his view.

Identity Formation 9

fessional football player" identity, but many other
factors in the system must also be accounted for. The
environment must provide a complex chain of events in
order for the genetic predisposition to be transformed
into a structural reality which, in turn, must experience specific modes of functioning in order to facili-
tate or maintain that structure. The individual must
be properly nourished in order to obtain the physique
and that physique must, from the beginning of development, experience a high level of function in order to
develop and maintain itself. All the while, a multitude of other factors in the system affect this identity choice. For example, even with all the physical
factors working in concert it is unlikely, given our
societal demands, that the "professional football
player" identity will emerge if the individual is female.

Valisner (1987) reminds us that the usual goal of
scientific study is to delineate the static aspects of
the phenomena under study. This is clearly erroneous
when one is examining the dynamic course of development. However, in order to avoid entering into a dis-
ordered world of dynamic relativism, it is important
to realize that every developmental process has outer
limits set by the context and the organism's own

state. One must also keep in mind that the temporal order of developmental events is critical as each event may redirect the course of development entirely.

This attention to the dynamic aspects of development is especially important to the understanding of identity formation wherein an individual moves from identity diffusion to identity achievement by actively exploring various alternatives. Grotevant and Cooper (1986) point out that in order to understand the role of relationships in identity development one must account for the fact that each individual in a relationship, as well as the relationship itself, changes over time. The importance of the temporal order of significant events in identity development is evident when an individual reaches a state of foreclosure. If people take on identities presented to them, without considering the alternatives, because of some salient event occurring previous to a personal commitment, they will very likely enter a stage of foreclosure. It is easy to become overwhelmed at the infinite number of possible developmental events and the infinite number of temporal orders in which these events may occur, but it is just this multitude of possibilities that negates static conceptualizations of development.

The last of Valisner's (1987) issues to be exam-

Identity Formation 11

ined here is that of intra-class uniformity versus variability. Empirical psychologists most often attempt to eliminate any variability from their theoretical consideration, usually through the processes of averaging or prototyping. However, Valisner (1987) promotes "the idea that generality is evidenced in variability, rather than in uniformity, of behavior and thinking" (p. 23). In this perspective, variability is seen as an indicator of psychological processes and a generator of psychological outcomes. The function of these processes and outcomes is to adapt the individual to the environment and to accommodate the environment to the individual. It has long been accepted that genetic variability increases the possibility of a species to adapt to new environments, so it should not be hard to accept the adaptive advantages of psychological variability.

CONCLUSIONS

The existence of intra-individual variability must be recognized when examining identity formation. For example, it should not be assumed that by labeling two people as being identity diffused they are identical people, or that even the aspects which earned them that identity diffused label are free from variability. The purpose of Marcia's (1966) four identity sta-

Page number must be given for direct quotations. (See page 261.)

tuses is to give a way of describing a particular region of the developmental continuum of identity. Individual variability will seriously affect the entire process.

A developmental systems approach is not an easier way to tackle the empirical study of identity formation, but a more correct way. Marcia's (1966) identity statuses do offer a conceptual framework by which to view the basic forms of identity that a person may be experiencing. However, the processes by which identity develops are complex. Finally, one must keep in mind that these processes occur in a developmental context, in a dynamic fashion, and with a considerable amount of intra-individual variability.

> A clear conclusion that restates the paper's thesis.

References

Adams, G. R. (1977). Personal identity formation: A
    synthesis of cognitive and ego psychology. Adoles-
    cence, 12 (46), 151–164.

Archer, S. L., & Waterman, A. S. (1983). Identity in
    early adolescence: A developmental perspective.
    Journal of Early Adolescence, 3 (3), 203–214.

Bernard, H. S. (1981). Identity formation during late
    adolescence: A review of some empirical findings.
    Adolescence, 16 (62), 349–358.

Gottlieb, G. (1976). Conceptions of prenatal develop-
    ment: Behavioral embryology. Psychological Review,
    83 (3), 215–234.

Grotevant, H. D. (1983). The contribution of the fam-
    ily to the facilitation of identity formation in
    early adolescence. Journal of Early Adolescence, 3
    (3), 225–237.

Grotevant, H. D., & Cooper, C. R. (1986). Individua-
    tion in family relationships: A perspective on in-
    dividual differences in the development of identity
    and role taking skill in adolescence. Human Devel-
    opment, 29 (2), 82–100.

Marcia, J. E. (1966). Development and validation of
    ego identity status. Journal of Personality and So-
    cial Psychology, 3, 551–558.

Marcia, J. E. (1983). Some directions for the investi-
    gation of ego development in early adolescence.
    Journal of Early Adolescence, 3, 215–223.

Title the page "References." Double-space throughout. Alphabetize by author's last name. (See pages 263–67.)

Two works by the same author are ordered by publication date. (See page 263.)

Identity Formation 14

Sabatelli, R. M., & Mazor, A. (1985). Differentiation, individuation, and identity formation: The integration of family system and individual developmental perspectives. Adolescence, 20 (79), 619-633.

Valisner, J. (1987). Culture and the development of children's actions: A cultural-historical theory of developmental psychology. New York: Wiley.

Waterman, A. S. (1984). Identity formation: Discovery or creation? Journal of Early Adolescence, 4 (4), 329-341.

CBE (Council of Biology Editors) Style

The *CBE Style Manual* (5th ed., 1983) provides guidelines for writers in biology and related fields such as anatomy, botany, zoology, and genetics.

In-Text Citations

Give author and year (plus precise page numbers when quoting) within the text according to the guidelines presented under APA style on pages 260–63. Authors may be mentioned in a sentence with the year following in parentheses, or both author and year may be placed in parentheses, as the following excerpt illustrates:

> In the case of apple leaf wax, it is known that the
> dihydrochalcone phloridzin is present. Although this
> is used by the apple aphid as a signal to feed, it is
> known to be repellent to the pea aphid Acyrthrosiphon
> pisi (Klingauf, 1971). There is also evidence that the
> constituents of the leaf wax may, on occasion, be
> repellent to insects. Certain varieties of Sorghum are
> distasteful to Locusta migratoria, because of the
> presence of leaf alkanes of chain length C_{19}, C_{21}, and
> C_{23} and of fatty acid esters of chain length C_{12}-C_{18}.
> These and other effects of surface wax constituents
> on insects are reviewed by Woodhead and Chapman
> (1986).

References

CBE style for citing references differs somewhat from APA style, most notably in the placing of the year at the *end* of each bibliographic citation rather than after the author's name. Start references on a new page, after the text but before any tables or figures, and title the page "Literature Cited" or "References Cited." Arrange citations alphabetically by author's last name. Two formats are found: (1) begin each new citation flush with the left margin and indent second and subsequent lines two spaces, or (2) alphabetize but also number each citation, placing numbers flush left and aligning second and subsequent lines with the first word of the first line. The first pattern is illustrated in examples provided with the explanation of forms for books and articles. The second pattern is illustrated in the sample "Literature Cited" page.

Form for Books

1. Give the author's name, last name first and initials, followed by the title (and subtitle, if there is one), *not* underlined. Capitalize only the first word of the title (and subtitle) and any proper nouns:

   ```
   Trinkaus, J. P. Cells and organs: The forces that shape
       the embryo.
   ```

2. Give edition information, or name(s) of editor(s), as appropriate:

   ```
   Trinkaus, . . . embryo. 2nd ed.
   ```

3. Provide the facts of publication: place of publication, followed by a colon; publisher, followed by a semicolon; and the date:

   ```
   Trinkaus, J. P. Cells and organs: The forces that shape
       the embryo. 2nd ed. Englewood Cliffs: Prentice Hall;
       1984.
   ```

4. For multivolume works, give only the volume(s) containing the material cited. If citing a section, or specific pages used, place the information after the year, preceded by a colon. Total book pages are not usually given.

   ```
   Rothschild, M. Secondary plant substances and warning
       colouration in insects. In van Emden, H. ed. Insect-
       plant interactions. Oxford: Oxford Univ. Press; 1973:
       pp. 69-102.
   ```

Form for Articles

1. Cite the author, last name first and initials, and then give the article title, *not* in quotation marks, capitalizing only the first word and any proper nouns:

   ```
   Lentz, T. L.; Trinkaus, J. P. Differentiation of the
       junctional complex of surface cells in the developing
       Fundulus blastoderm.
   ```

2. Give the journal title, *not* underlined, using standard abbreviations:

   ```
   Lentz, . . . blastoderm. J. Cell Biol.
   ```

3. Cite the volume number, followed by a colon; the article's inclusive page numbers, followed by a semicolon; and the year of publication:

   ```
   Lentz, . . . J. Cell Biol. 48: 455-472; 1971.
   ```

4. For journals that page each issue separately rather than consecutively throughout the issues in one year, add the issue number in parentheses following the volume number:

   ```
   Rice, A. L. Decapod crustacean larvae collected during
       the International Indian Ocean Expedition. Bull. Br.
       Mus. (Nat. Hist.) Zool. 21(1): 1-24; 1970.
   ```

Sample References. Use the following sample references for preparing citations according to CBE style:

```
                        Literature Cited
1. Day, M. Omohuman skeletal remains. Nature. 222: 1135-
   1138; 1969.
2. Ehrlich, P. R.; Raven, P. H. Butterflies and plants: A
   study in coevolution. Evolution. 18: 586-608; 1964.
```

3. Munro, P. M. G. Comparative ultrastructure of red and white muscle fibres of roach. Ph.D. thesis, University of London; 1986.

4. Passano, V. T. The regulation of crustacean metamorphoses. Am. Zool. 1: 89–95; 1961.

5. Rathbun, M. J. Stalk-eyed crustaceans collected at the Monte Bello Islands. Proc. Zool. Soc. London: 653–664; 1914.

6. Sibly, R. M.; Smith, R. H., eds. Behavioural ecology: Ecological consequences of adaptive behaviour. 25th symposium of the British Ecological Society 1984. Blackwell: Oxford; 1985.

7. Willis, R., trans. The works of William Harvey. (London 1847.) Sources of science no. 13. Ed.-in-chief H. Woolf. New York: Johnson Reprint; 1965.

USGS (U.S. Geological Survey) Style

In its *Suggestions to Authors of the Reports of the United States Geological Survey* (7th ed., Washington, DC: Department of the Interior, 1991), the USGS establishes guidelines for its geologists' papers. You should know, however, that the variations of APA style found in *Suggestions to Authors* are not used in many of the journals relevant to geologists, including the *Journal of the Geological Society,* perhaps in part because of the close connection between geology and many applied sciences that use other styles. When preparing papers in geology courses, determine each professor's preference for APA style, CBE style, USGS style, or the number style.

In-Text Citations

In-text citations should provide author, year, and page references (unless the work cited is a dictionary or glossary). "And others" is preferred to "et al." when a citation refers to three or more authors.

References

Title the alphabetical list of sources "References Cited" or "References." The order of information is as follows: author, last name first followed by initials or by first name if only one name is used; year of publication, *not* in parentheses; title of work, *not* underlined, followed by a *colon*. Then, for books: the city of publication, the name of the publisher, and the number of book pages. And, for articles: the name of the periodical, capitalized but not underlined; volume and issue numbers in arabic numerals, *not* underlined; and inclusive page numbers. Commas are used between the elements of a citation except for the colon after the source's title. Each citation ends with a period. Here are several examples in USGS style:

Brindze, Ruth, 1972, Charting the Oceans: New York, Vanguard Press, 108p.

Eggers, A. A., 1987, Residual gravity changes and eruption magnitudes: Journal of Volcanology and Geothermal Research, v. 33, p. 201-216.

Heymsfield, A. J., and Miloshevich, L. M., 1991, Limit to greenhouse warming?: Nature, v. 351, no. 6321, p. 14-15.

Huybrechts, Philippe, Letreguilly, Anne, and Reeh, Neils, 1991, The Greenland ice sheet and greenhouse warming: Global and Planetary Change, v. 3, no. 4, p. 399-412.

Ryan, P. J., Halleman, D. R. F., and Stolzenbach, K. D., 1974, Surface heat loss from cooling ponds: Water Resources Research, v. 10, p. 930-938.

Tarrant, J. R., 1990, World food prospects for the 1990s: Journal of Geography, v. 89, no. 6, p. 234-238.

Van der Veen, C. J., 1986, Ice sheets, atmosphere CO_2 and

   sea level: Thesis, Univ. Utrecht, 185p.

World Bank, 1988, The World Bank Atlas, 1988: Washington,

   DC.

FOOTNOTE/ENDNOTE STYLE

As observed at the beginning of this chapter, instructors in history, philosophy, and the arts frequently prefer the footnote or endnote form of documentation to any form of parenthetical documentation. There are two chief guides to footnote and endnote style: the *MLA Handbook* (3rd ed., 1988) and the *Chicago Manual of Style* (13th ed., 1982). The required information and the order of that information in a footnote are the same in these two style manuals, but they differ in minor ways in format.

Since both style manuals recommend some form of parenthetical citation rather than footnote or endnote style, students who are advised to follow one of these two style manuals must first be certain that the instructor so advising actually wants them to use either footnotes or endnotes. (An instructor requiring MLA style *probably* wants the author/page style presented in Chapter 5; an instructor requiring adherence to the Chicago style *may* want the author/year style *or* footnotes or endnotes.) If footnote/endnote style is requested, then determine if the instructor has a preference. The *MLA Handbook,* for example, advises writers to use endnotes unless specifically requested to use footnotes, and the *Chicago Manual* also prefers endnotes. Some instructors, however, are now expecting footnotes rather than endnotes, perhaps on the assumption that students are preparing their papers on word processors, for footnotes are much easier to prepare on word processors than on typewriters. Finally, if you are using the footnote or endnote style, ascertain your instructor's preference with regard to a bibliography in addition to documentation notes. Because the first footnote or endnote reference to a source contains complete bibliographic information for the source, a list of works cited or bibliography is not necessary. Still, some instructors want both complete documentation notes and the alphabetized works cited page(s) following the text (with footnotes) or after the endnotes.

The guidelines below for preparing footnotes and endnotes adhere to the *Chicago Manual of Style.* The few differences in presentation found in the *MLA Handbook* are explained where appropriate.

In-Text Citation

Use a raised (superscript, such as this[2]) arabic numeral immediately following all material from a source, whether the borrowed material is
quoted or paraphrased. The number follows all punctuation except the
dash, and it always follows, never precedes, material needing documentation. Number footnotes or endnotes consecutively throughout the paper,
beginning with "1." Study the following brief excerpt from Everard H.
Smith's study of the Civil War, as an example:

> A cautious scholar, Clausewitz was unwilling to predict whether the
> democratic nationalism unleased by Napoleon would lead to even
> more violent future wars. Yet he was not hopeful, for he believed
> that the passions of the people, once engaged, could not easily be
> restrained.[61] Alexis de Tocqueville, who toured the United States
> during the same period, reached similar conclusions about the rela-
> tionship of warfare to popular will. A democracy, he surmised, would
> fight with irresistible determination because of the totality of its in-
> volvement: "War . . . in the end becomes the one great industry,
> and every eager and ambitious desire sprung from equality is focused
> thereon."[62]

Use the same care to present material from sources with introductory
tags and with a placing of superscript numbers so that readers can tell
where borrowed material begins and where it ends. Regularly placing citation numbers only at the ends of paragraphs will not result in accurate
documentation.

LOCATION AND PRESENTATION OF FOOTNOTES

1. Place footnotes on the same page as the borrowed material. You
   need to calculate the number of lines needed at the bottom of the
   page to complete all the footnotes for that page. If you miscalculate,
   retype the page. (A word processor will make these calculations for
   you.)

2. Begin the first footnote four lines (two double spaces) below the last
   line of text.

3. Indent the first line of each footnote five spaces. Type the superscript
   numeral that corresponds to the one in the text, leave one space, and
   then type the reference information. (This is the most common practice in research papers, but the *Chicago Manual* shows online nu-

merals followed by a period—for example: 1. Chicago style can be found in books and some journals, especially with endnotes.)

4. If a footnote runs to more than one line of text, single-space between lines and begin the second line flush with the left margin.

5. If more than one footnote appears on a page, double-space between notes.

Location and Presentation of Endnotes

1. List endnotes in consecutive order corresponding to the superscript numbers in the text.

2. Indent the first line of each endnote five spaces. Type the raised number, leave one space, and then type the reference. (Again, this is the traditional pattern in research papers, but the *Chicago Manual* shows an on-line number followed by a period. See the alternative example below.)

3. If an endnote runs to more than one line, double-space between lines and begin the second line flush with the left margin.

4. Double-space between endnotes.

5. Start endnotes on a new page titled "Notes." Endnotes follow the text and precede a list of works cited, if such a list is included.

Footnote/Endnote Form: First (Primary) Reference

Each first reference to a source contains all the necessary author, title, and publication information that would be found in a list of works cited or list of references. Subsequent references to the same source use a shortened form. Prepare all first-reference notes according to the following guidelines.

Form for Books

1. Cite the author's full name in signature order, followed by a comma.

2. Cite the title of the book, and underline it. Include the complete subtitle, if there is one, unless a list of works cited is also provided. No punctuation follows the title.

3. Give the facts of publication in parentheses: city of publication fol-

lowed by a colon, publisher followed by a comma, and year of publication.

4. Give the precise page reference. Do not use "p." or "pp." *MLA Handbook* style: Use no punctuation between the closing parenthesis and the page reference. The *Chicago Manual:* Place a comma after the closing parenthesis, before the page number.

> ¹ Daniel J. Boorstin, The Americans: The Colonial Experience (New York: Vintage-Random, 1958), 46.

(The most common footnote/endnote pattern uses a superscript number and a comma after the closing parenthesis.)

Alternative

1. Daniel J. Boorstin, The Americans: The Colonial Experience (New York: Vintage-Random, 1958), 46.

(If you use this less common style, do not indent the first line of the note, as the alternative example illustrates.)

FORM FOR ARTICLES

1. Cite the author's full name in signature order, followed by a comma.
2. Cite the title of the article in quotation marks, and place a comma *inside* the closing quotation mark.
3. Give the facts of publication: the title of the journal, underlined; the volume in arabic numerals; and the date followed by a colon. Citations of scholarly journals require the volume number followed by the date in parentheses; citations of popular magazines and newspapers eliminate the volume number, giving the date only, not in parentheses.
4. Provide a precise page reference following the colon, without using "p." or "pp." All notes end with a period.

> ² Everard H. Smith, "Chambersburg: Anatomy of a Confederate Reprisal," American Historical Review 96 (April 1991): 434.

Sample Footnotes/Endnotes

Additional information must be added as necessary to the simplest examples given above. Some of the most common variations are illustrated here. Note that the examples are presented as endnotes; that is, the lines of each note are double-spaced. Remember that footnotes are single spaced *within* each note but double-spaced *between* notes. The traditional style of indenting the first line, using a raised numeral, and placing a comma after the facts of publication in a book citation has been followed in these examples.

A WORK BY TWO OR THREE AUTHORS

[3] Charles A. Beard and Mary R. Beard, The American Spirit (New York: Macmillan, 1942), 63.

A WORK BY MORE THAN THREE AUTHORS

[4] Lester R. Brown et al., State of the World 1990: A Worldwatch Institute Report on Progress Toward a Sustainable Society (New York: W. W. Norton, 1990), 17.

AN EDITED WORK

[5] The Autobiography of Benjamin Franklin, ed. Max Farrand (Berkeley: University of California Press, 1949), 6-8.

(Begin with the title—or the editor's name—if the author's name appears in the title.)

[6] Bentley Glass, Orvsei Temkin, and William L. Straus, Jr., eds., Forerunners of Darwin: 1745-1859 (Baltimore: Johns Hopkins Press paperback edition, 1968), 326.

A TRANSLATION

[7] Allan Gilbert, trans. and ed., The Letters of Machiavelli (New York: Capricorn Books, 1961), 120.

⁸ Jean Jacques Rousseau, <u>The Social Contract and Discourses</u>, trans. with an introduction by G. D. H. Cole (New York: Dutton, 1950), 42–43.

A Preface, Introduction, or Afterword

⁹ Ernest Barker, introduction, <u>The Politics of Aristotle</u>, trans. and ed. Ernest Barker (New York: Oxford University Press, 1962), xiii.

A Book in Two or More Volumes

¹⁰ Paul Tillich, <u>Systematic Theology</u>, 3 vols. (Chicago: University of Chicago Press, 1951–63), 1:52.

(Make the page reference first to the volume number, followed by a colon, and then the page number.)

A Book in Its Second or Subsequent Edition

¹¹ George Vernadsky, <u>A History of Russia</u>, 4th ed. (New Haven: Yale University Press, 1954), 124–25.

A Book in a Series

¹² Charles L. Sanford, ed., <u>Benjamin Franklin and the American Character</u>, Problems in American Civilization (Lexington, MA: D. C. Heath, 1955), 4.

A Work in a Collection

¹³ George Washington, "Farewell Address, 1796," in <u>A Documentary History of the United States</u>, ed. Richard D. Heffner (New York: New American Library, 1965), 64–65.

An Encyclopedia Article

¹⁴ <u>The Concise Dictionary of American Biography</u>, 1964 ed., s.v., "Anthony, Susan Brownell."

(Do not cite a page number for reference works arranged alphabetically; rather, cite the entry in quotation marks after "s.v." [*sub verbo*— "under the word"]. The edition number or year is needed, but no other facts of publication are required for well-known reference works.)

An Article in a Scholarly Journal

^{15} Ellen Fitzpatrick, "Rethinking the Intellectual Origins of American Labor History," American Historical Review 96 (April 1991): 426.

An Article in a Popular Magazine

^{16} Robert B. Reich, "Dumpsters: The End of an Unfair Trade Practice," The New Republic, 10 June 1991: 9.

An Editorial

^{17} "The Third World's Peace Dividend," editorial, Washington Post, 28 May 1991: A18.

A Review

^{18} Gabriel P. Weisberg, "French Art Nouveau," rev. of Art Nouveau in Fin-de-Siècle France: Politics, Psychology, and Style by Deborah Silverman, Art Journal 49 (Winter 1990): 427.

Footnote/Endnote Form: Short Forms

After the first full documentary footnote or endnote for a source, subsequent references to the same source should be shortened forms. The simplest short form for any source with an author or editor is the author's or editor's last name followed by a comma and a precise page reference; thus: ^{19}Fitzgerald, 425. If there is no author cited, use a short title and page number. If two sources are written by authors with the same last name, then add first names or initials to distinguish between them. For example, if you used "The Tendency of History" by Henry

Adams and *The Founding of New England* by James T. Adams, then the
short forms would be as follows:

> [20] Henry Adams, 16.
>
> [21] James T. Adams, 252.

More typically, if you use two or more sources by the same author,
then add a short title to the note; thus:

> [22] Boorstin, *American Politics*, 167.
>
> [23] Boorstin, *The Americans*, 65-66.

The Latin abbreviations *loc. cit.* and *op. cit.* are no longer recommended, and Ibid. is almost as obsolete, usually replaced now by the
simple short form of author's last name and page number. Remember
that Ibid. can be used only to refer to the source cited in the immediately
preceding note. The following footnotes, appearing at the bottom of a
page from a history paper, illustrate the various short forms.

Sample Footnotes from a History Paper

While mid-twentieth century historians may be more
accurate, they may have lost the flavor of earlier
American historians who had a clear ideology that shaped
their writing.[20]

[11] William Bradford, <u>Of Plymouth Plantation</u>, in <u>The
American Puritans: Their Prose and Poetry</u>, ed. Perry Miller
(New York: Anchor-Doubleday, 1956), 5.

[12] Daniel J. Boorstin, <u>The Americans: The Colonial Ex-
perience</u> (New York: Vintage-Random, 1958), 16.

[13] Ibid., 155.

[14] James T. Adams, 136.

[15] Henry Adams, <u>The Education of Henry Adams</u>, ed. D.
W. Brogan (Boston: Houghton Mifflin, 1961), 342.

[16] Boorstin, <u>American Politics</u>, 167.

[17] Henry Adams, "The Tendency of History," 16.

[18] Ibid., 71.

[19] Henry Adams, Education, 408.

[20] John Higham, "The Cult of the 'American Consensus': Homogenizing Our History," Commentary 27 (Feb. 1959): 94-96.

NUMBER STYLE

As noted at the beginning of this chapter, the number style of documentation requires that each source used be given a number as it is referred to and that only the number appear, in parentheses within the text, whenever reference is made to the source. The in-text citation by number is supported by a complete list of references organized (usually) in the order in which the sources are referred to in the paper. (A variation of this pattern is to organize the reference list alphabetically.) The following paragraph from a paper on the global tectonics of Venus illustrates one version of number-style in-text citation:

> One of the principal hypotheses concerning the nature of Venusian tectonics is that it is dominated by the effects of convective plumes rising in the mantle, impinging on the lithosphere, and producing hot spots—areas of volcanism and uplift created by the magmatic, thermal, and dynamic effects of the plumes *(3, 5, 6)*. Two major elements of this model are (i) that large-scale horizontal motion of the lithosphere does not take place or is, at most, a minor process *(6, 7)* and (ii) that Venus loses most of its heat through lithospheric conduction, which is enhanced at the thin lithosphere associated with hot spots *(6, 8)*.

The *Chicago Manual of Style* describes the number system as tedious for readers, particularly when several numbers are cited together but no authors' names are mentioned in the text. Not surprisingly, some journals relevant to the fields that use the number style (chemistry, physics, mathematics, computer science, and the medical sciences) have now switched to, or allow as an alternative, the author/year style of documentation. The American Chemical Society, for example, in its manual for writers, now lists the author/year style as one option. To add to the confusion, experts in some special fields in the earth sciences must employ the number system in some of the interdisciplinary journals for which they write. The paper on Venus, for example, was written by two geologists and published in the journal *Science*. For student researchers, the only advice must be to ascertain the instructor's preference and then follow that preferred format as explained in this text. The rest of this section illustrates patterns of in-text citation with numbers and, then, the styles for citing references according to the American Chemical Society, (*ACS Style Guide,* 1986), the American Institute of Physics (*AIP Style Manual,* 4th ed., 1990), and the American Mathematical Society (*A Manual for Authors of Mathematical Papers,* rev. ed., 1990).

In-Text Citation

1. Select the appropriate pattern of number citation, according to your field or your instructor's preference:
   A superscript number[2]
   An on-line number in parentheses (2)
   An on-line number in parentheses either in italic type *(2)* or underlined in the manuscript (2)
   An on-line number, usually in italic type, placed within square brackets [2]

2. Place the number immediately after the author's name

```
Head and Crumpler (3) have proposed . . .
```

OR

```
Head and Crumpler³ have proposed . . .
```

or after a sentence, clause, or phrase that contains the borrowed material:

```
In this model, lithospheric convergence is taking

place at Ishtar Terra, with accretion of buoyant

plateau material (13) or underthrusting of normal

thickness crust (14) . . .
```

3. When citing several sources at once, place numbers in ascending order:

```
in the literature (2, 3, 6)

in the literature²,³,⁶
```

(Note that superscript numbers are separated by commas with no spaces between commas and numbers.)

ACS (American Chemical Society) Style

IN-TEXT CITATION

The *ACS Style Guide* lists 11 journals requiring superscript numbers for in-text citation, 5 journals (plus books published by ACS) requiring on-line italic numbers, and 3 requiring author/year citations. References should be listed in the order of in-text citation when the writer is using numbers, alphabetically when using the author/year style.

REFERENCES

Most journals in the field follow a style of beginning each reference with its number and repeating the form of the number that was used in the text; that is, if superscript numbers were used in the text, then each reference begins with a superscript number, and the references are in consecutive order, beginning with "1." In the *ACS Style Guide,* however, no number is shown at the beginning of a reference, and there is no indenting of either the first line or the second and subsequent lines of each reference. Follow these guidelines for preparing references:

1. Begin your list of references on a new page after the text but before any tables or illustrations. Title the page "References."
2. Cite authors by last name and initials, last name first for all authors. Separate multiple authors' names with a semicolon:

```
Littman, M.; Yeomans, D. K.
```

Form for Books

1. Cite the book title, with normal capitalization, in italics (underlined), followed by a semicolon:

```
Comet Halley: Once in a Lifetime;
```

2. Provide publication information in this order: publisher first, followed by a colon; place, followed by a comma; and date:

```
American Chemical Society: Washington, DC, 1985.
```

3. Specific volume, chapter, and/or page numbers are often cited, if only one part of the book is used. If many pages throughout a book

have been cited in the text, then exclude specific pages from the reference. When citing portions of a book, use the following abbreviations or spelled-out forms, noting capitalization when used:

Abstract

Chapter

ed. (for *edition,* but Ed. or Eds. for *editor* or *editors*)

No. (for *number*)

p. (for *page*); pp (for *pages*—no period used)

Part

Vol. (for a specific volume); vols. (for number of volumes)

Example

Armstrong, G. W. et al. In Analytical Chemistry of the Elements; Kolthoff, I. M.; Elving, P. J., Eds.; Interscience-Wiley: New York, 1961; Part 2, Vol. 7.

Form for Articles

1. Do not give the title of the article. Cite the *journal* title after the author's name, in abbreviated form and in italics (underlined):

Bercovici, D.; Schubert, G. Science

2. Cite the year in bold type, indicated by a wavy line under the year. (If you are using a word processor, use the bold function key for the year.) There is no punctuation between the journal title and the year; a comma follows the year.

Bercovici, D.; Schubert, G. Science 1989,

OR

Bercovici, D.; Schubert, G. Science **1989,**

3. Without spacing, cite the volume number, in italics (underlined), followed by a comma:

Bercovici . . . Science 1989,244,

4. Without spacing, cite either the initial page of the article or, preferred by ACS, the inclusive page numbers for the article:

   Bercovici . . . Science **1989,**244,950.

5. When citing references to articles in journals that are not paged continuously throughout the issues in a year, include the issue number in parentheses following the volume number. Note that there is no space between the volume number and the opening parenthesis or between the comma and the page numbers.

   Wilizek, F. Sci. Amer. **1991,**264(5),58–65.

6. Indicate when a reference is to an English translation of an article by adding "Engl. Transl." in parentheses after the journal title. Then, if possible, add a reference to the original article.

Sample References.   Use the following sample references as models for preparing citations for papers in chemistry:

References

Steudel, R. Chemistry of Nonmetals; deGruyter: Berlin, 1977; p. 15.

Smith, D. W. Inorganic Substances: A Prelude to the Study of Descriptive Inorganic Chemistry; Cambridge Univ. Press: Cambridge, 1990; Chapter 6.

Head, J. W.; Crumpler, L. S. Nature **1990,**346,525.

Wainscoat, R. J. In The World of Galaxies; Corwin, H. G.; Bottinelli, L., Eds.; Proceedings of the Conference "Le Monde des Galaxies," Paris, France; New York and Berlin: Springer-Verlag, 1989; pp 290-292.

Miller, W. H.; Schaefer, H. F.; Berne, J.; Segal, G. A. Modern Theoretical Chemistry; Plenum: New York, 1976; Vol. 1, Part A.

Grimm, R. E.; Phillips, R. J. J. Geophys. Res., in press.

AIP (American Institute of Physics) Style

IN-TEXT CITATION

The preferred style of documenting sources is the use of superscript numbers in consecutive order throughout the text supported by a list of references organized in the order of citation in the text. The AIP also recognizes the alternative of author/year citation but advises writers to get approval for this pattern of citation before using it in a paper submitted for publication.

REFERENCES

The list of references should be placed after the text and any appendices but before tables and figures. Title the page "References." Double-space throughout the list. Start each reference on a new line, beginning with the superscript number flush with the left margin. Subsequent lines are also flush with the left margin.

1. Give authors' names in signature form as they appear on the title page of the work cited and follow with a comma:

   [1]D. F. Shriver and M. A. Drezdzen,

   ### Form for Books

2. Cite the title of the book in italics (underlined), with normal capitalization:

   The Manipulation of Air-Sensitive Compounds

3. Add number of volumes or edition number, as necessary:

   The Manipulation of Air-Sensitive Compounds, 2nd ed.

4. Place publication information within parentheses—publisher first, then place, then date, each element separated by a comma:

   [1]D. F. Shriver and M. A. Drezdzen, The Manipulation of Air-Sensitive Compounds, 2nd ed. (Wiley, New York, 1986).

5. For edited books, first give the author(s) of the particular part used; give the editor(s) following the title:

```
²W. D. Grobman and E. E. Koch, in Photoemission in Sol-
ids II, edited by L. Ley and M. Cardona (Springer, Ber-
lin, 1979).
```

Form for Articles

6. Article titles are not usually given. Cite the journal title, in abbreviated form, *not* underlined, after the name(s) of the author(s):

```
³T. A. Germer and W. Ho, J. Chem. Phys.
```

7. Give the volume number in bold type, indicated in the manuscript with a wavy line. (If you are using a word processor, use the bold function key for the volume number.)

```
³T. A. Germer . . . Phys. 89 (OR: 89)
```

8. Place a comma *after* the volume number, then the *first* page number, and then the year of publication in parentheses:

```
³T. A. Germer and W. Ho, J. Chem. Phys. 89, 652 (1988).
```

9. When citing references to articles in journals that are not paged continuously throughout the issues in a year, include the issue number in parentheses following the volume number:

```
⁴Barbara Goss Levi, Phys. Today 44 (2), 17 (1991).
```

Sample References. Use the following sample references as models for preparing papers in physics:

```
                          References
¹S. K. Kurtz, in Laser Handbook, edited by F. T. Arecchi
and E. O. Schulz-Dubois (North-Holland, Amsterdam, 1972),
Vol. 1.
```

[2]K. Kubodera and H. Kobayashi, Mol. Cryst. Liquid Cryst. **182A,** 103 (1990).

[3]Lawrence Badash, ed., <u>Rutherford and Boltwood: Letters on Radioactivity</u> (Yale Univ. Press, New Haven, 1969), pp. 76–77.

[4]D. J. Adams and E. M. Adams, Mol. Phys. (1991), in press.

[5]S. W. deLeeuw, J. W. Perram, and E. R. Smith, Proc. R. Soc. London Ser. A **373,** 27 (1980).

[6]J. T. Spencer, P. A. Dowben, and V.-G. Kim, U.S. Patent No. 4,957,773 (18 September 1990).

[7]Callery Chemical Company, Technical Bulletin No. CM-070, 1971.

[8]R. B. Jackman and J. S. Foord, <u>Extended Abstracts, Laser, Chemical Processing of Semiconductor Devices</u>, Mat. Res. Soc. Symp. Proc., 67 (1984).

AMS (American Mathematical Society) Style

In-Text Citation

In its revised second edition of *A Manual for Authors of Mathematical Papers,* the AMS encourages the use of specific references that include page numbers. The reference citation number, followed by precise pages, is placed in *square brackets,* and the number is in bold-face:

    As Jones [**3,** pp. 15–17] has demonstrated . . .

References

The AMS *Manual* shows the listing of references consecutively by number as cited in the text. However, the manual does include the possibility of listing references alphabetically. When numbering consecutively, use an on-line number, *not* in boldface or brackets. Indent each number three spaces from the left margin. Subsequent lines in each reference are flush with the left margin.

1. Cite the author(s) by initial(s) and last name in signature order, followed by a comma:

   ```
   1. U. Grenander,
   ```

Form for Books

2. Give the title of the book in italics (underlined), capitalizing only the first word of the title (and subtitle, if there is one) and any proper nouns; place a comma after the title:

   ```
   1. U. Grenander, Lectures in pattern theory,
   ```

3. Add number of volumes, edition number, or series name and number, as appropriate:

   ```
   1. U. Grenander, Lectures in pattern theory,
   Applied mathematical sciences no. 33,
   ```

4. Give the facts of publication in the order of publisher, city of publication, and year, all elements separated by commas:

   ```
   1. U. Grenander . . . Springer-Verlag, New York,
   1981.
   ```

Form for Articles

5. Following the author's name, cite the article title, *underlined,* capitalizing only the first word and any proper nouns, and follow it with a comma:

   ```
   2. C. Lance, On nuclear C*-algebra,
   ```

6. Give the journal title, abbreviated and *not* underlined:

   ```
   2. C. Lance, On nuclear C*-algebra, J. Funct. Anal.
   ```

7. Follow the journal title with the volume number in boldface (indicated in the manuscript with a wavy line), the year in parentheses, a comma, and inclusive page numbers:

> 2. C. Lance, <u>On nuclear C*-algebra</u>, J. Funct. Anal.
> **12** (1973), 157–176.

Sample References.   Use the following sample references as models for preparing citations for papers in mathematics:

References

1. S. M. Ross, <u>Introduction to probability models</u>, 4th ed., Academic Press, Boston, 1989.

2. D. Knuth, <u>Semi numerical algorithms</u>, Vol. 2, <u>The art of computer programming</u>, 2nd ed., Addison-Wesley, Reading, MA, 1981.

3. C. Keutenauer, <u>Sèries rationnelles et algèbres syntactiques</u>, Thèse, Univ. Paris, VI (1980).

4. G. M. Seitz, <u>Maximal subgroups of exceptional algebraic groups</u>, Amer. Math. Soc. Memoirs **441** (1991), 1–197.

5. H. Azad, M. Barry, and G. Seitz, <u>On the structure of parabolic subgroups</u>, Comm. in Alg. **18** (1990), 551–561.

6. S. Richman, <u>A defect relation for quasi-meromorphic mappings</u>, Annals of Math, in press.

A List of
Abbreviations

You will see many of the abbreviations listed below in your college reading and research. Some of them will be appropriate in your research papers. In general, you are encouraged to use abbreviations or short titles of literary works and books of the Bible in parenthetical citations and content notes. Abbreviations are usually unacceptable in the texts of papers, however, except for those well known to readers in a given discipline (e.g., *MLA* for *Modern Language Association; REM* for *rapid eye movement; Btu* for *British thermal unit*). Further, Latin abbreviations, once regularly used in footnote or endnote citations, are now discouraged.

SCHOLARLY ABBREVIATIONS

abbr.	abbreviated, abbreviation
abr.	abridged, abridgment
anon.	anonymous
art.	article
b.	born

bk., bks.	book(s)
ca. *or* c.	circa (about) Used with approximate dates—e.g., "ca. 1850."
cf.	confer (compare) Do not use "cf." when "see" is meant.
ch., chs.	chapter(s)
chap., chaps.	chapter(s)
col., cols.	column(s)
comp.	compiled by, compiler
d.	died
diss.	dissertation
ed., eds.	edited by, edition(s), editor(s)
e.g.	*exempli gratia* (for example)
enl.	enlarged (e.g., "enl. ed.")
esp.	especially
et al.	*et alii* (and others)
et seq.	*et sequens* (and the following) Used with a page number, as in "p. 5 et seq.," to mean "page 5 and the following page."
f., ff.	and the following page(s) Exact references are better—e.g., "pp. 24–26" rather than "pp. 24 ff."
fig.	figure
ibid.	*ibidem* (in the same place) Used to cite a different page in the immediately preceding cited work; not acceptable in MLA style; discouraged in most style manuals.
i.e.	*id est* (that is)
illus.	illustrated by, illustrations, illustrator
incl.	includes, including, inclusive
inf.	infra (below) The phrase "see below" is preferred.
introd.	introduction
l., ll.	line(s) Do not use in text; no longer used in MLA parenthetical citations.
loc. cit.	*loco citato* (in the place cited) Not acceptable in MLA style.
MS, MSS	manuscript(s)
n., nn.	note(s)
N.B.	*nota bene* (mark well, take careful note)
n.d.	no date (of publication) given
n.p.	no place (of publication) given
n.s. *or* ns	new series

obs.	obsolete
op. cit.	*opere citato* (in the work cited) Not acceptable in MLA style.
o.s. *or* os	old series
p., pp.	page(s) Do not use "ps." for "pages."
pass.	*passim* (here and there, throughout the work)
pseud.	pseudonym
pt., pts.	part(s)
rev.	review, revised, revision
rpt.	reprint, reprinted
sec.	section
ser.	series
st., sts.	stanza(s)
sup.	supra (above) The phrase "see above" is preferred.
trans.	translated by, translation, translator(s)
v.	*vide* (see)
v., vv.	verse(s)
viz.	*videlicet* (namely)
vol., vols.	volume(s)
vs. *or* v.	versus (against)

ABBREVIATIONS OF PUBLISHERS' NAMES

Shortened forms for publishers' names are used in bibliographic citations in MLA style. See page 87 for abbreviations of university presses.

Abrams	Harry N. Abrams, Inc.
ALA	American Library Association
Allen	George Allen and Unwin Publishers, Inc.
Allyn	Allyn and Bacon, Inc.
Appleton	Appleton-Century-Crofts
Barnes	Barnes and Noble Books
Basic	Basic Books, Inc.
Beacon	Beacon Press, Inc.
Bobbs	The Bobbs-Merrill Co., Inc.
Bowker	R. R. Bowker Co.
Clarendon	Clarendon Press
Dell	Dell Publishing Co., Inc.

Dodd	Dodd, Mead, and Co.
Doubleday	Doubleday and Co., Inc.
Dutton	E. P. Dutton, Inc.
Farrar	Farrar, Straus, and Giroux, Inc.
Free	Free Press
Gale	Gale Research Co.
GPO	Government Printing Office
Harcourt	Harcourt Brace Jovanovich, Inc.
Harper	HarperCollins; formerly Harper & Row Publishers, Inc.
Heath	D. C. Heath and Co.
Holt	Holt, Rinehart, and Winston, Inc.
Houghton	Houghton Mifflin Co.
Knopf	Alfred A. Knopf, Inc.
Lippincott	J. B. Lippincott Co.
Little	Little, Brown, and Co.
Macmillan	Macmillan Publishing Co., Inc.
McGraw	McGraw-Hill, Inc.
Merrill	Merrill Publishing Co.
MLA	Modern Language Association
Norton	W. W. Norton and Co., Inc.
Prentice	Prentice-Hall, Inc.
Putnam's	G. P. Putnam's Sons
Random	Random House, Inc.
St. Martin's	St. Martin's Press, Inc.
Scott	Scott, Foresman and Co.
Scott/Little	Scott, Foresman/Little, Brown, Inc.
Scribner's	Charles Scribner's Sons
Simon	Simon and Schuster, Inc.

ABBREVIATIONS FOR MONTHS

Abbreviate the months as shown below. (*May, June,* and *July* are not shortened.) Use abbreviated forms in citations but not in the text.

Jan.	Apr.	July	Oct.
Feb.	May	Aug.	Nov.
Mar.	June	Sept.	Dec.

ABBREVIATIONS FOR STATES

Use the following postal abbreviations (without periods) when giving the state after a city in a citation. Do not abbreviate the names of states in the text.

Alabama	AL	Missouri	MO
Alaska	AK	Montana	MT
Arizona	AZ	Nebraska	NE
Arkansas	AR	Nevada	NV
California	CA	New Hampshire	NH
Colorado	CO	New Jersey	NJ
Connecticut	CT	New Mexico	NM
Delaware	DE	New York	NY
District of Columbia	DC	North Carolina	NC
Florida	FL	North Dakota	ND
Georgia	GA	Ohio	OH
Hawaii	HI	Oklahoma	OK
Idaho	ID	Oregon	OR
Illinois	IL	Pennsylvania	PA
Indiana	IN	Rhode Island	RI
Iowa	IA	South Carolina	SC
Kansas	KS	South Dakota	SD
Kentucky	KY	Tennessee	TN
Louisiana	LA	Texas	TX
Maine	ME	Utah	UT
Maryland	MD	Vermont	VT
Massachusetts	MA	Virginia	VA
Michigan	MI	Washington	WA
Minnesota	MN	West Virginia	WV
Mississippi	MS	Wisconsin	WI
		Wyoming	WY

ABBREVIATIONS FOR BOOKS OF THE BIBLE

Abbreviate books of the Bible in parenthetical references. Combine the abbreviations with chapter and verse citations as in this example: (Gen. 2.12). Do not underline titles or place them within quotation marks. All the books of the Bible are listed below; note that those of one syllable are not abbreviated.

OLD TESTAMENT (OT)

Gen.	Genesis
Exod.	Exodus
Lev.	Leviticus
Num.	Numbers
Deut.	Deuteronomy
Josh.	Joshua
Judg.	Judges
Ruth	Ruth
1 Sam.	First Samuel
2 Sam.	Second Samuel
1 Kings	First Kings
2 Kings	Second Kings
1 Chron.	First Chronicles
2 Chron.	Second Chronicles
Ezra	Ezra
Neh.	Nehemiah
Esth.	Esther
Job	Job
Ps.	Psalms
Prov.	Proverbs
Eccles.	Ecclesiastes
Song Sol.	Song of Solomon
Isa.	Isaiah
Jer.	Jeremiah
Lam.	Lamentations
Ezek.	Ezekiel
Dan.	Daniel
Hos.	Hosea
Joel	Joel
Amos	Amos
Obad.	Obadiah
Jon.	Jonah
Mic.	Micah
Nah.	Nahum

OLD TESTAMENT (OT)

Hab.	Habakkuk
Zeph.	Zaphaniah
Hag.	Haggai
Zech.	Zechariah
Mal.	Malachi

NEW TESTAMENT (NT)

Matt.	Matthew
Mark	Mark
Luke	Luke
John	John
Acts	Acts of the Apostles
Rom.	Romans
1 Cor.	First Corinthians
2 Cor.	Second Corinthians
Gal.	Galatians
Eph.	Ephesians
Phil.	Philippians
Col.	Colossians
1 Thess.	First Thessalonians
2 Thess.	Second Thessalonians
1 Tim.	First Timothy
2 Tim.	Second Timothy
Tit.	Titus
Philem.	Philemon
Heb.	Hebrews
Jas.	James
1 Pet.	First Peter
2 Pet.	Second Peter
1 John	First John
2 John	Second John
3 John	Third John
Jude	Jude
Rev.	Revelation

ABBREVIATIONS FOR LITERARY WORKS

When appropriate in parenthetical documentation, use abbreviations for the titles of literary works. In general, abbreviate by using the initial letters of the key words of a title (e.g., SL for The Scarlet Letter) or by using a short form of a one-word title (e.g., Can. for Candide). Note that these abbreviated titles are underlined, in contrast to the books of the Bible. Use the following abbreviations for Shakespeare's plays.

Ado	Much Ado About Nothing
Ant.	Antony and Cleopatra
AWW	All's Well That Ends Well
AYL	As You Like It
Cor.	Coriolanus
Err.	The Comedy of Errors
Ham.	Hamlet
1H4	Henry IV, Part 1
2H4	Henry IV, Part 2
H5	Henry V
1H6	Henry VI, Part 1
2H6	Henry VI, Part 2
3H6	Henry VI, Part 3
H8	Henry VIII
JC	Julius Caesar
Jn.	King John
LLL	Love's Labour's Lost
Lr.	King Lear
Mac.	Macbeth
MM	Measure for Measure
MND	A Midsummer Night's Dream
MV	The Merchant of Venice
Oth.	Othello
Per.	Pericles, Prince of Tyre
R2	Richard II
R3	Richard III
Rom.	Romeo and Juliet

Shr.	The Taming of the Shrew
TGV	The Two Gentlemen of Verona
Tim.	Timon of Athens
Tit.	Titus Andronicus
Tmp.	The Tempest
TN	Twelfth Night
Tro.	Troilus and Cressida
Wiv.	The Merry Wives of Windsor
WT	The Winter's Tale

Appendix B

Key Reference
Works by Discipline

The following list of reference works by discipline can aid your research in a specific field. Of course not all the works will be found in every library, and your library may have other, similar reference aids. In large college libraries many more works will be found than those listed here, arranged in the reference room by Library of Congress classification number, that is, grouped by subject field. This appendix begins with an index to the disciplines and then organizes works under the alphabetically arranged disciplines. For each discipline general works (including bibliographies, guides, encyclopedias, dictionaries, and histories) are listed first, followed by indexes to articles relevant to the discipline, and then several key databases for online searches. Your reference librarian can help with database searches and direct you to additional reference sources in your field.

INDEX TO LIST OF REFERENCE WORKS BY DISCIPLINE

World Literature (*see* Language and Literature, 330)

LIST OF REFERENCE WORKS BY DISCIPLINE

Art and Architecture

GENERAL WORKS
AND BIBLIOGRAPHIES

American Art Directory. New York: Bowker, 1952–present.

Annotated Bibliography of Fine Art. 1897. Rpt. Boston: Longwood, 1976.

Applied and Decorative Arts: A Bibliographic Guide. Ed. D. L. Ehresmann. Littleton, CO: Libraries Unlimited, 1977.

Art Books. 1950–1979. New York: Bowker, 1979. Supplement 1985.

Art Education: A Guide to Information Sources. C. Bunch. Detroit: Gale, 1977.

Art Library Manual: A Guide to Resources and Practice. Ed. Philip Pacey. New York: Bowker, 1977.

Bibliographic Guide to Art and Architecture. Boston: Hall, 1976–. Annual.

Britannica Encyclopaedia of American Art. Ed. M. Rugoff. Chicago: Encyclopaedia Britannica, 1973.

Contemporary Architects. 2nd ed. Chicago: St. James, 1987.

Contemporary Artists. 2nd ed. New York: St. Martin's, 1983.

Dictionary of American Painters, Sculptors, and Engravers. Ed. Mantle Fielding. New York: Editions, 1986.

Encyclopedia of World Art. 16 vols. New York: McGraw, 1959–1983. Supplement 1987.

Fine and Applied Arts Terms Index. Detroit: Gale, 1983.

Fine Arts: A Bibliographic Guide. Ed. D. L. Ehresmann. 2nd ed. Littleton, CO: Libraries Unlimited, 1979.

Gardner's Art Through the Ages. 8th ed. 2 vols. New York: Harcourt, 1986.

Guide to Art Reference Books. Chicago: ALA, 1959.

Guide to Basic Information Sources in the Visual Arts. Ed. Gerd Muehsam. Santa Barbara: ABC/Clio, 1977.

Guide to the Literature of Art History. E. M. Arntzen and R. Rainwater. Chicago: ALA, 1980.

A History of Architecture. F. Bannister. 18th ed. New York: Scribner's, 1975.

Larousse Dictionary of Painters. New York: Larousse, 1981.

Macmillan Encyclopedia of Architects. Ed. A. K. Placzek. 4 vols. New York: Free, 1982.

The New International Illustrated Encyclopedia of Art. 24 vols. New York: Greystone, 1967.

Oxford Companion to Twentieth Century Art. Ed. H. Osborne. Oxford: Oxford UP, 1981.

Pelican History of Art. 50 vols. in progress. Baltimore: Pelican, 1953–present.

Random House Library of Painting and Sculpture. 4 vols. New York: Beazley, 1981.

Research Guide to the History of Western Art. W. E. Kleinbauer and T. P. Slavens. Chicago: ALA, 1982.

INDEXES TO JOURNAL ARTICLES

Art Index. New York: Bowker, 1929–present.

Index to Art Periodicals. 11 vols. Boston: Hall, 1962. Supplements.

DATABASES

Architecture Database (RILA), DIALOG

Art Literature International (RILA), DIALOG

Arts & Humanities Search, BRS, DIALOG

Biological Sciences

GENERAL WORKS AND BIBLIOGRAPHIES

Bibliography of Bioethics. L. Walters. Detroit: Gale, 1975–. Annual.

Biological Abstracts. 1926–present. Semimonthly. Annual cumulations.

Biology Data Book. Eds. P. L. Altman and Dorothy S. Dittmer. 2nd ed. 3 vols. Madison: FASEB, 1972–1974.

Dictionary of the Flowering Plants and Ferns. J. C. Willis. 8th ed. New York: Cambridge UP, 1973.

Dictionary of Genetics and Cell Biology. N. Maclean. New York: New York UP, 1988.

Dictionary of Theoretical Concepts in Biology. K. E. Row and R. G. Frederick. Metuchen: Scarecrow, 1981.

Dictionary of Zoology. Ed. A. W. Leftwich. 3rd ed. New York: Van Nostrand, 1973.

Encyclopedia of the Biological Sciences. Ed. Peter Gray. 2nd ed. New York: Reinhold, 1970.

Guide to Sources for Agricultural and Biological Research. Eds. J. R. Blanchard and L. Farrell. Berkeley: U of California P, 1981.

Henderson's Dictionary of Biological Terms. S. Holmes. 9th ed. New York: Van Nostrand, 1979.

Information Sources in the Life Sciences. Ed. H. V. Wyatt. Stoneham, MA: Butterworth, 1987.

Library Research Guide to Biology: Illustrated Search Strategy and Sources. Ann Arbor: Pierian, 1978.

Macmillan Illustrated Animal Encyclopedia. Ed. P. Whitfield. New York: Macmillan, 1984.

Smith's Guide to the Literature of the Life Sciences. Ed. R. C. Smith et al. 9th ed. Minneapolis: Burgess, 1980.

INDEXES TO JOURNAL ARTICLES

Biological Abstracts. 1926–present.

Biological and Agricultural Index. New York: Wilson, 1947–present.

General Science Index. New York: Wilson, 1978–present.

DATABASES

BIOSIS Previews, DIALOG, BRS
Life Sciences Collection, DIALOG
Scisearch, DIALOG
Zoological Record Online, DIALOG

Business and Economics

GENERAL WORKS AND BIBLIOGRAPHIES

AMA Management Handbook. Ed. W. K. Fallon. 2nd ed. New York: American Management Assoc., 1983.

American Dictionary of Economics. Ed. Douglas Auld et al. New York: Facts on File, 1983.

American Economic and Business History: Information Sources. Detroit: Gale, 1971.

Basic Business Library: Core Resources. Ed. B. S. Schlessinger. Phoenix: Oryx, 1983–present.

Bibliographic Guide to Business and Economics. Boston: Hall, 1975–present. Annual.

Business and Economics Books, 1876–1983. 4 vols. New York: Bowker, 1983.

Business Information Sources. Ed. L. M. Daniells. 2nd ed. Berkeley: U of California P, 1985.

Business Publications Index and Abstracts. Detroit: Gale, 1983–present. Annual.

Dictionary of Banking and Financial Services. Ed. J. M. Rosenberg. New York: Wiley, 1985.

The Dictionary of Modern Economics. Ed. David Pearce. 3rd ed. Cambridge: MIT, 1986.

Dow Jones–Irwin Business and Investment Almanac. Ed. S. N. Levine. Homewood, IL: Jones-Irwin, 1977–. Annual.

Economic Handbook of the World. Ed. A. S. Banks et al. New York: McGraw, 1981.

Economics: Bibliographic Guide to Reference Books and Information Resources. Ed. Peter Melnyk. Littleton, CO: Libraries Unlimited, 1971.

Economics Books. Clifton, NJ: Kelley, 1974–. Annual.

Economics Information Resources Directory. Detroit: Gale, 1984–present.

Encyclopedia of American Economic History: Studies of the Principal Movements and Ideas. 3 vols. New York: Scribner's, 1980.

Encyclopedia of Business Information Sources. Ed. Paul Wasserman et al. 6th ed. Detroit: Gale, 1986.

Historical Bibliography of Administration, Business, and Management. Ed. D. D. Van Fleet. Monticello: Vance Biblios., 1978.

Information Sources in Economics. Ed. J. Fletcher. 2nd ed. London: Butterworth, 1984.

International Directory of Business. Eds. H. Johannsen and G. T. Page. Englewood Cliffs: Prentice, 1981.

Money, Banking, and Macroeconomics: A Guide to Information Sources. J. M. Rock. Detroit: Gale, 1977.

The New Palgrave: A Dictionary of Economics. Ed. J. Eatwell et al. 4 vols. New York: Stockton, 1987.

Select Bibliography of Modern Economic Theory, 1870–1929. Ed. H. E. Batson. 1930. Rpt. New York: Kelley, 1968.

Standard & Poor's Register of Corporations, Directors and Executives. New York: Standard, 1928–. Annual.

Where to Find Business Information. 2nd ed. New York: Wiley, 1982.

INDEXES TO JOURNAL ARTICLES

Accountants' Index. New York: AICPA, 1921–present.

Business Periodicals Index. New York: Wilson, 1958–present.

Journal of Economic Literature. Nashville: American Economics Assn., 1964–present.

The Wall Street Journal Index. New York: Dow Jones, 1958–present.

DATABASES

ABI/INFORM, BRS

D&B Dun's Financial Records Plus, DIALOG

D&B Electronic Business Directory, DIALOG

Disclosure Database, BRS, DIALOG

Economic Literature Index, DIALOG

Laborlaw I and II, DIALOG

Management Contents, BRS

Moody's Corporate News, DIALOG

PTS Prompt, DIALOG

Standard & Poor's Daily News, DIALOG

Trade and Industry Index, DIALOG

Chemistry

GENERAL WORKS AND BIBLIOGRAPHIES

Chemical Industries Information Sources. Ed. T. P. Peck. Detroit: Gale, 1979.

Chemical Publications, Their Nature and Use. 5th ed. New York: McGraw, 1982.

Encyclopedia of Chemical Technology. Ed. Herman F. Mark et al. 3rd ed. 24 vols. New York: Wiley, 1978–1984.

Guide to Basic Information Sources in Chemistry. Ed. Arthur Antony. New York: Wiley, 1979.

How to Find Chemical Information: A Guide for Practicing Chemists, Teachers, and Students. Ed. R. E. Maizell. 2nd ed. New York: Wiley, 1987.

Literature of Chemical Technology. E. T. E.
Singer and J. F. Smith. Washington:
ACS, 1968.
Miall's Dictionary of Chemistry. Ed. S. W.
A. Sharp. 5th ed. Harlow, Essex:
Longman, 1981.
Searching the Chemical Literature. Wash-
ington: ACS, 1961.
The Use of Chemical Literature. Ed. R. T.
Bottle. 3rd ed. London: Butterworth,
1979.
*Using the Chemical Literature: A Practical
Guide.* H. M. Woodburn. New York:
Dekker, 1974.
*Van Nostrand Reinhold Encyclopedia of
Chemistry.* Ed. D. M. Considine et al.
4th ed. New York: Van Nostrand,
1984.

INDEXES TO JOURNAL ARTICLES

Chemical Abstracts. Easton: ACS, 1907–
present. Weekly.
General Science Index. New York: Wilson,
1978–present.

DATABASES

Analytical Abstracts, DIALOG
CA Search, DIALOG, BRS
Chemical Industry Notes, DIALOG
Chemname, DIALOG
Compendex, BRS
Inspec, BRS
Ntis, BRS
Scisearch, DIALOG

Computer Science

GENERAL WORKS
AND BIBLIOGRAPHIES

AMC Guide to Computing Literature. An-
nually, 1978–present.
*Annotated Bibliography on the History of
Data Processing.* Ed. J. W. Cortada.
Westport: Greenwood, 1983.

Computer Dictionary for Everyone. Ed.
Donald Spencer. New York: Scrib-
ner's, 1981.
Computer Dictionary and Handbook. 4th
ed. Indianapolis: Sams, 1985.
*Computer-Readable Databases: A Directory
and Data Sourcebook.* Ed. M. E. Will-
iams et al. Chicago: ALA, 1985.
*Computing Information Directory: A Com-
prehensive Guide to the Computing Lit-
erature.* D. M. Hildebrandt. Federal
Way, WA: Pedoro, 1985.
Dictionary of Computing. Ed. V. Illing-
worth. New York: Oxford UP, 1986.
Encyclopedia of Artificial Intelligence. Ed.
S. C. Shapiro. 2 vols. New York:
Wiley, 1987.
*Encyclopedia of Computer Science and Engi-
neering.* Ed. A. Ralston. 2nd ed. New
York: Van Nostrand, 1983.
*Guide to Reference Sources in the Computer
Sciences.* New York: Macmillan, 1974.
*Historical Dictionary of Data Processing:
Technology, Biographies, Organizations.*
James W. Cortada. 3 vols. Westport:
Greenwood, 1987.
*Scientific and Technical Information
Sources.* Ed. C. Chen. Cambridge: MIT,
1987.

INDEXES TO JOURNAL ARTICLES

Applied Science and Technology Index. New
York: Wilson, 1958–present.
Computer Abstracts. London: Technical In-
formation, 1957–present.
Computer Literature Index. Phoenix: ACR,
1971–present.

DATABASES

Business Software Database, BRS
Computer Database, BRS
Inspec, DIALOG
Microcomputer Index, DIALOG

Education (including Physical Education and Health)

Bibliographic Guide to Education. Boston: Hall, 1978–present.

A Bibliographic Guide to Educational Research. Ed. D. M. Berry. 2nd ed. Metuchen: Scarecrow, 1980.

Digest of Education Statistics. Washington: GPO, 1962–present. Annually.

Education Journals and Serials. Ed. M. E. Collins. Metuchen: Scarecrow, 1988.

Encyclopedia of Educational Research. Ed. H. E. Mitzel. 5th ed. 4 vols. New York: Free, 1982.

Encyclopedia of Sports. F. G. Menke. 2nd ed. New York: Barnes, 1978.

Foundations of Physical Education. Ed. C. A. Bucher. 8th ed. Philadelphia: Lea, 1979.

A Guide to Sources of Educational Information. Ed. M. L. Woodbury. 2nd ed. Arlington, VA: Information Resources, 1982.

Handbook of Research on Teaching. Ed. M. C. Wittrock. 3rd ed. New York: Macmillan, 1986.

International Encyclopedia of Education. Eds. T. Husen and T. N. Postlethwaite. 10 vols. Elmsford, NY: Pergamon, 1985.

International Yearbook of Education. Paris: UNESCO, 1948–. Annual.

Library Research Guide to Education. Ed. J. R. Kennedy. Ann Arbor: Pierian, 1979.

The Philosophy of Education: A Guide to Information Sources. Ed. C. A. Baatz. Detroit: Gale, 1980.

Research Processes in Physical Education, Recreation, and Health. 2nd ed. Englewood Cliffs: Prentice, 1984.

Resources in Education (formerly *Research in Education*). Washington: ERIC, 1956–present.

Sports and Physical Education: A Guide to the Reference Resources. B. Gratch et al. Westport: Greenwood, 1983.

Subject Bibliography of the History of American Higher Education. Westport: Greenwood, 1984.

World Education Encyclopedia. Ed. G. T. Kurian. 3 vols. New York: Facts on File, 1988.

Current Index to Journals in Education. Phoenix: Oryx, 1969–present.

Education Index. New York: Wilson, 1929–present.

Physical Education Index. Cape Girardeau, MO: Oak, 1978–present.

Physical Fitness and Sports Medicine. Washington: GPO, 1978–present.

State Education Journal Index. Westminster, CO: 1963–present.

A-V Online, DIALOG
ERIC, DIALOG, BRS
Exceptional Child Education Resources, DIALOG, BRS
Sport Database, BRS

Environmental Studies

A Dictionary of the Environment. Ed. Michael Allaby. New York: Van Nostrand, 1977.

Encyclopedia of Community Planning and Environmental Management. Eds. M. S. Schultz and V. L. Kasen. New York: Facts on File, 1984.

Energy Abstracts for Policy Analysis. Oak Ridge, TN: TIC, 1975–present.

Energy Information Guide. Ed. D. R. Weber. Santa Barbara: ABC-Clio, 1982–1983.

Environment Abstracts. New York: Environment Information Center, 1971–present.

Environmental Impact Assessment: A Bibliography with Abstracts. Eds. B. D. Clark, R. Bisset, and P. Wathern. New York: Bowker, 1980.

Grzimek's Encyclopedia of Ecology. Ed. B. Grzimek et al. New York: Van Nostrand, 1976.

Handbook of Air Pollution Technology. Eds. Seymour Calvert and Harold M. Englund. New York: Wiley, 1984.

Pollution Abstracts. Washington: Cambridge Scientific Abstracts, 1970–present.

Selected Water Resources Abstracts. Springfield, VA: Ntis, 1968–present.

Water and Water Pollution Handbook. Ed. Leonard L. Ciaccio. 4 vols. New York: Dekker, 1971–1973.

INDEXES TO JOURNAL ARTICLES

Biological Abstracts. Philadelphia: Biblio-graphical Abstracts, 1926–present.

Environmental Index. New York: EIC, 1971–present.

General Science Index. New York: Wilson, 1978–present.

DATABASES

Biosis Previews, BRS, DIALOG
Compendex Plus, DIALOG
Environline, DIALOG
Environmental Bibliography, DIALOG
Pollution Abstracts, DIALOG, BRS
Water Resources Abstracts, DIALOG

Ethnic Studies

ASIAN-AMERICAN STUDIES

Asian American Studies: An Annotated Bibliography and Research Guide. Ed. Hyung-Chan Kim. Westport: Greenwood, 1989.

Asians in America: Filipinos, Koreans, and East Indians. H. B. Melendy. New York: Hippocrene, 1981.

The Chinese of America. Jack Chen. New York: Harper, 1982.

East to America: A History of the Japanese in the United States. R. A. Wilson and B. Hosokawa. New York: Quill, 1980.

Vietnamese Americans: Patterns of Resettlement and Socioeconomic Adaptation in the United States. Darrel Montero. Boulder: Westview, 1979.

BLACK AMERICAN STUDIES

Afro-American Reference. Ed. N. Davis. Westport: Greenwood, 1985.

Bibliographic Guide to Black Studies. Boston: Hall, 1975–. Annual.

A Bibliography of the Negro in Africa and America. Ed. M. N. Work. New York: Octagon, 1966.

Black Index: Afro-Americans in Selected Periodicals 1907–1949. R. Newman. New York: Garland, 1981.

Dictionary of American Negro Biography. Eds. R. W. Logan and M. R. Winton. New York: Norton, 1982.

Encyclopedia of Black America. Ed. W. A. Low. New York: McGraw, 1981.

The Negro Almanac: A Reference Work on the Afro-American. Eds. H. A. Plaski and J. Williams. 5th ed. Detroit: Gale, 1990.

Negro in the United States: A Research Guide. Ed. E. K. Welsch. Bloomington: Indiana UP, 1965.

A Pictorial History of Black Americans. Langston Hughes et al. 5th rev. ed. New York: Crown, 1983.

Who's Who among Black Americans. Northbrook, IL: WWABA, 1976. 3rd ed. 1981.

HISPANIC-AMERICAN STUDIES

Chicano Literature: A Reference Guide. Eds. J. A. Martinez and F. A. Lomeli. Westport: Greenwood, 1985.

Hispanics in the United States: A New Social Agenda. Eds. P. S. J. Cafferty and W. McCready. New Brunswick: Transaction, 1984.

Literature Chicana. Comp. R. G. Trujilo. Encino: Floricanto, 1985.

Manual of Hispanic Bibliography. Eds. D. W. Foster and V. R. Foster. 2nd ed. New York: Garland, 1976.

¿Quien Sabe?: A Preliminary List of Chicano Reference Materials. Los Angeles: U of California Chicano Studies Research Center, 1981.

Sourcebook of Hispanic Culture in the United States. Ed. D. W. Foster. Chicago: ALA, 1982.

Spanish-American Women Writers: A Bibliographical Research Checklist. Ed. L. E. R. Cortina. New York: Garland, 1982.

NATIVE AMERICAN STUDIES

American Indian Novelists: An Annotated Critical Bibliography. New York: Garland, 1982.

Guide to Research on North American Indians. Ed. A. B. Hirschfelder et al. Chicago: ALA, 1983.

Indians of North America: Methods and Sources for Library Research. M. L. Haas. Hamden, CT: Library Professional Pubs., 1983.

Studies in American Indian Literature: Critical Essays and Course Designs. New York: MLA, 1983.

INDEXES TO JOURNAL ARTICLES

Hispanic American Periodicals Index. Los Angeles: UCLA Latin American Center, 1974–present.

Index to Periodical Articles by and about Blacks. Boston: Hall, 1973–present.

MLA International Bibliography. New York: MLA, 1921–present. (For ethnic languages and literature.)

Sage Race Relations Abstracts. London and Beverly Hills: 1976–present.

Social Sciences Index. New York: Wilson, 1974–present. (For sociological and anthropological approaches to ethnic studies.)

DATABASES

America: History and Life, DIALOG
Population Bibliography, DIALOG
Social Scisearch, DIALOG, BRS
Sociological Abstracts, DIALOG, BRS

Film

GENERAL WORKS AND BIBLIOGRAPHIES

Concise History of the Cinema. Peter Cowie. 2 vols. New York: Barnes, 1971.

Dictionary of Film Terms. Frank E. Beaver. New York: McGraw, 1983.

Film: A Reference Guide. Robert A. Armour. Westport: Greenwood, 1980.

Film Facts. C. S. Steinberg. New York: Facts on File, 1980.

Film Research: A Critical Bibliography. Ed. P. J. Bukalski. Boston: Hall, 1972.

Film Review Digest. Millwood, NY: Kraus, 1975. Quarterly.

Film Study: A Resource Guide. Frank Manchel. Rutherford: Fairleigh Dickinson UP, 1973.

The Filmgoer's Companion. Ed. Leslie Halliwell. 8th ed. New York: Scribner's, 1984.

International Encyclopedia of Film. Ed. Roger Manvell. New York: Crown, 1972.

International Motion Picture Almanac. New York: Quigley, 1929–present. Annual.

The Macmillan Film Bibliography. George Rehrauer. 2 vols. New York: Macmillan, 1982.

New York Times Film Reviews 1913–1968. 10 vols. New York: New York Times and Arno, 1971–1972. Biennial supplements.

The Oxford Companion to Film. Ed. L. A. Bawden. New York: Oxford UP, 1976.

INDEXES TO JOURNAL ARTICLES

Film Literature Index. New York: Filmdex, 1973–present. Quarterly.
International Index to Film Periodicals. New York: Bowker, 1972–present. Annual.
The New Film Index: A Bibliography of Magazine Articles in English, 1930–1970. Eds. R. D. MacCann and E. S. Perry. New York: Dutton, 1975.

DATABASES

Magill's Survey of Cinema, DIALOG

Foreign Languages

FRENCH

An Annotated Bibliography of French Language and Literature. Ed. F. Bassan, et al. New York: Garland, 1975.
Concise Bibliography of French Literature. Ed. Denis Mahaffey. New York: Bowker, 1976.
Concise Oxford Dictionary of French Literature. Ed. J. Reid. Oxford: Clarendon, 1976.
Critical Bibliography of French Literature. Syracuse: Syracuse UP, 1947–1985. In progress.
Dictionnaire etymologique de la langue francaise. O. Block and W. Wartburg. Paris: Presses Universitaires de France, 1975.
French Literature: An Annotated Guide to Selected Bibliographies. Ed. R. Kempton. New York: MLA, 1981.
French Twenty Bibliography: Critical and Biographical References for the Study of French Literature since 1885. Ed. D. W. Alden. New York: French Institute, 1981.

Grand Larousse encyclopedique. 12 vols. Elmsford, NY: Maxwell, 1964. Supplements.
Oxford Companion to French Literature. Eds. Paul Harvey and Janet Heseltine. Oxford: Clarendon, 1959.

GERMAN

A Critical Bibliography of German Literature in English Translation: 1481–1927. B. Q. Morgan. 2nd ed. Metuchen: Scarecrow, 1965. Supplements.
Der Grosse Duden. Ed. R. Duden. 10 vols. New York: Adler's, 1971.
Deutsches Woerterbuch. Eds. Jacob Grimm and Wilhelm Grimm. 32 vols. New York: Adler's, 1973.
German Literature: An Annotated Reference Guide. Eds. U. K. Faulhaver and P. B. Goff. New York: Garland, 1979.
German Periodical Publications. Eds. G. Erdelyi and A. F. Peterson. Stanford: Hoover, 1967.
Introduction to Library Research in German Studies. Ed. L. Richardson. Boulder: Westview, 1984.
Lese der Deutschen Lyrik: Von Klopstock bis Rilke. Friedrich Burns. New York: Irvington, 1961.
Oxford Companion to German Literature. Ed. H. Garland. 2nd ed. New York: Oxford, 1986.
Reallexikon der deutschen Literaturgeschichte. Eds. W. Kohlschmidt and W. Mohr. 3 vols. New York: DeGruyter, 1958–1977.
Selected Bibliography of German Literature in English Translation: 1956–1960. Ed. M. F. Smith. Metuchen: Scarecrow, 1972.
Who's Who in Germany: A Biographical Dictionary. 2 vols. New York: IPS, 1978. Supplements.

LATIN

Cambridge History of Classical Literature.
New York: Cambridge UP, 1982–
present. In progress.

*The Classical World Bibliography of Roman
Drama and Poetry and Ancient Fiction.* New York: Garland, 1978.

*Introduction to Medieval Latin Studies: A
Syllabus and Bibliographical Guide.* M.
R. McGuire and H. Dressler. 2nd ed.
Washington: Catholic UP, 1977.

Latin Literature. J. W. Mackail. New York:
Ungar, 1966.

Oxford Companion to Classical Literature.
Ed. P. Harvey. 2nd ed. New York: Oxford UP, 1937.

Oxford Latin Dictionary. Ed. P. G. Glare.
New York: Oxford UP, 1982.

*Studies in Roman Literature, Culture and
Religion.* Henrik Wagenvoort. New
York: Garland, 1978.

RUSSIAN

*Basic Russian Publications: A Bibliographic
Guide to Western-Language Publications.* Ed. P. L. Horecky. Chicago: U
of Chicago P, 1965.

*Basic Russian Publications: A Selected and
Annotated Bibliography on Russia and
the Soviet Union.* Ed. P. L. Horecky.
Chicago: U of Chicago P, 1962.

*Bibliography of Russian Literature in Eng-
lish Translation to 1945.* Ed. M. B.
Line. 1963. Rpt. Totowa, NJ: Row-
man, 1972.

Dictionary of Russian Literature. Ed. W. E.
Harkins. 1956. Rpt. Westport: Greenwood, 1971.

*Guide to Bibliographies of Russian Litera-
ture.* Eds. S. A. Zenkovsky and D. L.
Armbruster. Nashville: Vanderbilt UP,
1970.

Guide to Russian Reference Books. K. Mai-
chel. 5 vols. Stanford: Hoover Institute Press, 1962–1967.

Handbook of Russian Literature. Ed. V.
Terras. New Haven: Yale UP, 1985.

*Introduction to Russian Language and Lit-
erature.* R. Auty and D. Obolensky.
New York: Cambridge UP, 1977.

*Literature of the Soviet Peoples: A Historical
and Biographical Survey.* Harri Junger.
New York: Ungar, 1971.

*The Modern Encyclopedia of Russian and So-
viet Literature.* Ed. H. B. Weber. Gulf
Breeze, FL: Academic International,
1971–present. In progress.

*Russia, the USSR, and Eastern Europe: A
Bibliographic Guide to English Language Publications, 1975–1980.* Littleton, CO: Libraries Unlimited, 1982.
Supplements.

SPANISH

Bibliography of Old Spanish Texts. Ed. Anthony Cardenas et al. 3rd ed. Madison: Hispanic Seminary, 1984.

Diccionario de la literatura latinoamerica.
Washington: OAS, 1958.

*Dissertations in Hispanic Languages and
Literatures: An Index of Dissertations
Completed in the United States and
Canada.* Eds. J. R. Chatham and C.
C. McClendon. Lexington: UP of
Kentucky, 1981.

Handbook of Latin American Literature.
Comp. D. W. Foster. New York: Garland, 1987.

Handbook of Latin American Studies.
Gainesville: U Press of Florida, 1935–
present.

*Historia de la literatura española e hispan-
oamerica.* E. Diez-Echarri. Madrid:
Aguilar, 1983.

Historia de la literatura hispanoamericana.
E. Anderson-Imbert. 2 vols. Mexico:
Fondo, 1974.

*The Literature of Spain in English Transla-
tion: A Bibliography.* Comp. R. S.
Rudder. New York: Ungar, 1975.

Modern Spanish and Portuguese Literatures.
Eds. M. J. Schneider and I. Stern.
New York: Ungar, 1988.

Oxford Companion to Spanish Literature.
Ed. F. Ward. Oxford: Clarendon,
1978.

A Sourcebook for Hispanic Literature and Language. D. W. Bleznick. Metuchen: Scarecrow, 1983.

Spanish and Spanish-American Literature: An Annotated Guide to Selected Bibliographies. Ed. H. C. Woodbridge. New York: MLA, 1983.

INDEXES TO JOURNAL ARTICLES

Humanities Index. New York: Wilson, 1974.

MLA International Bibliography. New York: MLA, 1921–present.

DATABASES

LLBA (Linguistics and Language Behavior Abstracts), BRS

MLA Bibliography, DIALOG

Geology

GENERAL WORKS
AND BIBLIOGRAPHIES

Bibliography of North American Geology. 49 vols. Washington: GPO, 1923–1971.

Catalog of the U.S. Geological Survey Library. Boston: Hall, 1964. Supplements.

Dictionary of Geology. J. Challinor. 6th ed. New York: Oxford, 1986.

The Encyclopedia of Applied Geology. C. W. Finkl, Jr. New York: Van Nostrand, 1984.

Encyclopedia of Field and General Geology. Ed. C. W. Finkl, Jr. New York: Van Nostrand, 1982.

Geological Reference Sources: A Subject and Regional Bibliography. Eds. D. Ward, M. Wheeler, and R. Bier. Metuchen: Scarecrow, 1981.

Glossary of Geology. Eds. R. L. Bates and J. A. Jackson. 3rd ed. Falls Church: AGI, 1987.

Guide to Information Sources in Mining, Minerals, and Geosciences. Ed. S. R. Kaplan. New York: McGraw, 1978.

McGraw-Hill Encyclopedia of the Geological Sciences. New York: McGraw, 1978.

Publications of the Geological Survey. Washington: GPO, 1979.

Sourcebook in Geology: Fourteen Hundred to Nineteen Hundred. Ed. K. F. Mather. Cambridge: Harvard UP, 1970.

Use of Earth Science Literature. Ed. D. N. Wood. New York: Archon, 1973.

INDEXES TO JOURNAL ARTICLES

Bibliography and Index of Geology. Boulder: AGA, 1933–present.

General Science Index. New York: Wilson, 1978–present.

DATABASES

Compendex, BRS
Geoarchive, DIALOG
Geobase, DIALOG
Georef, DIALOG

History

GENERAL WORKS
AND BIBLIOGRAPHIES

America: History and Life: A Guide to Periodical Literature. Santa Barbara: ABC-Clio, 1964–present.

Bibliography of British History. Oxford: Clarendon, 1928–present.

A Bibliography of Modern History. Ed. J. P. C. Roach. New York: Cambridge UP, 1968.

Cambridge Ancient History. 12 vols. New York: Cambridge UP, 1923–39. Revision in progress.

Cambridge Medieval History. 8 vols. New York: Cambridge UP, 1911–36. Revision in progress.

Dictionary of American History. 8 vols. New York: Scribner's, 1976.

Encyclopedia of American History. Ed. R. B. Morris. 6th ed. New York: Harper, 1982.

Encyclopedia of World History. 5th ed. Boston: Houghton, 1972.

Facts on File Yearbook. New York: Facts on File, 1946–present.

Guide to American Foreign Relations since 1700. Ed. R. D. Burns. Santa Barbara: ABC-Clio, 1983.

Guide to Historical Method. Ed. R. J. Shafer. 3rd ed. Chicago: Dorsey, 1980.

Handbook for Research in American History: A Guide to Bibliographies and Other Reference Works. F. P. Prucha. Lincoln: U of Nebraska P, 1987.

Harvard Guide to American History. Ed. F. Freidel. Cambridge: Harvard UP, 1974.

The Historian's Handbook. H. J. Pulton and M. S. Howland. Norman: U of Oklahoma P, 1986.

Historical Bibliography. Ed. D. Williamson. Hamden: Shoe String, 1967.

International Bibliography of Historical Sciences. New York: Wilson, 1930–present.

Library Research Guide to History. Ed. E. Frick. New York: Pierian, 1980.

The Modern Researcher. J. Barzun and H. F. Graff. 4th ed. San Diego: Harcourt, 1985.

Research in Archives: The Use of Unpublished Primary Sources. Ed. P. C. Brooks. Chicago: U of Chicago P, 1968.

Researching and Writing in History: A Practical Handbook for Students. F. N. McCoy. Berkeley: U of California P, 1974.

The Times Atlas of World History. Ed. J. Barraclough. London: Times/Maplewood, NJ: Hammond, 1984.

Writing History Papers. Eds. J. D. Bennett and L. H. Harrison. St. Louis: Forum, 1979.

INDEXES TO JOURNAL ARTICLES

American Historical Association. *Recently Published Articles.* 1976–present.

Historical Abstracts, 1955–present.

Humanities Index. New York: Wilson, 1974–present.

DATABASES

America: History and Life, DIALOG

Historical Abstracts, DIALOG

Journalism and Mass Communications

GENERAL WORKS AND BIBLIOGRAPHIES

An Annotated Journalism Bibliography: 1958–1968. W. C. Price and C. M. Pickett. Minneapolis: U of Minnesota P, 1970.

Annotated Media Bibliography. Ed. B. Congdon. Washington: ACC, 1985.

The Associated Press Stylebook. New York: AP, 1977.

Basic Books in the Mass Media. Eleanor Blum. 2nd ed. Champaign: U of Illinois P, 1980. (Third ed.: *Mass Media Bibliography.* E. Blum and F. G. Wiehart. 1990.)

Broadcasting Cablecasting Yearbook. Washington: Broadcasting Publications, 1982–present. Annual.

Encyclopedia of American Journalism. D. Paneth. New York: Facts on File, 1983.

Encyclopedia of Twentieth-Century Journalists. Ed. William H. Taft. New York: Garland, 1984.

Halliwell's Film and Video Guide. 6th ed. New York: Scribner's, 1987.

International Encyclopedia of Communications. Ed. E. Barnouw et al. 4 vols. New York: Oxford, 1989.

Journalism Biographies: Master Index. Detroit: Gale, 1979. Supplements.

Journalist's Bookshelf. Eds. R. E. Wolseley and I. Wolseley. 8th ed. Atlanta: Berg, 1985.

Les Brown's Encyclopedia of Television. New York: Zoetrope, 1982.

The Literature of Journalism: An Annotated Bibliography. Warren C. Price. Minneapolis: U of Minnesota P, 1959.

Media Law: A Legal Handbook for the Working Journalist. K. Galvin. Berkeley: Nolo, 1984.

Media Research: An Introduction. Eds. R. D. Wimmer and J. R. Dominick. Belmont: Wadsworth, 1982.

NAB Broadcasting Bibliography: A Guide to the Literature of Radio and Television. 2nd ed. Washington: National Association of Broadcasters, 1984.

News Media and Public Policy: An Annotated Bibliography. Ed. J. P. McKerns. 2 vols. New York: Garland, 1985.

Radio and Television: A Selected, Annotated Bibliography. Metuchen: Scarecrow, 1978. Supplements to 1982.

The Reporter's Handbook. New York: St. Martin's, 1983.

U.S. Television Network News: A Guide to Sources in English. Comp. M. J. Smith, Jr. Jefferson, NC: McFarland, 1984.

Violence and Terror in the Mass Media: An Annotated Bibliography. Westport: Greenwood, 1988.

INDEXES TO JOURNAL ARTICLES

Business Periodicals Index. New York: Wilson, 1958–present.

Communications Abstracts. Beverly Hills: Sage, 1978–present.

Humanities Index. New York: Wilson, 1974–present.

DATABASES

AP News, DIALOG
Newsearch, BRS

Reuters, DIALOG
Social Scisearch, DIALOG
UPI News, DIALOG

Language and Literature

GENERAL WORKS
AND BIBLIOGRAPHIES

Contemporary Authors. Detroit: Gale, 1962–present.

Contemporary Literary Criticism. Detroit: Gale, 1973–present.

Fiction Catalog. New York: Wilson, 1980. Annual supplements.

Goldentree Bibliographies in Language and Literature. Series. Northbrook, IL: AHM, 1968–1979.

Handbook to Literature. C. H. Holman. 5th ed. New York: Macmillan, 1986.

Literary Criticism Index. Eds. A. R. Weiner and S. Means. Metuchen: Scarecrow, 1984.

Literary Research Guide. C. Patterson. 2nd ed. New York: MLA, 1983.

Magill's Bibliography of Literary Criticism. Ed. Frank McGill. 4 vols. Englewood Cliffs Salem, 1979.

Research Guide for Undergraduate Students: English and American Literature. New York: MLA, 1985.

Selective Bibliography for the Study of English and American Literature. Eds. R. D. Altick and A. Wright. 6th ed. New York: Macmillan, 1979.

SF Bibliographies. Eds. Robert E. Briney and Edward Wood. Chicago: Advent, 1972.

Supernatural Fiction Writers: Fantasy and Horror. Ed. E. F. Bleiler. 2 vols. New York: Scribner's, 1985.

AMERICAN LITERATURE (*see also* Ethnic Studies)

American Bibliography. Ed. Charles Evans. 14 vols. Magnolia, MA: Smith, 1967.

American Literary Scholarship. Durham: Duke UP, 1963–present.

American Novel: 1789 to 1968. Eds. D. Gerstenberger and George Hendrick. Chicago: Swallow, 1961 and 1970.

American Writers. 4 vols. New York: Scribner's, 1961–1981. Supplements.

Backgrounds of American Literary Thought. R. W. Horton and H. W. Edwards. 3rd ed. New York: Meredith, 1974.

Bibliographical Guide to the Study of Literature of the USA. Ed. C. Gohdes et al. 5th ed. Durham: Duke UP, 1984.

A Bibliographical Guide to the Study of Western American Literature. Ed. R. W. Etulain. Lincoln: U of Nebraska P, 1982.

Bibliography of American Literature. Ed. G. N. Blanck. 7 vols. New Haven: Yale UP, 1955–1983. In progress.

Bibliography of Bibliographies in American Literature. Charles H. Nilon. New York: Bowker, 1970.

Cambridge Handbook of American Literature. Ed. J. Salzman. New York: Cambridge UP, 1986.

Eight American Authors: A Survey of Research and Criticism. Ed. James Woodress. Rev. ed. New York: Norton, 1971.

Guide to American Literature and Its Background since 1890. Eds. J. M. Jones and R. M. Ludwig. 4th ed. Cambridge: Harvard UP, 1972.

Literary History of the United States. Ed. R. E. Spiller et al. 4th ed. 2 vols. New York: Macmillan, 1974.

Modern American Literature. Ed. D. Nyren. 4th ed. New York: Unger, 1969–1976. Supplements.

Oxford Companion to American Literature. Ed. J. D. Hart. 5th ed. New York: Oxford UP, 1983.

Sixteen Modern American Authors: A Survey of Research and Criticism. Ed. J. R. Bryer. New York: Norton, 1969.

The Transcendentalists: A Review of Research and Criticism. Ed. Joel Myerson. New York: MLA, 1984.

Twentieth Century American Science Fiction Writers. Ed. C. C. Smith. New York: St. Martin's, 1981.

BLACK AMERICAN LITERATURE (*see also* Ethnic Studies)

Bibliographic Guide to Black Studies. Boston: Hall, 1980. Supplements.

A Bibliography of Neo-African Literature from Africa, America, and the Caribbean. New York: Grove, 1966.

Black American Fiction: A Bibliography. Eds. C. Fairbanks and E. A. Engeldinger. Metuchen: Scarecrow, 1978.

Black American Fiction since 1952: A Preliminary Checklist. Eds. F. Deodene and W. P. French. Metuchen: Scarecrow, 1970.

Black American Literature: A Critical History. R. Whitlow. Totowa, NJ: Littlefield, 1974.

Black American Writers: Bibliographic Essays. Ed. M. T. Inge et al. 2 vols. New York: St. Martin's, 1978.

Black American Writers Past and Present: A Biographical and Bibliographical Dictionary. Ed. T. G. Rush et al. 2 vols. Metuchen: Scarecrow, 1975.

Black Americans in Autobiography: An Annotated Bibliography of Autobiographies and Autobiographical Books Written since the Civil War. Durham: Duke UP, 1984.

Black Literature Resources. New York: Dekker, 1975.

Blacks in America: Bibliographic Essays. Ed. James P. McPherson et al. New York: Doubleday, 1971.

Conjuring: Black Women, Fiction, and Literary Tradition. Bloomington: Indiana UP, 1985.

The Negro in American Literature and Bibliography of Literature by and about Negro Americans. Ed. Abraham Chapman. Oshkosh: Wisconsin Council of Teachers of English, 1966.

Poetry of the Negro: 1746–1970. Eds. Langston Hughes and Arna Bontemps. New York: Doubleday, 1970.

BRITISH LITERATURE

Anglo-Irish Literature: A Review of Research. Ed. Richard J. Finneran. New York: MLA, 1976. Supplement 1983.

Bibliographical Resources for the Study of Nineteenth Century English Fiction. Ed. G. N. Ray. Folcroft, PA: Folcroft, 1964.

British Writers. Ed. Ian Scott-Kilvert. 8 vols. New York: Scribner's, 1979–1983.

British Writers and Their Works. 10 vols. Lincoln: U of Nebraska P, 1964–1970.

Cambridge Bibliography of English Literature. Ed. F. W. Bateson. 5 vols. New York: Cambridge UP, 1941–1957.

Cambridge Guide to English Literature. Ed. M. Stapleton. New York: Cambridge UP, 1983.

Cambridge History of English Literature. Eds. A. W. Ward and A. R. Waller. 15 vols. Cambridge: Cambridge UP, 1907–1933.

A Descriptive Catalogue of the Bibliographies of Twentieth Century British Poets, Novelists, and Dramatists. Ed. E. W. Mellown. 2nd ed. Troy, NY: Whitson, 1978.

Dictionary of Literary Biography. Detroit: Gale, 1983–1985.

The English Romantic Poets: A Review of Research and Criticism. 4th ed. New York: MLA, 1985.

Garland Shakespeare Bibliographies. 18 vols. New York: Garland, 1980–present. In progress.

History of the English Novel. Ernest A. Baker. 11 vols. 1967. Rpt. New York: Barnes, 1975.

McGraw-Hill Guide to English Literature. 2 vols. Eds. K. Lawrence, B. Seifter, and L. Ratner. New York: McGraw, 1985.

Modern British Literature. 4 vols. Literary Criticism Series. New York: Ungar, 1966–1975.

New Cambridge Bibliography of English Literature. 5 vols. New York: Cambridge UP, 1969–1977.

Oxford Companion to English Literature. Ed. M. Drabble. 5th ed. Oxford: Clarendon, 1985.

Oxford History of English Literature. Oxford: Clarendon, 1945–present.

Romantic Movement: A Selective and Critical Bibliography. New York: Garland, 1980–present.

The Shakespeare Companion. G. L. Evans and B. Evans. New York: Scribner's, 1978.

Victorian Fiction: A Second Guide to Research. Ed. G. H. Ford. New York: MLA, 1978. (Covers 1963–1974.)

DRAMA AND THEATER

American Drama Criticism: Interpretations, 1890–1977. Ed. F. E. Eddleman. Hamden: Shoe String, 1979. Supplement 1984.

Catalog of the Theatre and Drama Collections. Boston: Hall, 1967. Supplements.

Contemporary Dramatists. Ed. J. Vinson. 4th ed. New York: St. Martin's, 1987.

Critical Survey of Drama. Ed. F. N. Magill. 6 vols. Englewood Cliffs: Salem, 1982. Supplement 1987.

Cumulated Dramatic Index. 2 vols. Westwood: Faxon, 1965.

Drama Criticism. 2 vols. Denver: Swallow, 1970.

Dramatic Criticism Index. Eds. P. F. Breed and F. M. Sniderman. Detroit: Gale, 1972.

A Guide to Reference and Bibliography for Theatre Research. J. Bailey. 2nd ed. Columbus: Ohio State UP, 1983.

Index to Full Length Plays: 1895–1964. 3 vols. Westwood: Faxon, 1956–1965.

Index to Plays in Periodicals. Metuchen: Scarecrow, 1979.

McGraw-Hill Encyclopedia of World Drama. 2nd ed. 5 vols. New York: McGraw, 1984.

Modern Drama: A Checklist of Critical Literature on 20th Century Plays. Metuchen: Scarecrow, 1967.

New York Times Theatre Reviews, 1870–1919. 6 vols. New York: New York Times and Arno, 1975.

Oxford Companion to the Theatre. 4th ed. Fair Lawn: Oxford UP, 1984.

Play Index. 6 vols. New York: Wilson, 1953–present.

A Survey and Bibliography of Renaissance Drama. 4 vols. Lincoln: U of Nebraska P, 1975–1978.

LANGUAGE STUDIES

American Literature and Language: A Guide to Information Sources. Detroit: Gale, 1982.

Cambridge Encyclopedia of Language. Ed. D. Crystal. New York: Cambridge, 1988.

A Concise Bibliography for Students of English. 5th ed. rev. by W. E. Coburn. Stanford: Stanford UP, 1972.

A Dictionary of American English on Historical Principles. Eds. W. Craigie and J. R. Hulbert. 4 vols. Chicago: U of Chicago P, 1938–1944.

Dictionary of American Regional English. Ed. F. Cassidy. Cambridge: Harvard UP, 1985–present. In progress.

Oxford English Dictionary. 2nd ed. 20 vols. New York: Oxford UP, 1989.

The World's Major Languages. Ed. B. Comrie. New York: Oxford UP, 1987.

MYTHOLOGY AND FOLKLORE

American Folklore: A Bibliography. Metuchen: Scarecrow, 1977.

The Arthurian Encyclopedia. Ed. N. J. Lacy. New York: Garland, 1984.

Arthurian Legend and Literature: An Annotated Bibliography. E. Reiss et al. 2 vols. New York: Garland, 1984–. In progress.

Bibliography of Greek Myth in English Poetry. Ed. H. H. Law. Folcroft, PA: Folcroft, 1955.

Bullfinch's Mythology. New York: Avenel, 1978.

Dictionary of Classical Mythology. P. Grimal. New York: Blackwell, 1986.

Fable Scholarship: An Annotated Bibliography. Ed. Pack Carnes. New York: Garland, 1982.

The Facts on File Encyclopedia of World Mythology and Legend. A. S. Mercatante. New York: Facts on File, 1988.

Folklore and Literature in the United States: An Annotated Bibliography. Ed. S. S. Jones. New York: Garland, 1984.

The Golden Bough. Sir James Frazer. 3rd ed. 12 vols. New York: St. Martin's, 1955.

Guide to Folktales in the English Language. D. L. Ashlimar. Westport: Greenwood, 1987.

Handbook of American Folklore. Ed. Richard M. Dorson. Bloomington: Indiana UP, 1983.

Historical Atlas of World Mythology. Joseph Campbell. San Francisco: Harper, 1983–. In progress.

Index to Fairy Tales, Myths, and Legends. Ed. M. H. Eastman. 2nd ed. Westwood: Faxon, 1926. Supplements.

Mythological and Fabulous Creatures: A Source Book and Research Guide. Westport: Greenwood, 1987.

Storyteller's Sourcebook. Detroit: Gale, 1982.

The Study of American Folklore. J. H. Brunvand. 3rd ed. New York: Norton, 1987.

Women and Folklore: A Bibliographic Survey. Ed. Francis A. DeCaro. Westport: Greenwood, 1983.

THE NOVEL

American Fiction: A Contribution Toward a Bibliography. Ed. Lyle H. Wright. 3 vols. San Marino: Huntington Library, 1969, 1979.

American Fiction 1900–1950: A Guide to Information Sources. Ed. James Woodress. Detroit: Gale, 1974.

The American Novel. Ed. Christof Wegelin. New York: Macmillan, 1977.

The American Novel 1789–1959: A Checklist of Twentieth Century Criticism. Denver: Swallow, 1961.

American Novel Through Henry James. C. H. Holman. Arlington Heights: Davidson, 1973.

British Novel: Conrad to the Present. P. L. Wiley. Arlington Heights: Davidson, 1973.

British Novel: Scott Through Hardy. Ian Watts. Arlington Heights: Davidson, 1973.

The Contemporary English Novel: An Annotated Bibliography of Secondary Sources. Eds. H. W. Drescher and B. Kahrmann. New York: IPS, 1973.

The Contemporary Novel: A Checklist of Critical Literature on the British and American Novel since 1945. Eds. I. Adelman and R. Dworkin. Metuchen: Scarecrow, 1972.

The Continental Novel: A Checklist of Criticism in English, 1900–1960. Metuchen: Scarecrow, 1968. Supplements 1967–1983.

Critical Survey of Long Fiction. Ed. F. N. Magill. 8 vols. Englewood Cliffs: Salem, 1983. Supplement 1987.

English Novel Explication: Criticism to 1972. Eds. H. Palmer and J. Dyson. Hamden, CT: Shoe String, 1973. Supplement 1976–present.

POETRY

American and British Poetry: A Guide to the Criticism. Athens, OH: Swallow, 1984.

Critical Survey of Poetry. Ed. F. N. Magill. 8 vols. Englewood Cliffs: Salem, 1982.

English Poetry: Select Bibliographical Guides. Ed. A. E. Dyson. New York: Oxford UP, 1971.

Granger's Index to Poetry. Ed. W. J. Smith. 8th ed. New York: Columbia UP, 1986.

Poetry Explication: A Checklist of Interpretations since 1925 of British and American Poems Past and Present. Boston: Hall, 1980.

Princeton Encyclopedia of Poetry and Poetics. Ed. Alex Preminger et al. Princeton: Princeton UP, 1974.

THE SHORT STORY

American Short-Fiction Criticism and Scholarship, 1959–1977: A Checklist. Ed. Joe Weixlmann. Athens: Ohio UP, 1982.

Critical Survey of Short Fiction. Ed. F. N. Magill. 7 vols. Englewood Cliffs: Salem, 1981. Supplement 1987.

Short Story Index. Eds. D. E. Cook and I. S. Monro. New York: Wilson, 1953. Supplements.

Twentieth-Century Short Story Explication. Ed. W. S. Walker. 3rd ed. Hamden, CT: Shoe String, 1977. Supplements.

WORLD LITERATURE

Benet's Reader's Encyclopedia. 3rd ed. New York: Harper, 1987.

Columbia Dictionary of Modern European Literature. Eds. Jean-Albert Bede and William Edgerton. 2nd ed. New York: Columbia UP, 1980.

Encyclopedia of World Literature in the 20th Century. Ed. L. S. Klein et al. 2nd ed. 4 vols. New York: Ungar, 1981–1984.

Reader's Companion to World Literature. Ed. L. H. Horstein. Rev. ed. New York: NAL, 1973.

INDEXES TO JOURNAL ARTICLES

Abstracts of English Studies. Urbana: NCTE, 1958–present.

Abstracts of Folklore Studies. Austin: U of Texas P, 1962–1975.

MLA International Bibliography of Books and Articles on Modern Language and Literature. New York: Modern Language Association, 1921–present. Annually.

DATABASES

Book Review Index, DIALOG
MLA Bibliography, DIALOG

Mathematics

GENERAL WORKS AND BIBLIOGRAPHIES

Annotated Bibliography of Expository Writing in the Mathematical Sciences. Eds. M. P. Gaffney and L. A. Steen. Washington: Mathematics Association, 1976.

Bibliography and Research Manual of the History of Mathematics. Ed. K. L. May. Toronto: U of Toronto P, 1973.

Current Information Sources in Mathematics: An Annotated Guide to Books and Periodicals: 1960–72. Ed. E. M. Dick. Littleton, CO: Libraries Unlimited, 1973.

Encyclopedic Dictionary of Mathematics. Ed. K. Ito. 2nd ed. 4 vols. Cambridge: MIT Press, 1987.

How to Find Out in Mathematics. Ed. J. E. Pemberton. 2nd ed. Elmsford, NY: Pergamon, 1970.

International Catalogue of Scientific Literature: 1901–1914. Section A: Mathematics. Metuchen: Scarecrow, 1974.

Mathematics Encyclopedia: A Made Simple Book. Garden City: Doubleday, 1977.

Omega Bibliography of Mathematical Logic. Eds. G. H. Muller and W. Lenski. 6 vols. New York: Springer-Verlag, 1987.

Use of Mathematical Literature. Ed. A. R. Darling. Stoneham, MA: Butterworth, 1977.

Using the Mathematical Literature: A Practical Guide. Ed. B. K. Schaefer. New York: Dekker, 1979.

The VNR Concise Encyclopedia of Mathematics. Ed. W. Gellert et al. Florence, KY: Reinhold, 1977.

INDEXES TO JOURNAL ARTICLES

General Science Index. New York: Wilson, 1978–present.

Mathematical Reviews. Providence: AMS, 1940–present.

DATABASES

Mathsci, DIALOG

Music

GENERAL WORKS AND BIBLIOGRAPHIES

Baker's Biographical Dictionary of Musicians. 7th ed. New York: Schirmer, 1984.

Contemporary American Composers: A Biographical Dictionary. Ed. Ruth Anderson. 2nd ed. Boston: Hall, 1982.

Dictionary of Music. Eds. A. Isaacs and E. Martin. New York: Facts on File, 1983.

The Encyclopedia of Opera. Ed. Leslie Orrey. New York: Scribner's, 1976.

Encyclopedia of Pop, Rock, and Soul. Ed. Irwin Stambler. New York: St. Martin's, 1977.

General Bibliography for Music Research. Ed. K. E. Mixter. 2nd ed. Detroit: Information Coordinators, 1975.

Information on Music: A Handbook of Reference Sources in European Languages. 3 vols. Littleton, CO: Libraries Unlimited, 1975–1984.

International Cyclopedia of Music and Musicians. Ed. Bruce Bohle. 11th ed. New York: Dodd, 1985.

Library Research Guide to Music. Ed. J. Druesdow. Ann Arbor: Pierian, 1982.

Music Reference and Research Materials: An Annotated Bibliography. Ed. V. Duckles. 3rd ed. New York: Free, 1974.

Musica: Sources of Information in Music. Ed. J. H. Davies. 2nd ed. Elmsford, NY: Pergamon, 1969.

New College Encyclopedia of Music. Eds. J. A. Westrup and F. L. Harrison. New York: Norton, 1981.

New Grove Dictionary of American Music. Eds. H. Hitchcock and S. Sadie. 4 vols. New York: Grove, 1986.

New Grove Dictionary of Music and Musicians. Ed. Stanley Sadie. 20 vols. New York: Macmillan, 1980.

New Harvard Directory of Music. Ed. Willi Apel. Cambridge: Harvard UP, 1986.

New Oxford Companion to Music. New York: Oxford UP, 1983.

New Oxford History of Music. London: Oxford, 1957–present. In progress.

Popular Music: An Annotated Index of American Popular Songs. 6 vols. New York: Adrian, 1964–1973. In progress.

Source Readings in Music History. Ed. Oliver Strunk. 5 vols. New York: Norton, 1950.

INDEXES TO JOURNAL ARTICLES

Music Article Guide. Philadelphia: Information Services, 1966–present.

Music Index. Warren, MI: Information Coordinations, 1949–present.

DATABASES

Music Literature International (RILM): *(Repertoire Internationale de Litterata Musicale),* DIALOG

Philosophy

GENERAL WORKS
AND BIBLIOGRAPHIES

A Bibliographical Survey for a Foundation in Philosophy. Ed. F. E. Jordack. Lanham, MD: UP of America, 1978.

A Bibliography of Philosophical Bibliographies. Ed. Herbert Querry. Westport: Greenwood, 1977.

The Classical World Bibliography of Philosophy, Religion, and Rhetoric. New York: Garland, 1978.

Dictionary of the History of Ideas. Ed. P. Wiener. 5 vols. New York: Scribner's, 1974.

A Dictionary of Philosophy. Ed. P. A. Angeles. New York: Harper, 1981.

Dictionary of Philosophy. Ed. A. R. Lacey. New York: Paul/Methuen, 1987.

Encyclopedia of Philosophy. Ed. P. Edwards. 8 vols. New York: Macmillan, 1967–1968.

A Guide to Philosophical Bibliography and Research. Ed. R. T. DeGeorge. New York: Appleton, 1971.

A History of Philosophy. Frederick Copleston. 9 vols. Garden City: Doubleday, 1977.

Philosophy: A Guide to the Reference Literature. H. E. Bynago. Littleton, CO: Libraries Unlimited, 1986.

Philosophy: A Select, Classified Bibliography of Ethics, Economics, Law, Politics, Sociology. Ed. S. A. Matczak. Jamaica, NY: Learned, 1970.

Philosophy and Psychology: Classification Schedule, Author and Title Listing. 2 vols. Cambridge: Harvard UP, 1973.

Research Guide to Philosophy. Eds. T. N. Tice and T. P. Slavens. Chicago: ALA, 1983.

Research in Philosophy. H. J. Koren. Pittsburgh: Duquesne UP, 1966.

World Philosophy: Essay Reviews of 225 Major Works. Ed. Frank Magill. 5 vols. Englewood Cliffs: Salem, 1982.

INDEXES TO JOURNAL ARTICLES

Humanities Index. New York: Wilson, 1974–present.

Philosopher's Index. Bowling Green: Bowling Green UP, 1967–present.

DATABASES

Philosopher's Index, DIALOG

Physics

GENERAL WORKS AND BIBLIOGRAPHIES

American Institute of Physics Handbook. Ed. D. E. Gray. 3rd ed. New York: McGraw, 1972.

Annual Review of Nuclear Science. Palo Alto: 1952–present.

Concise Dictionary of Physics and Related Subjects. Ed. J. Thewlis. 3rd ed. New York: Oxford UP, 1986.

The Encyclopedia of Physics. Ed. Robert Besancon. 3rd ed. New York: Van Nostrand, 1985.

Encyclopedia of Physics. Eds. Rita G. Lerner and George L. Trigg. Reading, MA: Addison, 1981.

How to Find Out about Physics. Ed. Bryan Yates. New York: Pergamon, 1965.

Information Sources in Physics. Ed. D. F. Shaw. 2nd ed. London and Boston: Butterworth, 1985.

An Introductory Guide to Information Sources in Physics. Ed. L. R. A. Melton. New York: Inst. of Physics, 1978.

Physics Literature: A Reference Manual. R. H. Whitford. 2nd ed. Metuchen: Scarecrow, 1968.

Solid State Physics Literature Guides. New York: Plenum, 1972–present.

Sources of History of Quantum Physics. Ed. T. S. Kuhn et al. Philadelphia: APS, 1967.

Use of Physics Literature. Ed. H. Coblans. Stoneham, MA: Butterworth, 1975.

INDEXES TO JOURNAL ARTICLES

Applied Science and Technology Index.

Current Papers in Physics. London: IEE, 1966–present. Bimonthly.

Current Physics Index. New York: AIP, 1975–present. Quarterly.

DATABASES

SciSearch, DIALOG

SPIN (Searchable Physics Information Notices), DIALOG

Political Science

GENERAL WORKS AND BIBLIOGRAPHIES

Basic Documents on Human Rights. Ed. I. Brownlie. 2nd ed. Oxford: Clarendon, 1981.

Blackwell Encyclopedia of Political Institutions. Ed. V. Boddanor. Oxford: Blackwell, 1987.

The Book of the States. Chicago: Council of State Governments, 1935–present. Biennial.

Communism in the World since 1945. Ed. S. K. Kimmel. Santa Barbara: ABC-Clio, 1987.

Dictionary of Modern Political Ideologies. Ed. M. A. Reff. New York: St. Martin's, 1987.

A Dictionary of Political Thought. R. Scruton. New York: Harper, 1982.

A Guide to Reference Materials in Political Science: American Government. Ed. C. E. Vose. Washington: APSA, 1975.

Handbook of Political Science Methods. David G. Garson. 2nd ed. Boston: Holbrook, 1976.

Information Sources of Political Science. F. L. Holler. 4th ed. Santa Barbara: ABC-Clio, 1986.

International Bibliography of Political Science. New York: IPS, 1979. Supplements.

The Literature of Political Science: A Guide for Students, Librarians, and Teachers. C. Brock. New York: Bowker, 1969.

Monthly Catalog of U.S. Government Publications. Washington: GPO, 1895–present.

Political Handbook of the World. New York: McGraw, 1975–present. Biennial revisions.

Political Research and Political Theory. Ed. O. Garceau. Cambridge: Harvard UP, 1968.

The Presidents: A Reference History. Ed. H. F. Graff. New York: Scribner's, 1984.

Sources of Information in the Social Sciences. W. H. Webb. 3rd ed. Chicago: ALA, 1986.

The Statesman's Yearbook. New York: St. Martin's Press, 1964–present. Annually.

The Study of International Relations: A Guide to Information Sources. Robert L. Pfaltzgraff, Jr. Detroit: Gale, 1977.

Yearbook of the United Nations. Lake Success: United Nations, 1947–present.

INDEXES TO JOURNAL ARTICLES

ABC: Pol Sci. Santa Barbara: ABC-Clio, 1969–present.

PAIS Bulletin. New York: Public Affairs Information Service, 1954–present.

Social Sciences Index. New York: Wilson, 1974–present.

DATABASES

Congressional Record Abstracts, DIALOG
PAIS, DIALOG, BRS
U.S. Political Science Documents, DIALOG
Washington Presstext, DIALOG
World Affairs Report, DIALOG

Psychology

GENERAL WORKS
AND BIBLIOGRAPHIES

American Handbook of Psychiatry. Ed. S. Arieti. 2nd ed. 8 vols. New York: Basic, 1974–1981.

Annual Reviews of Psychology. Palo Alto: Annual Reviews, 1950–present.

Bibliographic Guide to Psychology. Boston: Hall, 1975–. Annual.

Bibliography of Aggressive Behavior: A Reader's Guide to the Research Literature. Eds. J. M. Crabtree and K. E. Mayer. New York: Liss, 1977.

Counseling: A Bibliography with Annotations. Eds. R. S. J. Freeman and H. A. Freeman. Metuchen: Scarecrow, 1964.

Cumulated Subject Index to Psychological Abstracts: 1927–1960. 2 vols. Boston: Hall, 1966. Supplements.

Dictionary of Psychology. James P. Chaplin. Rev. ed. New York: Dell, 1985.

Encyclopedia of Psychology. Ed. R. J. Corsini. 4 vols. New York: Wiley, 1984.

Encyclopedic Dictionary of Psychology. Eds. R. Harré and R. Lamb. Oxford: Blackwell, 1983.

How to Find Out in Psychology. D. H. Borchardt and R. D. Francis. Oxford: Pergamon, 1984.

The Index of Psychoanalytic Writings. Ed. A. Grinstein. 14 vols. New York: International Universities, 1956–1971.

International Encyclopedia of Psychiatry, Psychology, Psychoanalysis, and Neurology. Ed. Benjamin B. Wolman. 12 vols. New York: Van Nostrand, 1977.

Library Use: A Handbook for Psychology. J. C. Reed and R. M. Baxter. Washington: APA, 1983.

Psychological Research: An Introduction. A. J. Bachrach. 4th ed. New York: Random, 1981.

Research Guide for Psychology. Ed. R. G. McInnis. Westport: Greenwood, 1982.

INDEXES TO JOURNAL ARTICLES

Child Development Abstracts and Bibliography. Chicago: U of Chicago P, 1927–present.

Psychological Abstracts. Lancaster, PA: APA, 1927–present.

DATABASES

Mental Health Abstracts, DIALOG
PsycALERT, DIALOG, BRS
PsycINFO, DIALOG, BRS

Religion

GENERAL WORKS
AND BIBLIOGRAPHIES

Books on Buddhism: An Annotated Study Guide. Yushin Yoo. Metuchen: Scarecrow, 1976.
Catholic Encyclopedia. Appleton, WI: Nelson, 1981.
Dictionary of American Religious Biography. Ed. Henry W. Bowden. Westport: Greenwood, 1977.
A Dictionary of Comparative Religion. Ed. S. G. F. Brandon. New York: Scribner's, 1970.
Encyclopedia of American Religions. Ed. J. G. Melton. 2 vols. Wilmington, NC: McGrath, 1978.
Encyclopedia Judaica. 16 vols. New York: Macmillan, 1972.
The Encyclopedia of Religion. Ed. M. Eliade. 16 vols. New York: Macmillan, 1987.
Guide to Hindu Religion. Ed. David J. Dell. Boston: Hall, 1981.
Guide to Indexed Periodicals in Religion. J. J. Regazzi and T. C. Hines. Metuchen: Scarecrow, 1975.
Guide to Islam. Ed. D. Ede et al. Boston: Hall, 1983.
Harper's Bible Dictionary. Ed. Paul W. Aachtmeier. 2nd ed. New York: Harper, 1985.
The International Standard Bible Encyclopedia. Ed. G. W. Bromley. Grand Rapids: Eerdmans, 1979–1982. In progress.
Introduction to Theological Research. Ed. Cyril J. Barber. Chicago: Moody, 1982.

Library Research Guide to Religion and Theology. R. Kennedy. Ann Arbor: Pierian, 1974.
Lives of the Saints. Ed. Thurston Attwater. 4 vols. Westminster: Christian Classics, 1976.
New Catholic Encyclopedia. 17 vols. New York: McGraw, 1977–1979.
Oxford Dictionary of the Christian Church. Eds. F. L. Cross and E. A. Livingstone. 2nd ed. New York: Oxford UP, 1974.
Philosophy of Religion: A Guide to Information Sources. Ed. Donald Capps et al. Detroit: Gale, 1976.
A Reader's Guide to the Great Religions. Ed. C. J. Adams. 2nd ed. New York: Free, 1977.
Reference Works for Theological Research: Annotated Selective Bibliographical Guide. Ed. Robert Kepple. 2nd ed. Lanham, MD: UP of America, 1981.
Religions: A Select, Classified Bibliography. Ed. J. F. Mitros. New York: Learned, 1973.
Religious Books and Serials in Print. New York: Bowker, 1978. Biennial.
Research Guide to Religious Studies. Eds. J. F. Wilson and T. P. Slavens. Chicago: ALA, 1982.

INDEXES TO JOURNAL ARTICLES

The Catholic Periodical and Literature Index. New York: Catholic Library Association, 1934–present.
Religion: Index One: Periodicals, Religion and Theological Abstracts. Chicago: ATLA, 1949–present.

DATABASE

Religion Index, DIALOG, BRS

Sociology and Social Work

GENERAL WORKS
AND BIBLIOGRAPHIES

Dictionary of Sociology and Related Sciences.
Ed. Henry Pratt Fairchild. Totowa,
NJ: Littlefield, 1977.
Encyclopedia of Social Work. Ed. John
Turner. 2 vols. New York: NASW,
1977. Annual supplements.
Encyclopedia of Sociology. 2nd ed. Guilford,
CT: DPG Reference, 1981.
*A Guide to Information Sources for Social
Work and the Human Services.* H. N.
Mendelsohn. Phoenix: Oryx, 1987.
*International Encyclopedia of the Social Sci-
ences.* Ed. D. E. Sills. 18 vols. New
York: Macmillan, 1968–1980.
*Library Research Guide to Sociology: Illus-
trated Search Strategy and Sources.*
Eds. P. McMillan and J. R. Kennedy.
Ann Arbor: Pierian, 1981.
*Reference Sources in Social Work: An Anno-
tated Bibliography.* Ed. James H. Con-
rad. Metuchen: Scarecrow, 1982.
*Sociology of America: A Guide to Informa-
tion Sources.* Charles Mark and Paula
F. Mark. Detroit: Gale, 1976.
*Sociology: Classification Schedule, Author
and Title Listing, Chronological List-
ings.* 2 vols. Cambridge: Harvard UP,
1973.
Student Sociologist's Handbook. Eds. P. B.
Bart and L. Frankel. 3rd ed. Glenview:
Scott, 1981.

INDEXES TO JOURNAL ARTICLES

Social Work Research and Abstracts. New
York: NASW, 1977–. Quarterly.
Sociological Abstracts. New York: Sociologi-
cal Abstracts, 1952–present.

DATABASES

Child Abuse and Neglect, DIALOG
Family Resources, DIALOG, BRS

Population Bibliography, DIALOG
Social Scisearch, DIALOG
Sociological Abstracts, DIALOG, BRS

Women's Studies

GENERAL WORKS
AND BIBLIOGRAPHIES

*American Women and Politics: A Selected
Bibliography and Research Guide.* New
York: Garland, 1984.
*American Women Writers: An Annotated
Bibliography.* Ed. B. A. White. New
York: Garland, 1976.
*Bibliographic Guide to Studies on the Status
of Women: Development and Popula-
tion Trends.* Paris: UNESCO, 1983.
*Bibliography on Women: With Special Em-
phasis on Their Roles in Science and So-
ciety.* A. B. Davis. New York: Science
History, 1974.
*Feminist Resources for Schools and Colleges:
A Guide.* Ed. A. Chapman. Westbury,
NY: Feminist Press, 1986.
Films for, by, and about Women. Kaye Sulli-
van. Metuchen: Scarecrow, 1980.
Index-Directory of Women's Media. Wash-
ington: Women's Institute for Free-
dom of the Press, 1975–present.
*New Feminist Scholarship: A Guide to Bibli-
ographies.* Ed. Jane Williamson. Old
Westbury, NY: Feminist Press, 1979.
*The Status of Women: A Selected Bibliogra-
phy.* New York: United Nations, n.d.
Who's Who of American Women. Chicago:
Marquis, 1958–present.
*Women in America: A Guide to Informa-
tion Sources.* Ed. V. R. Terris. Detroit:
Gale, 1980.
*Women Today: A Multidisciplinary Ap-
proach to Women's Studies.* Ed. M. A.
Baker et al. Monterey: Brooks/Cole,
1979.
*Women and Work: Paid and Unpaid: A Se-
lected Annotated Bibliography.* Ed. M.
A. Ferber. New York: Garland, 1987.

The Women's Rights Movement in the Seventies. Ed. Albert Krichmar et al. Metuchen: Scarecrow, 1977.

Women's Studies Abstracts. Honeoye: Rush, 1972–present. Quarterly with annual index.

Women's Studies: A Recommended Core Bibliography. Eds. E. Stineman and C. Loeb. Littleton, CO: Libraries Unlimited, 1979.

INDEXES TO JOURNAL ARTICLES

Social Sciences Index. New York: Wilson, 1974–present.

DATABASES

Social Scisearch, DIALOG, BRS
Sociological Abstracts, DIALOG, BRS

Acknowledgments

Figures 4 and 5, from Lawrence Lundgren, *Environmental Geology,* © 1986, pp. v, 569. Prentice Hall, Englewood Cliffs, New Jersey.

Figure 7, excerpt from *Magazine Index,* © 1991 Information Access Company.

Figure 8, reprinted with permission from "Propaedia" of *Encyclopaedia Britannica,* 15th Edition, © 1988 by Encyclopaedia Britannica, Inc.

Figure 9, reprinted with permission from the Index of *Encyclopaedia Britannica,* 15th Edition, © 1988 by Encyclopaedia Britannica, Inc.

Figure 10, reprinted with permission from "Prohibition" in *Encyclopaedia Britannica* 15th Edition, © 1988 by Encyclopaedia Britannica, Inc.

Figure 17, excerpt from *Subject Guide to Books In Print, 1989–1990.* © Reed Publishing, Inc.

Figure 18, excerpt from *Bibliographic Index,* 1984. Reprinted by permission of The H. W. Wilson Company.

Figure 19, excerpt from *Essay and General Literature Index.* Reprinted by permission of The H. W. Wilson Company.

Figure 20, Excerpt from *Reader's Guide to Periodical Literature.* Reprinted by permission of The H. W. Wilson Company.

Figure 21, excerpt from *The New York Times Index 1981.* Copyright © 1981 by The New York Times Company. Reprinted by permission.

Figure 23, excerpt from *Social Sciences Index.* Reprinted by permission of The H. W. Wilson Company.

Index

340